SHE WHO WAS LOST
IS REMEMBERED

SHE WHO WAS LOST IS REMEMBERED

HEALING FROM INCEST THROUGH CREATIVITY

EDITED BY LOUISE M. WISECHILD

THE SEAL PRESS

Cover and text design by Clare Conrad

Acknowledgements:
Heidi Eigenkind, "Cunt Song." Originally published in *Contemporary Verse 2,* Vol. 11 No. 1. Roseann Lloyd, "*Insect* is an Anagram for *Incest,*" "Oh," and "Exorcism of *Nice.*" Originally appeared in *Tap Dancing for Big Mom* (Minneapolis: New Rivers Press, 1986). Reprinted by permission of the publisher. Marie-Elise Wheatwind, "Living Hand-to-Mouth." Originally appeared in *Chicana Lesbians: The Girls Our Mothers Warned Us Against,* edited by Carla Trujillo (Berkeley: Third Woman Press, 1991). Reprinted by permission.

Library of Congress Cataloging-in-Publication Data
She who was lost is remembered : healing from incest through
    creativity / edited by Louise Wisechild.
        p.   cm.
    ISBN 1-878067-09-5
        1. Incest--United States.   2. Incest victims--United States-
-Biography.   3. Incest in literature.   I. Wisechild, Louise M.
HQ72.U53S49   1991
306.877--dc20   91-21464
                                                          CIP

Printed in the United States of America
First printing, October 1991
10   9   8   7   6   5   4   3   2   1

Foreign Distribution:
In Canada: Raincoast Book Distribution, Vancouver, B.C.
In Great Britain and Europe: Airlift Book Company, London

Editor's Acknowledgements

I have been inspired and encouraged by many people during the past two and a half years of gathering material for this anthology. It has been an honor and a pleasure to work with each of the contributors to this anthology. Each time I read their words and viewed their art I emerged feeling passionate about the importance of this work. I am grateful as well for their patient and good humored responses to my editorial requests.

I conceived this project following a conversation with Alice Miller. Her pioneering work on childhood and creativity has greatly influenced my thinking and commitment to the role of creativity in healing.

One hundred and sixty women bravely sent me their work in answer to my intial call for submissions — the range and depth of their work was a constant reminder of the power of creativity to transform both the creator and her audience. I am also grateful to the women I have seen as clients over the past twelve years as well as those in my workshops and healing through art groups. They continually remind me of the uniqueness of each woman's journey to reclaim herself from childhood sexual abuse. I thank all of these women for sharing with me their courage, wisdom and dedication to healing.

Laura Davis, Sandra Butler, Vickie Sears, Marguerita Donnelly, SDiane Bogus and Gallerie Publications were particularly helpful in assisting me in distributing my call for submissions.

Jane Klassen, Betsey Beckman, Sarah Herd, Helen Tevlin, Ginny NiCarthy, Ruth Crow, Gail Fairfield, Deb Clark and Cara Newoman gave me emotional support, laughter and timely good advice during this project. Marilyn Grey rented me a studio next door to my home, enabling me to move these many papers from the table and sofa of our one room house into a beautiful, peaceful place of their own.

The women at Seal Press have once again been wonderful to work with. Their enthusiasm and commitment to this project fueled my vision and gave the loose threads a form. My editor, Barbara Wilson, gave me much good help and wisdom at all stages of this work. Her sensitivity, humor and thoughtfulness were a great gift throughout our work together. I am thankful as well to Clare Conrad, the graphic design artist at Seal, for her many hours of viewing, reproducing and arranging the art that appears in this book. Meredith Waring did a fine job of copyediting the final manuscript as well.

Lastly, I thank my partner, Marianne Twyman, for her listening, hugging, patience, insight and love.

Louise M. Wisechild

Contents

Preface
Margaret Randall

It hasn't been that many years—ten?—five?—since incest was still the best-kept family secret. A taboo, they said. But should a practice so pervasive, that crosses the lines of class, race and culture, really be called a taboo? In fact, the taboo was the speaking out, the telling. Our patriarchal society still tries to protect the perpetrators of incest while ignoring, disbelieving or punishing the victims who dare to break the silence.

I say that our society still *tries* to protect the perpetrator because, although all the cultural and legal mechanisms of protection remain in place and most often continue to operate, many of us—in the great majority women—are reclaiming our memories and our power. Feminist theory and feminist therapy have created the context in which we can remember, speak, share and heal. It is out of this context that we have built such solid and supportive communities.

The title of this anthology is explicit: *She Who Was Lost Is Remembered: Healing From Incest Through Creativity*. The strong, healthy, whole, creative being who was lost by virtue of the crime committed against her, is remembered, reclaimed, found. Memory brings back the creative child, precursor to the creative adult. If creative power is crippled or lost through violation, it is unleashed through healing. And, not at all paradoxically, it also gives birth to creativity. The creative act is a healing experience for artist and viewer, writer and reader, singer and sung to.

Enforced silence has claimed so many unknown voices. The journey from silence into speech also breaks the barriers of shame. Shame is of course a constant in the life of the abused: *it was my fault . . . I asked for it (or liked it) . . . if I tell I will die . . . or mother will die . . . or the family will fall apart . . . or no one will believe me anyway. . . .*

So breaking through the shame demands and unleashes a tremendous creative energy. For many, survival itself is the creative act. For some—among them the women in this book—an artistic expression is freed, its subject matter often the very experience of incest or its healing.

Make no mistake. It is we who have created this context, this space, this community. And that in itself has been a monumental act of creativity. The Freudian psychiatrists and others who were there to help us survive (read: adapt) only pushed us deeper into the confusion which results from society's tolerance for and protection of the abuser. We were fantasizing, they said. We were confused. We were hysterical. We needed help. Theirs.

Our society is permeated, at every level, with this tolerance, this protection. Look for a moment at our wars of aggression. Vietnam. Nicaragua. Grenada. Panama. The Persian Gulf. Violation is the name of the game, aggression by the powerful against those with less power. What we are asked to accept, indeed be proud of at the national level, repeats itself on a reduced scale in the home, at school, on the street.

We have had to free ourselves from an abuse we were told did not take place, or in any case was "natural," "unavoidable," "just the way things are." And as with every struggle for freedom, we have done this step by step, piece by piece. There were the first voices, those courageous women who told their stories when no one believed them, simply because they had to. Surrounded by suspicion, if not outright hostility, they made our way easier. We heard them, and it helped us hear ourselves. Together, slowly, we created community, a safe place where we can articulate the horror, the fear, the anger—and the relief.

Anger. That's been an important piece. For when we are finally able to release the anger, when we can pronounce it and channel it—not against ourselves but against the perpetrators and the system that protects them—then we can begin to unleash that creativity stifled by fear. Misused power and control are always silencing forces. Rebellion frees the voice.

Naming is also essential in the creative act of healing. By naming the perpetrator, we strip him of his protection. We force him to accept responsibility for his abuse. And as with all true art, the work in this anthology is also and eloquently about naming.

It is important for us to understand how generations of (mostly) women have been silenced by being forced to "keep the secret." Protect the perpetrator. Maim and kill our own potential for expression. In a society in which credibility, prestige, protection is always on the side of the abuser, silence becomes one of the victim's survival tools. We may have *had* to remain silent in order to stay alive. But in our journey from victim to survivor, we have often had to take that which once enabled us to live and reconceptualize it as something to be broken through, a crutch from which we must liberate ourselves in order to take back our creative power.

The women in this book have taken the risk of this painful

but liberating step. What's more, they are willing to share with us the "story behind the story." In each essay there is a history, one of millions. With the women/artist/survivor who has broken her bonds, we are able to retrieve the memory, unfold the meaning, reclaim the self. And in each case the essay is followed by the work itself—a story, a poem or series of poems, a drawing. We hear the voices, see and touch the pain and power.

Because abuse is a silencing, and the reclaimed voice a shared strength, these last few years of incest work (personal and group therapy, the support structures, the workshops, the conferences and books) have included an increasing number of projects by artists and writers who are survivors. With our art we create a chain of experience; one voice is heard by another and urges that other to speak as well. A word, an image, a corporal movement—any and all of these may elicit recognition: *This also happened to me . . . this is my story too. . . .*

Most artists and writers who decide to go public with our story of abuse and healing face a double jeopardy: the initial pain of accepting a reality quite possibly hidden from our prior consciousness, and the pain that may come from family or friends when we insist upon splitting shame down the middle. We have exposed the family secret, "washed our dirty laundry in public," often forcing others to examine their own lives in ways they may not be ready or willing to endure.

But art moves reality into multidimensional realms. In a poem, image or song, *the truth* may acquire a life of its own. The expressive form touches us in ways an article or statistical analysis rarely can. This is the magic. This is what art is about.

This anthology is about women refusing to be silenced, fighting their way through shame, and using both sides of their history—the experience of violation as well as the journey of healing—in art fueled by contagious power. It is about memory, reclaimed and transformed. And it is about process, something to which women have always paid attention.

The *when* and *why* and the *how* and the *how difficult* can be found in the essays. The poetry and prose and the visual art offer up a product that is also, and powerfully, infused with process. The combination is a collection both immediate and far reaching. And this is a growing genre. One day it will be as basic a part of our literary canon as those *hundred great books*—so overrated but incomplete a part of the human experience.

Introduction
Louise M. Wisechild

Every incest survivor learned not to tell. We learned this in the midst of the most intimate violence delivered at the hands and whims of someone bigger and older than ourselves, someone whom we were supposed to have been able to trust.

In daring to tell, we tug at the roots of violence concealed in the mythology of the "perfect family." We confront, as women, what has made us feel helpless, isolated and wrong. As we tell, we speak the truths that have been neglected. In telling, we honor ourselves as women and girl-children.

Yet telling is a complex act. Healing requires more than an occasional sentence; it involves a commitment to ourselves, to the value of our voices and to the invention of ways of living and communicating that are a far cry from what we saw around us as children and from what most of us have lived with as adults. Healing is the task of creating ourselves.

In editing this anthology, I have witnessed the power of creativity to enable us, as survivors, to heal. Through creativity, we are able to go deeply into the difficult emotions we encounter on our journeys to reclaim ourselves. By creating from metaphor, memory and emotion, we are literally making something of our lives. We are taking our voices and our own stories seriously. Making art not only allows us to tell, but to create something new and strong from what was experienced when we were small. In addition, the poetry, drama, music and visual art that comes from this place of the personal has a rare power to move, validate and inspire others who witness it.

Many of the professional writers and artists in this book told me of the difficulty they had in finding publishers and galleries willing to publish or exhibit work on the subject of incest and abuse. They were told that their work was "too painful" and "too personal"—as if art came from a mysterious impersonal place that has little to do with the experience of the artist. In her book, *The Untouched Key: Tracing Childhood Trauma in Creativity and Destructiveness,* Alice Miller examines this myth by exploring childhood trauma in the lives of well-known artists. She suggests that artists are intuitively compelled to find an expression for what they were forbidden to speak as children. Yet, for the artists she cites, these childhood influences on their creativity were expressed unconsciously, without insight as to the connection between the content of their work and the experiences of their lives.

In compiling this anthology, I was interested in not only presenting the creative work of survivors, but also in hearing directly from these poets, visual artists, performers, writers and musicians about what they had discovered about the relationship between their art and their healing from childhood abuse. Work from all corners of the country as well as from other countries came in response to my call for submissions. I became known at my local post office as "the woman who gets all that mail."

I received packages of crayon drawings and poetry, sketches in pen and pencil, paintings, stories, performance pieces and music. Each with a story of abuse by fathers, uncles, brothers, stepfathers, mothers, baby-sitters, neighbors, preachers, teachers and cults.

I received work from women of all class backgrounds, religious upbringings and cultures, each one finding image and language to speak what was prohibited. Women such as Judy Grahn, Jacqueline Carr and Ayofemi Folayan who clung to creativity like a life-jacket through childhood. Women like Heidi Eigenkind, Vickie Sears and Julie Blackwomon, who reclaimed their creative voice after others tried to take their creativity from them. Women who fell into periods of silence and self-destruction, and then emerged into lives of tremendous creative energy like Roseann Lloyd, Linda Ness and Jena.

So it was that I read and re-read the work of these survivors: women finding voice in clay and ink, photographs and performance. Some days I was moved and inspired by the volume and honesty of this work. On other days I had to stop, to grieve and rage at the enormity of what has been done to us and the struggle to make ourselves whole. Yet always, when I returned, this work heartened and encouraged me.

In choosing work for this anthology, I looked for art and writing that reached below the surface to give voice to the complex emotions and experiences that incest survivors face. I wanted creative work that honestly confronted the reality of childhood. Work that spoke to the diversity of women's experiences—both in childhood and in recovery. I was interested in art that suggested metaphors and images which might lead us on this path of expressing and transforming our experience as incest survivors. Creative work that might validate and inspire other women by its truth, power and honesty.

I included work by women who define themselves as professional creative artists and those who do not. As Kim Newall said about working in a survivor-artist group, "We share similar issues even though we have different levels of experience with our craft." Yet I also looked for craft—for creativity involves revision and concentration; it entails a serious devotion to finding and experimenting with styles and developing meaning from layers of experience and metaphor. Creativity involves crafting a form to hold the intensity of experience. I looked for work that moved me, inspired me and made me look again. As Linda Ness says, work which "stops the eye and haunts the mind, until there is a spark of understanding."

So, slowly, I gathered together the work in this anthology. I came to see that even though the work represents a variety of creative media by women with diverse experiences, yet there are themes that underlie this expression.

I found that much of work, as Nancy Redwine says, took the survivors to "a place we cannot occupy without our bodies." Incest is violence perpetrated upon the body and healing often involves a physical reclaiming. Kim Newall, Katherine F. H. Heart and Laurie York talk about the bodily act of making visual art from their experiences. Judy Grahn, Debby Earthdaughter, Cheryl Marie Wade and Catherine Houser describe a process of finding words and images by working with the metaphors and symptoms of abuse they found by listening to their bodies. Other artists made their own body the focus of their art—such as the self-portrait work of Patti Levey and Laurie Williams's conscious transformation of her own appearance.

These women, as creative artists, also give voice to the experience of girl-children. Incest is an act perpetrated upon us as children. For too long, work about children has been sentimentalized and filtered through accepted adult standards that have little to do with the actual experiences of girls. In this collection, many women continue giving voice and image to their experience as children, refuting the myth that childhood is separate from our experience as adults, but is rather an ongoing part of who we are. These women honor this connection to she who is child in themselves. Judy Bierman writes poems with her left hand so that the child can speak through a hand that replicates the early awkwardness in learning to write. Beryl-Elise Hoffstein writes fiction about a child's experience being hospitalized because of abuse. Vickie Sears writes from a child's point of view in an orphanage. Becky Birtha writes a poem for her inner child titled, "You Are Not Broken." Janvier Rollande draws intricately detailed pencil portraits of herself and the child within her. In this work, these women not only speak for the child, but also reconnect with the creativity that is an integral part of childhood.

Some of the women in this book found that their creativity spoke in images and words they did not recognize as indicators of past abuse until years later. In this way, creativity often proceeds the process of memory and insight. "In my early art work there were signs of incest which I never really saw," Bonnie Martinez says. "I'm sure that all these images helped prepare me for the final realization of the terrible abuse that had been done to me as a child." Becky Birtha and Lynn Yamaguchi Fletcher both describe how their poetry leads them in their search to piece together their memory as they learn to listen and trust what their art tells them about themselves.

In this collection are also many stories of women who traded addiction and self-destruction for the paintbrush, the hammer and the pen. As these women speak in their work and their essays, they often describe an explosion of energy that compelled them to express what happened to them—even though confronting their memories was difficult, emotionally challenging and disruptive within the context of their lives. Still, as each woman followed her creative impulse, she found healing and a new home in her own expression.

In claiming this healing, survivors give voice to that which gives us inspiration and hope. Heidi Eigenkind chants, "What was taken from her is given back/ Her name is spoken/ Her deeds are recalled/ Her wounds are tended/ She is welcomed/ She is made whole."

Many women in this book invoke the power of the natural world, calling on the elements of fire, air, water and wind. From the natural world, where what is left of wildness grows unfettered, women claim the power of jellyfish, blackberry vines, mountains and lions. They make pictures of themselves giving birth to themselves. They paint and hammer and sculpt safe places so that we might see what safety looks like.

"I have heard my voice, my own voice defending me, so I can trust myself, more," Judy Grahn says about her experience in hearing her performance tape, *March to the Mother Sea,* on the radio. So do many of the women in this book speak not only of the connection between their own creativity and their personal healing, but also to their commitment in being public with this work; not only as individual artists, but in joining with other artists in group shows throughout the country. Lalla Lepeshkin tells of her experience in organizing two Recovery Shows in Santa Fe, New Mexico, of celebrating, "the release of our shame to a deeper healing and trust in our own being, our right to express. . . and to take up space in the world."

But the most remarkable feature of this work is the beauty and power that these women have fashioned from the horror and ugliness of incest. In their creativity, these women express their survival, strength and resilience even as they remember that which made them feel lost, defeated and helpless. This work encourages every survivor to reach for her crayons, paints, clay and pens. It reminds us that she who was lost returns to speak with a bold and impassioned voice that changes us as we create and as we witness the creative work of each other.

SHE WHO WAS LOST
IS REMEMBERED

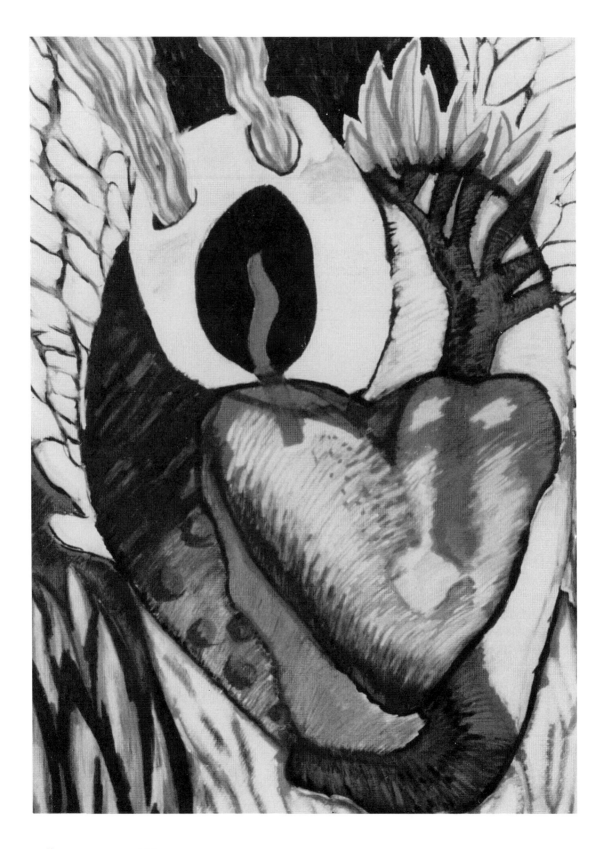

KIM NEWALL

My Body's Language

Kim Newall

A WAIST-HIGH RED brick wall runs horizontally across my upper back. It scratches my insides. Every muscle strand cinches tightly. Whenever I stand in a kitchen, any kitchen, doing dishes, I am afraid someone is approaching me from behind. My chest clenches into a knot. Breathing is no longer involuntary. I must consciously and with great effort force air in and out of my lungs.

Making art is escape, is retreat, is connection. Making art is to make a wall of my own to live behind, and making art is the ladder of connection over the wall.

I introduce you now to my right arm. It draws these pictures. It is an amazing part of my body and with it I have the most developed relationship that I have with any part of my body.

Along with memories, both visual and kinesthetic, I have these pictures. They document my healing process. They are my body's language of revelation. Altogether, the pictures I've drawn comprise my body of evidence indicting my father and all the others, known and unknown, for the incest, sexual assault and torture I was subject to as a child. I do not have video tapes or confessions to assist me in believing myself. I do have these pictures. They draw themselves through my right arm. They surprise and frighten me. Always they offer me a picture of my healing.

I have been remembering for over two years. I have had amnesia longer than I have had my memory and now I am beginning to have my body. Drawing is learning my body's language. My right arm bypasses the why and how of abuse, giving me the what: what happened to me, what it looks like inside my body, inside my pysche, what it did to me and what it looks like as it heals.

The pictures I draw surround me on the walls of my studio, in my bedroom and on the walls of the homes of the women I care for. I am in an old isolation when I make them, and they connect me to others who see them. As a child growing up, I always drew pictures. I filled notebooks with pictures of stories of men with

Left, *Passionate Angel,* 1988, 28″ × 35″, crayon on paper

guns and fists having adventures on horseback. I practiced anatomy, perspective, technique and composition as I pretended myself into powerful scenarios. I rarely used color. Through the act of drawing, I created a world to live in and I created myself as an artist. It was the act that anchored me to my daily life. I had a place to put myself, a nurturing prison.

Creativity seeks its own truth, like water finding a crack, cracking the rock, prying secrets, finding the core to release the power of a woman, of me. Holding and hiding secrets had hardened me into an inability to expose. The creative waters travel throughout my body, collecting my stories and revealing them to me. My pictures tell the secrets and dissolve their power to silence me.

My body, my experience, my courage and my drive to make something from, and in response to my life come together in an act of translation and evolution. I piece together the legend of my life from an aerial view of where I've been, where the rivers of my life originate, and the course to my destination. To be carried to such a height is the emergence of the observer. The observer is the part of myself who watches my evolution without interference. She is compassion toward myself and self-empathy. The observer allows my visual images to come forth uncensored. She then carefully deciphers and translates them with the help of inner voices who come into existence via specific, often traumatic events. Her listening ear invites these voices to speak.

The Liar sits next to me as I write this essay. The Liar is me at seven years of age. Her backside is the wall. She is unclothed and it is dark, wet and cold. At seven she has mastered the split between what is hidden "back there" and the unreachable future "out there." She is never fully either place. She is stuck in-between the two worlds I live in. She protects the secrets of the unseen side.

The Liar puts on a good front of confidence and capability. She is my father's safety. She is my mother's ignorance. She is the gatekeeper of the confused mind. She protects me from knowing the truth that would split me open: the integration that would kill me. The Liar speaks to me:

You don't know anything. You write from no place where no one else was and you were not seen there. Every word you write will make you more invisible. Though your body tells you its truth, I will make it unrecognizable by laughing at you. I can confuse you because you know I know what happened, yet what I am telling you is that nothing happened. I am your body protecting your mind. As you try to dissolve the wall I have created, you seek to split me into the parts I am made of, destroying me. I won't let you do this. I am the combination of you and your father.

My Father's Two Selves and Me Makes Two, 28" × 40", crayon on paper

The Liar stands behind me anytime I do dishes in anyone's kitchen. The Liar is my father. His hands are so large and mine so small that both my wrists are held in the vise of his thumb and forefinger. By the time my wrists are too big for this grip, he no longer needs it. I know how to remove my pants, underpants, socks and shoes in one fast gesture of submission and compliance. As a thirty-one-year-old woman I still undress this way. I stop breathing as I do it.

As I talk to the Liar, pains shoot down my right arm and I am unable to grip anything. In writing this essay, I have forgotten my pictures. There exists an uncomfortable relationship between my self and my pictures. The Liar discounts my body's stories, the body of evidence made by my right arm. The words used by the Liar to confuse me, designed to undermine self-belief, are stronger than the silent imploring images that picture my truth. So specific and symbolic, so quiet, my pictures don't yell at me the way the Liar does. It is the difference between a still, silent child whose body, face and posture say all that is needed, and the talking, yelling adult whose descriptions and justifications create a reality no one questions. The lying voice is louder than my pictures. Do I trust the silence in which my pictures are seen and heard? I am choosing to believe the child, to believe my silent screaming pictures that demand the space of how my truth looks.

I am beginning to understand my process of disbelief. I begin a dialogue with the Liar:

"What is your pain?"

"You seek to split me apart and destroy me."

"Don't you have two parts? Aren't you leaving the scared part behind?"

"I am powerful in the secrets I maintain."

"Your smiles and smugness belong to him."

"Who is he?"

"Our father. He carries a sickness. He deposited it into us."

"We were available and we belong to him. We reminded him of himself."

"I am me."

"You keep his secret."

"I choose."

I remind the Liar: "He chose us. You were a little girl who could hide your fear. He thought girls were easier to destroy."

"Not in my case."

"You were very strong but you had no choice. Now you can tell your whole story."

"No one to tell."

"Tell me. I can bring you back from there. Your strength can now come from the full knowledge of what you have survived. This is how you can grow up, detach your backside from the wall. Do you trust me to hear your stories?"

"You sometimes don't believe me."

"Do you ever embellish the truth of your experiences for sympathy or self-pity?"

"I can barely tell you the truth." My father begins to separate from the entity of my seven year old.

I live inside a wall. The wall is my body. The Liar has emerged in dialogue because of my intention to dissolve the wall. The wall divides the split between the daytime self my mother

saw and the truth I lived with my father. I float inside the wall suspended in numbness. The thickness of the wall extends just beyond my outstretched arms, expanding and contracting with the perceived safety of my immediate environment.

The length of the wall extends along the trajectory of my body's movement. It traces every place I've ever been. It snakes together all the images of all the events that occurred in every location occupied by my body at every age. Different parts of me live in sections of the wall. The Liar lives in the section now in the process of dissolving. The sections vary in length and density, depending on what is held in the stones of the wall. The stones hold stories. They release their images, sounds and body sensations when conditions are right. The insistent waters of creative and healing intention split them open.

From left to right: *Inner Narrative,* 1, 2 and 3, 1988, 20″ × 30″, woodcut

The wall came into existence to ensure dis/integration. To consciously know both the abuse at night and the liar-rapist father I lived with during the day would have destroyed me. Now I can choose to integrate the two parts of my life as a child. This means the revolution of the function of the wall. It must now disintegrate so that I can become whole. I do this slowly, section by section. So many stones, holding so many stories. The gatekeepers of each section protect the stories and I, the observer of myself, approach cautiously so as not to re-abuse myself. To try dissolving the sections quickly would destroy the parts of me that insured my survival. These parts of me—the Liar, the Grave-Seed Self and the Psychic Self—are my self-knowing, the wisdom I have from what happened to me.

The wall served as a nurturing prison. Within it, I survived, became an artist. The wall served as a separation from an incomprehensible reality. Love and hatred couldn't live above ground together in such close proximity. I could drop into the center of the wall like a lead seed when I was being raped. In this deep place, I am so small that I am surrounded by miles of dark, safe space. No one can touch me there. When I am there, no other part of me exists and I am safe and alone, even though I am actually in much danger without protection. This part I call the Grave-Seed Self. It is a self that came out of a place. It is a place like death.

I am the seed in the bottom center of the picture entitled *Psychic Self Floating in the Insulation of the Grave-Seed Self.* Originally my intention was to draw the vast distance between the Grave-Seed Self and the surface of my body. The wrapped shapes at the top of the picture are my fingers. When I become tiny (as I still occasionally do), my hands become numb and I could drive a truck through the hugeness of each finger. During the making of this picture, a face drew itself in between my tinyness and the surface of my body: as though all that space gave birth to a new part of me. I recognized this face. It would sometimes float behind my eyes during meditation and would show me the past or future if my questions were apropriate and specific enough, and if I had time to listen. This self, called Psychic Self, evolved out of a vast inner space of retreat—the insulation of the inner wall. There is a great silence in numbness, and this part can hear with its eyes in complete darkness.

Making images of the devastation of child-rape and torture is currently the content of my work. Looking at and evolving from the events in my past, showing my inner life to others is the intention and context of my work. Making with my hands is the water that sustains me, that keeps me from drying out. It moves over what I do and do not yet know, combining the two, growing me green. Making pictures and sculpture, and writing give expression and outlet to the intense approach to life my body was born with. Making art is also the expulsion of the poison deposited into my body by my father and others. My father's words created imaginary pictures he called reality, and these pictures were like a quickly growing weed, spreading over the surface of my life, of my body, to choke me, to make me ground for him instead of a self of my own. I externalize the effects of the poison, so the weeds don't grow huge.

Why undergo the process of re-memory? Walking along in my life, I found myself continually tripping on unseen roots. Intimate relationships caused a panic of life-and-death-proportions. I panicked whenever I entered a roomful of people or any unfamiliar place. Tripping over and over in the same places, I looked

Psychic self floating in the insulation of the grave-seed self, 1988, 28″ × 40″, crayon on paper

down. I strained my eyes. I saw exposed roots and decided to follow them down to an underground place that wanted to speak. An insistent voice sent the root above ground to find me and bring me back to the source of my tripping. Buried alive where the roots originate are abandoned parts of myself, parts I left behind when I exited my body for safety, when I identified with the abusers instead of myself. Some parts lie horizontal, some wander empty places, finding safety in the isolation of my deserted past, unreachable except by my desire to return and my intention to heal.

Why remember when it is so painful and disruptive? Because of the insistent roots tripping me, turning into the hands of my younger selves, grabbing at my ankles, sending their screams up from under my feet. The ground is never still enough for me to relax. I walk with the perpetual sense that I am walking all over myself, stepping on my own reaching-out hands, snapping finger bones. The pain inspires me to the effort of reclamation. I reach my hands down and pull myself up. I learn to hold myself.

First Person, Present Tense: Writing as an Act of Faith

Marie-Elise Wheatwind

I AM FOUR YEARS old. *My brother has taken the yellow school bus to kindergarten, my aunt is doing the breakfast dishes and I have decided it's time for me to learn how to read. I know that words on the page hold wonderful stories, because I've heard my aunt read them aloud to me. I also know that my aunt's magical glasses are a necessary part of understanding how these mysterious words work. So I go to my aunt's sewing room and find her reading glasses, then put them on. They make everything bigger, which makes perfect sense to me: It means that their magic is working, even though the glasses hardly fit my small face. But when I hold them over the morning newspaper, and then try to look through them at some of my aunt's storybooks, the glasses do not seem to help me read. I try several more books, and then finally take off the glasses and scrutinize them. They are thick and scratched, and they have a horizontal crack in the center of each oval lens. No wonder I can't read with these, I think. They're broken. Their magic has escaped through these cracks.*

I take the glasses, the newspaper and some matches out to the brick incinerator at the far end of my aunt's garden and make a fire. It is a glorious fire, which momentarily takes my mind completely off my failed attempt to read. I am held spellbound by the heat and glow of the flames until my aunt finds me, spanks me unmercifully and hauls me into the house. Later she finds me in whatever chair or corner I've been installed in, and she shakes two pieces of glass at me, their plastic frames melted, their horizontal cracks gray with ash. She threatens a new beating, demanding an explanation. I tell her the truth. For this I am rewarded, that very afternoon, with my first reading lesson.

My aunt's motivations for teaching me to read were no doubt selfish. I was a curious and mischievous child, a "holy terror," my aunt called me. She was an older woman robbed of a peaceful retirement by the inquisitive energy of two small children. Giving me books to read kept me occupied, quiet and content for hours. But books also gave me worlds beyond the small world of my aunt's garden, and later they were a means for escaping and surviving far worse punishments than my aunt's scoldings and spankings.

When I was five and my brother was six, we went to live for the first time with my mom, her new husband and our little sister. I started school then, going straight into first grade since I could already read and write, in both English and Spanish. I must have decided pretty early that I was going to be a writer; I published my first poems in the school newsletter when I was in the third grade. Later, at a different grammar school, I wrote for the school gazette, and in the sixth grade I wrote a two-act play about a pioneer family. When my teacher, Miss Miller, decided to produce this play (complete with a one-room cabin that we built in our bungalow as a stage set), my heart was set on playing the female lead. This part was given to April Fernandez, a shy but beautiful classmate who no one could possibly hate, least of all me. So I wrote an additional part for my play: the narrator. And since I was the only one who knew her words, I was allowed to chatter to my heart's content on our small dusty stage.

During those grammar-school years, I lived in two different worlds, or time zones. There was school, and there was home. At school I believed I was smart, that I could do anything. This is not to say I was an "A" student. I worked hard at the subjects that interested me and made a barely passing effort in classes I didn't like. Nevertheless, my teachers took the time to praise and encourage my writing and thinking, while my parents made me feel no matter how hard I tried, I would never be good enough.

At school I was an average, normal child, small for my age, with a few close friends. At home my role was never clearly defined, and changed on demand. I was always expected to obey and respect my elders. To my unpredictable mother, or an alcoholic neighbor, or visiting relatives, or constantly changing babysitters, I was alternately wicked, or a blessing, or a plaything, or a co-conspirator. As I grew older, expectations merged into accusations and then assumptions. Through all this, I somehow managed to believe in myself, but I also believed in my inherent worthlessness.

I am twelve, almost thirteen. It is summer. My mother has packed my things suddenly and is taking me the twenty-odd miles across town to stay with my grandparents. My great-grandmother is bedridden and sick, so I am going to help my grandmother take care of her. I don't mind any of this; I love my grandparents and look forward to the time I will have alone with them. My mother leaves after having coffee with Gram, but calls a few hours later to say she is coming to get me. She has found a diary that I had abandoned, and after reading about my fantasy boyfriend and an imagined first kiss, she has decided I don't deserve to stay there.

We drive in the hot Los Angeles smog downtown, into a neighbor-

hood I don't recognize. We park on South Arlington, near Pico and Wilshire Boulevards, and walk up concrete steps into a building that has been there for at least a century. My mother has brought me to the Convent of the Good Shepherd. She asks to see Sister Saint Germaine, the Mother Superior. I am surprised that this nun and my mother know each other. To my knowledge, my mother has never set foot inside any church. My mother reminds the Mother Superior of her stay there when she was sixteen, but the kind-faced, elderly nun waves aside my mother's appeals to leave me here now. Instead, she chastises my mother for not looking out for my emotional and spiritual well-being.

Walking back to the car, my mother hisses that I'm obviously "too far gone" to stay with the nuns. When she accuses me of cheap and loose behavior, I refuse to defend myself. I know that nothing I could say would change her opinion of me. We drive in angry silence back to my grandparents'. She leaves me there once again, giving them strict instructions about my curfews and privileges. I wait for days for a time when I can be alone, unwatched and unsupervised. When the opportunity arrives late one afternoon, I rip my diary to shreds, then use an entire box of fireplace matches to burn the pages and scorch the clothbound cardboard cover. I sweep the ashes into a paper bag and stuff the bag into the trash can. I vow never to keep a diary again. It is a promise that I keep for over ten years.

In high school, I took the required literature classes, plus electives like journalism, Shakespeare, art and creative writing. The creative writing teacher was a young woman in her early twenties who had graduated from UCLA with master's degrees in both literature and psychology. I don't remember how I found this out, but it was important to me.

My teacher's name was Jann Lobenstein. In my three years in high school, I was in seven of her classes and often ate my lunches in her room as well, ostensibly to do homework, or to work on the school literary magazine with members of the Writers' Club. This was the mid-sixties, and education in the L.A. city schools was probably at a liberal peak as far as progressive ideas or relaxed standards were concerned. We addressed some of our teachers by their first names and occasionally arrived late or missed classes altogether without penalty, as long as we showed up with creative work or a creative excuse for the time not spent in the classroom. But more often than not, I was in class. I would share the surreal images from the landscapes of my dreams, and Jann would interpret them matter-of-factly, with uncanny intuition.

Most of my efforts in creative writing classes were poems: first person, unrhymed, unpunctuated attempts at insight or introspection. Required prose or short story assignments were often dashed off during boring lectures in other classes, in bright-colored inks, and slipped into Jann's "In" box after school the day they were due. It's a telling fact that in the seven classes I took with Jann, I always received "B's" from her on my semester report cards. "I know you're capable of so much more than this," she often wrote on my papers.

One short story that I wrote then stands out clearly in my memory. It was written in third person and was about a girl who was about to graduate from high school. She has decided to run away from home, and as she packs the few books and clothes she intends to take with her, she unpins posters and photos and poems from her walls. Then she discovers scenes from her childhood that suddenly appear on the walls as if they are projected onto giant movie screens. She decides she does not want to leave these images up on the walls for anyone to see once she's gone. But each time she successfully peels one of these scenes away, it is replaced by a different, older scene. The box of things she has packed soon becomes buried under layers of ripped wallpaper—pointillist puzzle pieces, like large grainy blow-ups of black-and-white photographs of her life. When the walls start to reveal obscene pictures, she fears her family or friends suddenly will barge in before she can destroy them, and she panics. She sets fire to the piles of paper in the center of the room and watches mesmerized as everything burns, realizing as the flames destroy her past that she has nothing to take with her, and nowhere to go but through those flames to the door that opens out into her uncertain future.

I was terrified to share this story with my classmates, afraid they wouldn't understand it and even more afraid they would understand it, and would demand more details from me, more descriptions of the things that I didn't want everyone to see. But my classmates were incredibly gentle with me and managed to fill the entire class period with a discussion that always referred to my character as "she," never once suggesting that "she" was me. It would be years before I would find the words that would link that validating experience to what I knew I still needed.

I am twenty-three years old, my son is almost two, and I have just run away from my marriage. We are living in a small converted garage next to the railroad tracks on the west side of Santa Barbara. I write every day in a journal, not for literary reasons, but because I think I am crazy, and I think by recording my various mood swings or studying the differences in handwriting, I will be able to prove not only my suspicions, but the intimations of others as well. I've been told I will turn out "just like my mother," who has been in and out of mental health care programs for years now.

I have started therapy for the third time in as many months, trying to find someone I can trust, trying to feel comfortable with the process of re-vealing intimate secrets about myself to a qualified expert. This time I am in group therapy, attempting to "work things out" with my ex-husband, two hip psychologists named Al and Eleanor, and a dozen troubled strangers. We sit on paisley pillows in a brightly painted room and talk about "what's happening" with our feelings. There is abstract art on the walls by Al and Eleanor's former clients. The sessions always feel inter-minably long to me. After one of the sessions, Al approaches me as I'm putting on my hiking boots and tells me he really wants to hear more from me in the group.

"The beauty of this space is that it gives you a safe environment in which to say anything you want," he says to me in a reassuring voice.

"Maybe I just need to listen for a while," I reply.

He thinks about this for a moment and is reminded of a quiet young friend of his adolescent daughter.

"I'm sure she must be learning a lot just by listening to us," he muses. "In fact, my daughter told me that her friend had never heard an adult use the word 'fuck' in everyday conversation before meeting us," he laughs incredulously. "Can you imagine? I told her she's free to use any four-letter words around us that she wants. They are not dirty words in our house."

"And has she?"

"Oh no!" he laughs again. "The more I say 'fuck' around her, the more shocked she becomes. It will take her a while before she accepts that it's just a word, and nothing to be afraid of." He gives me a philosophical shrug, and is about to turn away, when I suddenly become angry.

"What if she doesn't want to accept it as just a word?"

Al raises one eyebrow in surprise, and before he can respond I say in a rush, "I mean, what if the word already has its own meaning for her, and what if hearing it makes her think of what she thinks 'fuck' is, instead of what it doesn't mean to you? Do her feelings count?"

Al has apparently never considered this, and from out of nowhere, Eleanor appears saying, "Of course her feelings count, and perhaps what you've just shared with Al tells him something she might never have said herself."

I decide that day to drop out of the group and start seeing Eleanor alone. She works intensely with me for almost three years, doing art ther-apy, hypnosis and body work, all the while encouraging me to write.

While in therapy, I started attending the local community col-lege, taking general undergraduate requirements and English classes. I was often required to keep a journal for the English classes, but I didn't write about my daily life and feelings. I re-corded my son's dreams and conversations, described the sunlight through the curtains, responded to the books I was reading, delighted or despaired over whomever I was currently in love with, and reassured myself, over and over, that I was not crazy and that I was not going to fail in reaching any of my goals. The writing in my journals became a testament of my faith in myself, of the life I had chosen to live.

I wrote believing that someone was listening to every word I said, and that listener believed in me, without judgment or reservation. I wrote as if my life depended upon it, and often it did. When I joked in my journal about "being too busy to commit suicide," my feelings resurfaced later in a poem, offering "Advice" to others who might feel the same way. When I felt overwhelmed with responsibilities, isolated and alone, I tried to write about the other side of that loneliness: the peace and calm that comes from solitude. "Graveyard Shift" is a short short story that attempts to establish how the everyday routine of one's life can also be a ritual in the process of healing. It "recovers" one of the important aspects of that time in my life: to be able to leave a letter or journal out on the table, and come home later to find it undisturbed, and to feel safe as a result of that simple act.

Now, at forty, I feel I am just beginning to deal with my life as a whole. I remember as a teenager hearing people say, "Child abuse and sexual abuse have lifelong repercussions for the victim." Knowing my own history of abuse, I listened, but defiantly thought, "Not me. I'm going to put my experiences behind me and get on with my life and not let it get to me." And in some ways, I did put the abuse behind me, conveniently blacked it out from my memory and got on with my life.

But the repercussions were still there, lurking in the shadows. Who I am is forever linked to how I have been treated, and has affected my ability to trust and choose friends, my sexual relationships and my self-esteem. For a time, it made me dependent on drugs and alcohol.

Who I am today is also shaped by words—not only the written words that provided me with imaginary landscapes and fictional friends, but also the unspoken words of my experience. These were words that were discounted, ignored, used against me or never shared to begin with. So I write, still hesitantly, about my feelings and experiences, not only for the listener who believes in me, but for those who may feel ashamed or afraid or unwilling to speak for themselves. I write to you, and for you, as an act of faith. I believe you have survived, like me, for a reason. I believe that our lives belong to us now, and we will make the best of this life, in spite of everything.

Living Hand-to-Mouth

The deaf say it best without words. Fingertips to lips, palm cradling an ear: eat and sleep, sign language for home. For me, there's no place to go back to. They're all dead, anyway: ashes scattered over an ocean slick with oil, thick with trash. And what could they tell me, if they were still here? Just the same old thing. I was a mistake. My father, that handsome Mexican bastard, left my mother with a three-month-old son, and me on the way. Left her ten dollars to get an abortion. Imagine, my aunts and grandparents would all say. Then mother would strike her best Joan Crawford pose. She had me anyway. And I'm not the least bit grateful.

We lived hand-to-mouth. You know what that means? Not just the backslap sting for sassing, but also the wrist grabbed to put it back. On payday the money went fast: There was food on the table and fruit in the bowl, but you couldn't ask if friends could have some. What there was had to last. So you learned not to bring anyone home. You kept silent when your friends were called no-good, worthless, a bad influence. If you tried to escape, the blame would shift and you'd be thrown in with them, nameless: cheap, slut, bitch, whore. Deny any of it and they'd call you a liar, the oldest four-letter word in the book.

One of my aunts liked to tell this story in Sunday School: Jesus was traveling along with all his groupies, and the crowd was getting out of hand. He wanted to weed out all the starfuckers from the true blues. (Okay, so she didn't tell it exactly the way I'm telling it.) But anyway, Jesus comes to this river and says, "Drink up, it's a long dry road ahead." He watches as the princes on their high horses order their handmaidens to dip silver chalices and bring water back to them. We know how far they'll go. Then Jesus watches as others, eager to please, throw themselves on the shore, lapping at the water like dogs, muddying their clothes. This isn't going to help his reputation, hanging out with dumb slobs. Then his chosen ones go to the water's edge and kneel. They cup their hands, dip them into the water and bring their makeshift vessels to their mouths, drinking their fill. I never understood the point of this parable. The aunt who told this story left her alcoholic husband and then killed herself. And we all know where Jesus ended up.

I'll tell you what living hand-to-mouth really means. He opens his pants and hands it to you. You open your mouth. This is not a pretty story. There's no happy ending. By the time you take your hand away from your mouth to say "No," or "Goodbye," there's no one but yourself to spit at. Once he's done, it's over; you're good at keeping quiet. But either way, you know he'll be back.

The Babysitter
a fragment from a work in progress

"You can choose the pictures this time."

It had been weeks since he'd brought out the picture box, so I'd forgotten how many things were in there. Not just photographs of men and women with no clothes on. There were flip books you could flutter to make an animated hand move; up and down on a man's penis. John said these were called "jack-off books." There were cartoons, just like the ones in the Sunday funnies, only these comics showed Mickey Mouse putting his penis up Minnie's dress, or Blondie on her knees, sucking ice cream off Dagwood's enormous prick.

My brother and I had laughed the first time he'd shown these to us.

"Oh, nasty," we had said. I understood then why we had to wait till after my little sister's bedtime to be allowed this secret privilege.

"This is what your mommy and daddy do in bed," our babysitter had told us. At first it had been hard to believe, but my brother convinced me.

"Just listen," my brother had whispered to me. "That's how they make the bed squeak."

Tonight John was letting me look in the picture box all by myself. He had given my brother two magazines, which he wouldn't let me see, and had chased him off to bed. I was sitting in front of the forbidden, late-night TV, hours past my bedtime.

"Go ahead," he'd said. "You know you want to."

He was right. I felt curious, mischievous. I wanted to know all the adult secrets, to understand now what I was told I wouldn't understand until I was older. He let me leaf through the box for quite awhile, until the late hour or the sameness of the photos made me feel bored, tired.

"Where's my goodnight kiss?" he'd asked when I finally decided to go to bed. He was sitting on one of the bar stools, a mock look of rejection in his eyes. I let him pull me onto his lap, and I ran my hands through his hair as he bent forward slightly for our ritual kiss. I always pretended I was an actress in a mushy movie, but John knew I was just practicing for the real thing, with someone my own size, my own age. After all, John was over six feet tall, and I was only ten.

Soon the pictures were supplemented by games. We all took

turns modeling my mother's lace bras and garter belts. John did it the best, prancing around in her high heels, bending forward so we could see the apples or oranges concealed in her "D" cups. He swung his blue-jeaned hips at us and snapped the elastic garters loudly as he imitated Betty Boop. We laughed and screamed.

Later at night, when John and I played alone, I was given more choices.

"We could do this," he'd say, selecting a few photographs, "or I can do this to you, or you could do this to me. . . . " I may have started off saying "no" to all his suggestions, but eventually I remember feeling curious, and then trapped. We were locked in the bathroom. He was leaning against the door.

"Don't you want to pet my friend?" he'd asked me one night. He was always playful and quiet, caressing me with an unfamiliar gentleness. Sometimes his hands would massage me until I became flushed, breathless. But when I refused to let him take my clothes off, he always stopped, saying, "I don't want to force you to do anything you don't want to do, but you could do something nice to me. . . . "

One time he sat me down and opened his pants in front of my face. He'd put something on the end of it. Was it cough syrup? It was sticky and sweet; maybe it was jam or chocolate syrup from the kitchen.

"Lick it off." His hands showed me where to put my hands, to keep him from choking me, but still he pushed his body toward me, moving in and out of my mouth. And then he would whisper things: that he liked me, that it felt good, I was so nice, he was almost done, it wouldn't take long. It was no use trying to move my head to the side to get away from him. His hands would cradle my face, even after he'd pulled out and pressed against my pajama top. Or if he'd turned away to spill himself into the sink, loud and streaming with running water, he'd just as quickly turn back toward me, smoothing my hair, zipping himself up, saying softly, "I like you. I'm sorry if I hurt you. Here. Let me get you something nice to drink. . . . "

Graveyard Shift

You do what you can to stay awake those last few hours. The bar rush always puts you into high gear: They come in all at once, taking up every booth and stool, each one expecting you to fill his cup first. Some of them order bacon and eggs, or something to soak up the booze in their blood; chicken-fried steak, patty melts, bar-b-que beef. You work fast and friendly, coffee pots in both hands, menus under one arm, water pitcher ready to grab. You've stocked the station with a stack of filters, premeasured full of coffee, but they always drink it faster than you can switch pots. You give smiles to the ones who are patient, brisk service to those who are are loud, demanding, obnoxious.

Sometimes a booth will stay awhile, filling the ashtrays three or four times, writing poems and drawing roses on the napkins, or making bets off the serial numbers of one dollar bills. But one by one they eventually pay up, throw some change on the table and drag themselves home to their old ladies or greasy magazines.

Then you let out a sigh and start your side work: topping the sugars, salts and peppers; shining and filling the napkin dispensers, pouring the ketchups together, cleaning their lips and caps with hot water from the kitchen. The cook makes you something on the sly and you eat it standing up, watching the door for early risers or late drivers. You can hear the dishwasher's radio turned up high, almost drowning out the muzak that plays over and over, night after night.

Somewhere around 4:30 a.m. you feel like the only soul awake, which you know isn't so. You can hear the cook scraping grease off the grill, but you've got your back to the shiny stainless of his food counter. Your eyes stare back from one of the booth's black windows, tired, wary, alone.

By 5:30, the morning regulars start drifting in with the rising sun: postal workers, policemen, bus drivers. Some of them don't have to say a word. They give you a nod or throw the cook a look, and then wait for you to bring them their coffee, their eggs sunny side up or poached light on wheat toast. They leave their bills on the counter and don't bother telling you to keep the change.

Finally the morning girls come in, clucking about the cold, grabbing for the coffee pot, tossing jokes over their shoulders at the "breakfast chef." You punch your time card, pull handfuls of change from your pocket, throw the coins in a pouch in your knapsack, find your coat and keys and walk the five blocks to your apartment. It's past dawn. The light is creamy yellow. There is an occasional car or a paper boy on a whizzing ten-speed, but the streets are safe. You feel good. The brisk cold snaps you awake. You take long strides, walking the straight line toward your locked place, your own haven.

You've left lights on, or the clock radio has clicked on in the kitchen, just loud enough to sound normal, homey. The cats cry to be fed, rubbing back and forth against your legs. You take off the apron, the uniform, your slip, all smelling of sweat, grease, cigarettes. You throw them in the hamper and make sure the bathroom door is locked before you peel off your pantyhose, underwear, bra. The water is hot by now, steaming up the mirror, so you step into the shower and scrub your face, your shoulders, your armpits, your breasts. You adjust the spray to needle sharp and soap yourself again while the water massages your neck and back. The towels are soft and slightly damp from the steam when you finally reach for them, dripping clean, relaxed and sleepy.

Hanging from a hook are your favorite clothes: some well-worn corduroys, or for today, your faded jeans, button-fly, narrow-legged and snug, but not too tight. Just soft enough to be comfortable. You pull on a cotton tank-top, and over that, a sweatshirt. Then you unroll a pair of cotton socks over each foot.

You drift tiredly to your room, with its small altar of seashells, rocks and dried flowers on the windowsill, and its narrow bed. Morning light filters through the thin white curtains. You part them slightly to allow the sun to hit the crystal prisms hanging on strings from the ceiling. On the table next to your bed are some books, your journal, some letters to answer. You often turn to them in this early quiet, but this morning your bones feel too heavy for the chair, your eyelids droop, your arms couldn't lift the pen.

So you throw yourself on the bed and pull a faded quilt around you. Here and there on the wall and ceiling, vivid crescents of color dance and scan as the prisms turn and catch the light. The cats curl at your side. Hours from now they might leap to the floor when the doorbell or phone rings, but you'll be dressed and ready for anything. For now, all you want is to surrender to the rock hard sleep of no dreams.

She Who Was Lost Returns

Heidi Eigenkind

A SENSE OF MY Self* as writer is something I've gained through a long and gruesome struggle with inner echoes of my father-rapist's voice. There have been times when my sense of desolation was unbearable, when I wanted to die in order to escape these echoes and my own impossible need to write. There were years when I wrote one or two poems. Most of the time, I couldn't write at all. Diary entries, attempts to record dreams or the details of my life were beyond me. I'd sit at my desk and feel my father's cock in my throat. I'd hear his voice inside my skull lacerating me in a German I no longer spoke, for my laziness, my weak will, my stubbornness, my decadence. I left my father's house over twelve years ago. Only in the last two years have I believed I am a writer.

I have memories of drawing as a child, and my mother once told me that she and my father couldn't keep me in paper. That two working-class immigrants would buy paper for their child still astounds me. But my father learned about culture (*Kultura*) from his fellow inmates—upper- and upper-middle-class Nazi officers—in a P.O.W. camp. He must have decided that drawing was a harmless and laudable activity for a young child.

For most of my childhood, I wanted to be an artist, especially after winning a year of free art classes in grade four. My art instructor was awful, but I was able to see a traveling exhibition of van Gogh's paintings. I vowed to dedicate my life to art after that. The harshness of van Gogh's life and his early suicide didn't deter me; my life was already hard, and I knew what wanting to die felt like. Art offered me purpose and hope.

My father allowed me the luxury of art until he realized the depth of my passion for it. Then, as always, he worked to destroy my exuberance, my spirit. By the time I was in high school, he had won. I no longer conceived of my Self as an artist. That was

---

* My use of "Self" is informed by Mary Daly's definition of this term as "the Original core of one's be-ing that cannot be contained within the State of Possession." *Webster's First New Intergalactic Wickedary of the English Language* (Boston: Beacon Press, 1987) p. 95.

for others; for people who were stronger, more talented and free of an endless, vicious battle to keep some part of their Selves intact. Art was not for the working class, was not for my father's daughter, was not for me.

I've drawn on and off all my life. In high school and university, I drew only occasionally. I no longer believed in what I drew. I did it because I had to, now and again. I moved more and more into words. Books had always offered me escape, and as I grew older teachers no longer echoed my grade five teacher's condemnation of me as illiterate. I began to be praised for my writing. My father raged against the library books I brought home (mostly fiction) and later against my decision to pursue an English Honors degree. But this time I persisted.

As an adolescent, I had discovered the secret of words: You could hide them in your head and no one need know. Only if you wrote things down was there any evidence. I made sure to write down only what my teachers requested. Later, I let myself write poems, but I hid them in my notebooks.

I escaped my father's death-grip when I was twenty-five. I left his house, the house in which he had continued to abuse me until months before my departure. It was my third attempt at leaving, and this time, with my lover's support, I succeeded. I had no blank spots, no missing memories, or so I thought. All the poetry I wrote was about incest. At first metaphorically. Later directly. Time and again over the next ten years, I utilized various therapies to explore the territories of my childhood, adolescence and early adulthood. Each time, I traveled deeper. In 1987, I once again entered therapy. I felt hopeless and out of control. On walks to and from work, oncoming traffic enticed me. I fantasized walking into a field of snow and freezing to death. It was a harsh, early winter. All I wanted was to die. Instead, I sought out a woman who could help me re-enter my body. I had done talk therapy many times. I knew that if I didn't find someone to help me do this work I would soon kill myself. I was thirty-five.

After a few sessions with this therapist, I went home and drew. All I had was typing paper and an old set of Laurentian colored pencils. I felt ten years old and hummed as I did my first drawing in more than a decade. A few months later, I began to draw in earnest. I drew almost every day. Some days, I did five, even six drawings. They were all about incest. They all had words on them. At first, I wrote captions, then brief stories, then extensive texts. Voices surfaced in the texts—the voices of child selves. Many of them. They told me stories about my body. About how I had survived what my father had done to me. I found gaps in my memory.

I entered places inside me I couldn't have imagined. I remem-

SHE WHO WAS LOST
IS RE-MEMBERED

SHE WHO WAS LOST
RETURNS
SHE WHOSE BODY WAS BROKEN
WHO WAS FED TO THE FIRE
WHO DIED UNATTENDED
BY ANY WHO KNEW HER
RETURNS

WHAT WAS TAKEN FROM HER
IS GIVEN BACK
HER NAME IS SPOKEN
HER DEEDS ARE RECALLED
HER WOUNDS ARE TENDED
SHE IS WELCOMED
SHE IS MADE WHOLE

THOSE
WHO FORGOT HER
CHANT HER BACK
INTO BEING
THOSE
WHO FORGOT HER
CHANT HER
HOME

SHE
WHO WAS
LOST
WEEPS
SHE WHO WAS LOST
RAGES
SHE WHO WAS LOST
REJOICES

SHE
WHO
WAS LOST
WHOSE NAME
WAS FORGOTTEN
SHE WHO WAS LOST
RETURNS

LONG
DID SHE WANDER
ALONE
AND
ABANDONED
LONG
DID SHE WAIT
FOR ONE VOICE
TO GREET HER

HER JOURNEY IS OVER
HER EXILE IS ENDED
SHE WHO WAS LOST
RETURNS

IN MEMORY OF WEDNESDAY NOVEMBER 1   NOVEMBER 5
1444

HE

bered back to my mother's womb and became a seven-week-old fetus who bargained for her life. I traveled further back, into what I reluctantly decided I could only understand as a previous life. I didn't want to know any of this. I didn't want more memory or other existences. This life was enough. But I went to these places anyway. And the only way I could record and explore what all this meant was through a melding of image and text. Neither one alone would do.

I am still doing this work. More and more, I sense an end coming. Recently, I've done drawings depicting a coming together, a return, both in terms of the selves living inside me and whoever else I once may have been. I have become aware of how complex a gift memory is, of the responsibilities this gift involves. How the sense of Self often referred to as "past life experiences" is not entertainment or a cosmically sanctioned means of avoiding personal and political realities. Memory remains a tool. How I use it is as important as the details it offers me. On one drawing, *She Who Was Lost Is Re-membered,* I've written a chant of home-coming, of restitution, of re-constitution. This chant addresses many of the aspects of my re-membering: the terror, the grief, the intense need to know, the unexpected and absolute joy in the regaining of what I often did not even know I had lost.

My drawings have helped return me to my Self. In them, I have been able to express layers of understandings, multiple senses of identity. These drawings are maps I have made in the midst of, during. Not before or after. They are maps of my searchings. I value them highly. Sometimes, despite the support of my partner and friends, I also discount them. I discount them because they are so personal, so obviously therapeutic, and because I know no one else who is doing anything like them. More often though, I acknowledge the drawings as gifts—as blessings I bestow on my Self and on all the Heidis I have ever been.

The child in me who once declared her Self an artist is ecstatic! At last she can draw whatever she feels, sees and knows. There are no rules. Nothing is forbidden. I am free to use whatever I want—words, images, memories, body sensations, dreams—and to invent my own symbols. I am creating a beauty and truth only I can give voice and shape to. I have returned home.

November, 1989

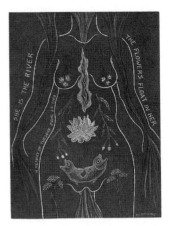

She is the River, 1989, 22″ × 30″, colored pencil on paper

Left, *She Who Was Lost Is Re-membered,* 1989, 22″ × 30″, colored pencil on paper

Cunt * Song

This is the place our stories come from—
tales of break and entry,
of who and where and how many times it was done.
This is the tongueless mouth that cries blood,
that sings to the moon.
This is where they who call us daughter, sister, cousin,
niece, baby search for treasure—
for the cherries, the rubies, the paydirt
buried inside us.

This is why they pry us open—
to find a home, a hole to spill want into,
a soft wall to ram against.
This is where again and again, they fail to find
what they desire,
for our tears, our cries (those they consent to hear),
our closed eyes, our rigid thighs indict them.
So over and over they come to plunder old ground,
to mine what isn't there.
Even when we mouth the words they teach us—
yes do it, I want it now, don't stop, please hurt me, oh
                    you're so big—
even then their cocks soften,
because cocks know you can't live in another's mouth
no matter how hard you try.

This is where the songs, pictures, poems
no one wants to know about happen—
here,
between our legs.
Some of them we bear among strangers too soon,
and they die—
their parentage lied about,
we, their fourteen-year-old mothers declared whores,
boy crazy, too wild to save.
Some of them we etch on our skin with razors, glass shards,
with paring knives—
tattoos no one admires,

---

* "Derivative of the Oriental Goddess as Cunti, or Kunda, the Yoni of the Universe... also cunning, kenning and ken: knowledge learning, insight, remembrance, wisdom." Barbara Walker, *The Woman's Encyclopedia of Myths and Secrets* (San Francisco: Harper & Row, 1983) p. 197.

art for which we are punished, fed pills, locked away.
Some of them we write down in diaries or draw on cheap paper
and show to people who call themselves friends,
but who call our work ugly, therapeutic, crude—
anything but strong or true.
Some of them stick in our throats,
where they roll around like the world's biggest pearl—
so we stutter, weep, are condemned as stupid, as being
beyond help,
until finally we stop making any sound at all.

This is where our stories come from—
from our bearded mouths.

No Longer Unspeakable

Becky Birtha

I AM NOT ABLE to call myself a survivor of incest. Reluctantly, I do say I am a victim of childhood physical abuse. Even to name it "child abuse" is hard—seems harsh and unfair to my parents, particularly my father, who was simply doing what his parents had done and what everyone else's parents did: overpowering a child with loud, angry, humiliating words, jerking her around, "spanking" with a hand, a switch, a belt, a ruler, or simply maintaining power by threatening to.

Over the years, I've come to realize that whatever my parents and other adults' beliefs were, either because of the time I was growing up (the 1950s and '60s) or because of ethnic traditions of childrearing in the African-American community, what happened to me was still abusive and painful—harsh and unfair to *me*—and left a lasting mark on my personality. The simple knowledge that I am still afraid to name that experience, afraid, in essence, of my parents, tells me how hurtful it was.

I am also able to say I am a rape survivor. That was a separate occurrence, one that happened after I was grown (or thought I was, at twenty) and supposedly in charge of my own life. I thought that the rape (by strangers, at gunpoint, in a sealed car at night) was my own fault. I realized that an experience like that could have the power to shatter me emotionally, so I dealt with it (or didn't deal with it) by deciding I was not going to let it take over my life, or accord it any importance at all. I pushed it into the background of my thoughts and feelings, never wrote about it, and went determinedly on with my life.

Both of these experiences left me with clear, concrete memories that I knew I could trust as real, even if, as in the case of the child abuse, everyone else in my family denied them. Though these experiences that I *can* clearly remember are not incest, it seems impossible to write about incest without including them. The reason is that they happened to the same person. And I am beginning to understand that all of these happenings are connected, that each has influenced my response to the others, and that what I have to live with and work my way through and resolve and heal from is the sum total of all that has happened to me.

All the same, incest is a whole other subject.

In the spring of 1989, I was on a leave of absence from my part-time job in order to write. Instead of the exhilarated sense of freedom and joy I had expected to feel at being liberated from having to work for someone else for a whole year, I was growing more and more directionless, unmotivated and depressed. I felt as if I had been laid off or fired—not given a prestigious award—and struggled with a frustrating sense of purposelessness. I was working on a book of poems about the break-up I'd gone through with my long-term lover two years earlier; it was slow, painstaking work. I was also seeing a therapist regularly, but still seeing no way out of the depression.

One night I had a dream, a nightmare that woke me up, horrified. In the dream, an abusive sexual act was being done to a small black baby doll. Yet, like so many other painful things in my life, I chose to put this dream aside and not accord it any importance. It was almost inadvertently that I happened to bring it up in a session with my therapist. Waking from the dream was scary and painful, but telling it was much more so. Yet telling someone was what cued me in to the dream's possible significance. My therapist suggested that it was not the dream itself, which she thought might have been easier for someone else to accept, but my reaction to it that flagged its importance for me. Even more than my reaction to the dream, it was my reaction to *the telling* that made me feel as though something was going on— that some sexual act had happened to me that I no longer remembered, but from which the dream was recalling my feelings.

The night after I told the dream, I was unable to sleep. By the time I realized what was happening, it was long past the hour when I could have called a friend, but I would not have felt safe telling anyone anyway. Alone in my house, crying and shaking, I tried to find a way to calm down. I needed to separate myself from the overwhelming feelings, and thought I could read something calming. Every book that I picked up seemed to be about sex. I remember one in particular that started out about two childhood friends, a boy and a girl. On the very second page, they were showing each other their genitals.

At last I turned to Gerard Manly Hopkins, William Butler Yeats and, eventually, William Wordsworth—male poets whose words I had memorized long ago and therefore knew I would not find disturbing. In the following days I began to write poems.

I remember writing the first of them while standing on a heavily populated corner, waiting for a bus downtown. I continued writing, scribbling rapidly in a spiral notebook, on the crowded bus. It was as if only the safety of that very public situation could provide me with the freedom I needed to touch such a painful personal issue without falling apart.

The first poems were about the dream. I wrote in the voice of the victim, and I wrote from "inside the mind of the oppressor." I wrote from the viewpoint of my parents, and I wrote out of the need to convince myself of my right to speak about such things. I also wrote, for the first time, about the rape I had survived twenty years earlier. New poems kept coming to me for several weeks. Though none of them are the kind of poems I needed and sought the night after I told the dream, eventually, some of them began to be loving poems toward myself.

There was still no reason to believe that I was an incest survivor—there was only this isolated dream and the feelings of shame, worthlessness, brokenness that it brought up. Yet the poems I was writing *sounded as though they had been written by an incest survivor.* I had to ask myself—why would anyone think such things, say such things, write such things, unless something had happened? No one *wants* to draw this kind of attention to herself. And there is still such a stigma attached to sexual abuse, no one wants to admit to having been its victim. *I* didn't want to have to call myself a survivor of sexual abuse. I didn't have any memories. But there were these poems, whose existence I couldn't explain any other way. In effect, the poems *are* the evidence.

Coming to terms with this knowledge has been a slow process. I couldn't bring myself to go to an incest survivors' group. So eventually I told my writing group. One week I took the poems in, asking that we not work on them in the usual, critical way, but explaining that I just needed to be heard. The response was overwhelmingly loving and accepting—instead of corrections and suggestions about line breaks and clarity, I got hugged and held while I cried. Other women in the group have brought in work dealing with similar painful places in their own lives.

It may be that supportive beginning that makes me feel a need to be public with these poems. Sometimes that publicity seems impossible. I feel ashamed of, and embarrassed by some of the content. And I remember how devastated my mother was over my reading, on a public radio broadcast, my poem called "A Father Hits His Two Children." I've often thought that the only time I could ever attempt to publish this work, especially the most explicit of the poems, would be after my parents' deaths.

But there is the urge to do it sooner, to do it despite how hard it will be—for me as well as for others in my family—despite how painful the work is to hear and read. I think that urge comes from

believing that these words can be of use to other women struggling with the same issues, and also from believing that being
public with this work, saying the poems out loud, putting them
down on paper, putting them out there in the world, is one more
step in the process of healing. Experiences written and heard, or
read, are no longer unspeakable.

I've learned to pay attention to other kinds of evidence as
well—bits and pieces of information like how young I was when I
left home and the fact that I never returned. I've noticed how uncomfortable I am with the subject of sexual abuse in general. Even
if it comes up as the theme of a song at a concert, I'll find myself
sitting in my seat with my knees drawn up and my arms hugged
tightly around them. I've begun to look at my attitudes and feelings about being a sexual person, period, to explore where they
came from, and to realize that they can be changed and become
much more positive. When my partner told me that she was
thinking of seeking a group for partners of survivors, I realized
that there was another piece of evidence. If she saw herself as a
partner of a survivor, I needed to start coming to terms with what
that made me.

Dealing with all of this has gone slowly for me. I've realized I
can't read or think about recovering all the time—that keeping
my focus on the subject was keeping me stuck in the depression
that seemed to have lasted my whole lifetime. The healing can't
happen all at once. I'm also aware that writing a poem about one
piece of my pain doesn't necessarily mean I have worked
through—or even touched—the feelings attached to it. Sometimes poems come much more easily than feelings.

My sense is that I still have a long way to go in this process. I
don't know if I will ever have any clear memories, or even another dream. I do trust that I will keep writing poems, each one
coming as I'm ready to handle whatever new information it contains for me. And I am committed to listening, to opening, to telling, to continuing this work.

I still cannot say that I am a survivor of incest. But I cannot
say that I am not.

The Parents' Pantoum

You remember wrong.
There was nothing the matter with us.
There was nothing the matter with our family.
You had the problem.

There was nothing the matter with us.
You were always too emotional.
You had the problem,
too sensitive, too selfish.

You were always too emotional.
You're being selfish now,
too sensitive, too selfish.
How do you think it makes us look?

You're being selfish now
to say such horrible things happened.
How do you think it makes us look?
How do you think it makes us feel

to say such horrible things happened?
We did everything we could for you.
How do you think it makes us feel?
Maybe we weren't perfect but

we did everything we could for you.
We did the best we knew how.
Maybe we weren't perfect but
we would never, never have done—

We did the best we knew how.
Anything to hurt you
we would never, never have done.
We would still do anything we could,

anything to hurt you,
to help you out.
We would still do anything we could.
It was always that way:

to help you out.
Those things you're making up—

it was always that way.
It could never have happened,

those things you're making up.
There was nothing the matter with us.
It could never have happened.
You were the problem.

There was nothing the matter with us.
There was nothing the matter with our family.
You were the problem.
You remember wrong.

Surveying the Extent of the Damage

Other people take their mothers out
for dinner on Mother's Day or on a Sunday afternoon
and they pay the bill. They send her
flowers, buy her a gift on her birthday.
They know what she likes.

Other people ask their fathers for a loan
to make the down payment on a house.
They feel fine if he co-signs. They ask
his advice about the roof, the terms,
the closing, the neighborhood.

Other people invite their parents over
for dinner. They're not afraid
they could never pull it off. They're not
afraid of what might get said at the table or how
they may be judged and found
hopelessly inadequate.

Other people wonder sometimes
how their parents are. They care. They want to
call them up. They want to see them.
And when it's been awhile,
they miss them.

Other people send their parents
money when they can. They
go with them to the doctor,
maybe spend a whole day at
the hospital, or every evening.
Other people take their aging parents
in to live with them.

Other people keep their parents' pictures
out in full view in their houses.
They show them to company.
They stop and look at the pictures
sometimes, during the day
with a rush of feeling that is neither
guilt nor fear.

Telling

Finally I begin to tell.
I do not know what I expected
but not this.
After I've told it all
after they have listened
after we question and answer, after talk
instead of going home
the women in my group
come up to me one by one
and each one takes me in her arms.
When the first woman touches me
I begin to cry
and cry and cry
while each woman one
after the other holds me and while they all
one after another, hold each other.
No one is repulsed by what I've
told, by what I've done.
No one is scandalized.
There is not even one who cannot bear
to touch me.
The room grows quiet except for,
without words,
each of the women telling
and telling me
I can still be loved.

You Are Not Broken

You are not broken, beautiful child.
Nothing about you is wrong.
Other people have made their mistakes
on you.
But you survived.

You are whole.
You will heal, you will be
all you ever wanted.
You no longer remain
the victim of those years.

Your body is yours.
You can fill it with joy.
Your thoughts are in your control.
Your feelings are free as
the sound of chiming bells.

You are loved,
you are lovable
beautiful child.
You always were.
You are forgiven.

A Raid on the Inarticulate: Writing and Its Role in Healing

Beryl-Elise Hoffstein

> *And so each venture*
> *Is a new beginning, a raid on the inarticulate*
> *With shabby equipment always deteriorating*
> *In the general mess of imprecision of feeling,*
> *Undisciplined squads of emotion*
> —T.S. Eliot *

WRITING "INTERROGATION" WAS embarrassing and enlightening, infuriating and empowering. But it was also surprising; it was the first time in years that I've been able to write an entire story of any kind, start to finish. I don't believe it was any accident that this particular story was the first one to break its way out.

In my childhood, I had what you might call a "speaker's block." I found it very difficult to speak (except to myself) and nearly impossible to talk in front of two or more people unless they were trusted friends. There were periods when I was silent for almost the entire day except for required speech such as answering questions in school.

The only problem I had with writing, however, was perfectionism. Everything, whether it was a sentence using the words on the daily spelling list or a story for the school newspaper, had to be exactly right, as though it were going to be reviewed later by the Nobel Prize Committee. However, once I could decide on a topic that would not offend the committee, I had no trouble putting words to paper. After all, who really cared what I had done on my summer vacation or why I wanted to be a doctor? These weren't secrets. These couldn't possibly make people view me with disgust. These were not the topics my mother meant when she warned me not to tell other people family business. The only remotely personal article I can remember writing as a child was when I was absolutely desperate for an idea and my mother sug-

---

* I want to thank Tanya Gardiner-Scott for pointing out the aptness of this quote.

gested I write a humorous piece about being overweight and my subsequent adversarial relationship with the doctor's scale in my father's office. Writing that piece was humiliating but not at all difficult. The words flowed easily. Using humor to appease the potentially hostile was, by then, an old trick. Also, when all was said and done, my weight was a secret to no one. It was certainly not a taboo subject; people talked to me about it anyway, whether I wanted them to or not. It may have caused me to be considered an ugly human being, but I was seen as a human being nonetheless. It did not shut me off irrevocably from others.

As I grew older, my problems reversed themselves; I learned how to make small talk, however awkwardly, but my ideas for writing started to enter dangerous and hidden territories. No matter what I started to write, even humor (still my preferred weapon to hold pain at arm's length), the story would eventually get around to sex, love, childhood, memories, sexual identity: all areas either forbidden to me or lost to me years ago. I was afraid. The forbidden areas might hurt someone, and I was the good little girl who would never hurt anyone for any reason, no matter what they might have done to me. I would betray my family, especially my mother for whom I had a kicked dog's loyalty. It would get me in trouble with my older brother, and who could predict what his reaction would be? I might not survive it. I would be removed even further from the human race than I already felt myself to be, and I would drown in shame. Perhaps everyone would see what I suspected in my worst moments: that being molested and tortured was all my fault, triggered by something sexually awful in me that could be perceived by others. Maybe it could even give other people the idea of assaulting me. I had never understood where this violence had come from in the first place. It seemed almost whimsical, abuse falling on me from out of the sky. My brother had hated me, obviously, but for no reason I could point to or name. Maybe it could descend on me again if I didn't stay absolutely quiet and keep my mouth shut.

As for the hidden areas, how can you write the truth about your life if you cannot remember large chunks of it? How do you know you aren't lying, making it all up to get attention, slandering the innocent? Unfortunately, the messages I had received from my family were not only to keep quiet but also to forget, and those orders had generalized to all areas of my life.

Through many years of trying, I found that if I couldn't write about my life, especially those parts that haunted me, I wouldn't be able to write about anything else either. I had ideas, titles, sometimes even first pages, but then each story would hit my writer's block like a pigeon flying into a glass door; stunned, it was unable to get up and go anywhere. So in addition to being shameful and weird, I also knew myself to be obsessed, untalented, a dilettante as a writer.

In the following years, while my unfinished stories lay stuffed into the backs of drawers, my own story slowly started getting clearer. I wasn't writing, but gradually and painfully, mostly in therapy, I started to be able to talk, at least sometimes and with some people. A few memories came back. I began to see my mother as neither monster nor goddess, but as a woman with many problems that I did not fully understand. She had my love and respect for trying to do the best she could, as well as my anger for not giving me what I needed so much, but either way, I did not owe her the loss of my voice. I learned that incest does not remove people from the human race. I had read the statistics that one in four women had been molested as children, and later, that approximately one in seven men had suffered similarly. However, nothing I'd read made the point quite so well as the time I attended a local women-only workshop for survivors and found myself in a room with most of my close friends and acquaintances. None of them had ever mentioned their incest experiences to me, even in our most intimate conversations, but there they sat, and they were not there to write a report for a college psychology class.

Eventually, I was even able to confront my older brother with what I knew. It wasn't a completely satisfying experience, but some of what he told me about our family and about childhood events of which I had no memories started to place his abuse of me in a context. It did not excuse it, but it made his behavior seem less random, less likely that it could happen again, that I could trigger it with some fearful unknown aspect of my body or personality.

With all of the changes in my life, I decided that maybe I could try writing again. At work I had the use of a computer, which made writing easier, and also less final than words written on a sheet of paper. If I didn't like what I had written, I could delete it or cut-and-paste it into a different order. I could just put down whatever thoughts I had, however unformed, and save them to edit and shape later. The computer gave me much more control over my writing and made it seem less frightening.

However, an odd thing happened. There I was, working away at a humorous story that had been rattling around in my mind for years, and suddenly the brick wall of writer's block went up again. Nothing more would come. I tried patience. I tried outwaiting it. I tried talking about it in therapy. Finally, sick of looking at the same damned computer screen for hours, I decided to write something else, anything else. How about describing something that had really happened to me? If nothing else, it would be practice in writing, and after all is said and done, what is a writer anyway? A writer is not someone who gets published. A writer is not someone who gets paid or wins a prize. A writer is someone who writes. Period.

So I started to write. And "Interrogation" came up on the screen almost effortlessly. It was one of those experiences that I had not had since childhood, of losing myself completely in a creation that welled up out of me without struggle or strain. It was complete, it was true, and it was good.

In order for me to tell anyone about anything worth hearing, I must first remove the original gag order that silenced me for so long and talk about the forbidden, the hidden, the painful. Otherwise all of my stories stay silenced. How else am I to become articulate when I have been mute for so long, except by stammering, stuttering and stumbling through the story of how I became mute in the first place? And then the ordinary everyday magic of writing begins, for by putting my thoughts, feelings and experiences down on paper, I can begin to see clearly what I think, what I need, who I was then and who I am now. The "undisciplined squads of emotion" have been outflanked and I've begun to get at my truth, my story.

Interrogation

I'm glad I got to pick out my clothing myself this morning. At least I'm not wearing some stupid pink dress or skirt or something. None of that lacy stuff my Aunt Florence keeps sending me for birthdays. Of course, I really ought to be wearing some of Daddy's old Army stuff from World War II, but Mommy probably wouldn't have let me wear it anyway. And anyway, I didn't really know this morning where I was going.

Oh, they told me I was going to the hospital several days ago, but it's why I'm going that's really important. They said that the doctors were going to find out why I kept getting sick all the time, but that's just some of it. I didn't figure out the rest until just now. At least I'm wearing pants and a long-sleeved turtleneck sweater. I feel better and stronger when I'm all covered up. I don't know why. I just do. And I feel better in boys' clothes too. That gets people like my Aunt Florence mad, but I don't care.

They've put me in the waiting room again. This is the third time. They keep taking me to different offices, examining me and asking questions, then bringing me back to the waiting room. I think they're mad at me but I don't care any more. I saw that John Wayne movie several nights ago on TV, and I had the dream again last night that I always have. I know what I have to do.

Everyone's mad at me anyway now. We just got back from a medical convention in New York City that my Daddy had to go to, and I spoiled it all for everyone by getting sick again. I asked Mommy if I could just stay by myself in the hotel room while she and Daddy and my brother saw the sights. I like being by myself and the bathroom was right next door. I could have just stayed in there. But Mommy said no, I couldn't be left alone there, so I had to go walking with them and we had to stop every block to try to find a bathroom and it hurt. Daddy got madder and madder at me. Couldn't I hold it for a little while? Then my brother laughed and called me a real little pisspot. But I was afraid I was going to have an accident right in the middle of downtown, so we went into buildings and restaurants on every single block. When we came back, Mommy called the doctor.

They've taken my blood and all the stuff they did when I got my tonsils taken out, but this time it's different. They try to pretend it's just like anybody going to the hospital but I know better now. I figured it out the third time they examined me.

All the doctors looked at me down there. Then they asked the questions. What made it creepy was that they all asked the same questions in the same order and with the same tone of voice. The last question they always asked very cautiously and they were also very careful not to look right at me. The third doctor left the room after he asked the questions and then his nurse came in and asked the very same questions in the very same way. That's when I knew.

The first question was normal: When did you first start having pain down there? I always let Mommy answer that because I don't remember, it's been so long. Then, what does the pain feel like? It was awful talking about myself down there but I was beginning to get used to it. It burned all the time, especially when I went to the bathroom, and I always felt like I had to go to the bathroom really bad even when I didn't or only had to go a little bit. Well then, did I know how to wipe myself the right way after I went to the bathroom? Of course I did! My mommy taught me that when I was very little, and I'm always careful: front to back, and never the other way around. Then they all nodded, they all took a big breath, and looking to the side or at the top of my head, they all asked the question they had been leading up to, the only real, important question: Have you been doing something else that would cause this?

That's when I thought of John Wayne and what he would do if the enemy asked him questions. No matter who asked or what they did to him, he would be strong and not tell them anything. It was like in my dreams, when I was a Marine. If I could just be strong and hold out against the pain, I would win. So I always said I didn't know what they were talking about, even though we *all* knew what we were talking about. I would not tell. I don't know what they would do to me if I told, but the needles and blood tests and things I'm getting right now are bad enough. I'm afraid of needles. Nurses always curl their lips at you and say in a voice that's supposed to be kind, "It doesn't hurt, dear. It's just a tiny prick and then it's all over." I know that! It's what it makes me think of that scares me, so I always try to run out of the doctor's office. I don't want to think about it right now.

Now here's the nurse and my parents coming to take me up to the children's ward. The nurse says in a jolly voice that she is going to give me the grand tour, but her face still looks stiff and funny. I am careful not to talk too much about anything at all.

First I'm shown the playroom and told about all the toys and kids in there I can play with. I know I won't, though. I want to stay by myself where no one will ask me anything and I can just sit quietly. I brought plenty of books to read and my teddy bear to keep me company.

Then I am shown to my room and introduced to my roommate, a girl in a lacy pink nightgown who looks several years older than I am.

"She's very brave," says the nurse, smiling at her. "She's been in here several weeks and has to have blood tests every day and she never complains."

The girl sits up in bed looking pink and pale, smiling smugly. I bet she's a real sissy, probably tells them everything they want to know and lets them do anything they want to do. I decide I'm not saying a single word to her for the whole time they keep me here.

That night, I have the dream again. I'm a boy named Johnny. Even though I'm just a kid, I'm a Marine on special assignment against the Communists. I have won several medals for being strong and brave and being able to take torture. This time I have to go behind enemy lines to deliver a message, but there is a traitor in the ranks and I am discovered and captured. I am taken to a prison cell where I am chained to the bare white walls and tortured, but I refuse to give them any information besides my name, rank and serial number. In the next room, I hear a girl crying. She's an American and I realize I have to rescue her. I get away from my guards for a few minutes and go to her cell door where I tell her who I am and not to worry. I'm going to break out and take her with me. In the meantime, she has to hold out and not tell anybody any secrets. She says that she knows who I am and that she has nothing to fear now. She'll wait for me to rescue her. I look through the bars at her before I go back to my cell. She looks a lot like my hospital roommate, only stronger and a lot prettier. Then my chance comes and I pick the lock of my cell. I open the door of the girl's cell, too, and we head for the prison gate.

Then the dream changes. Usually I escape and return home to be awarded a few more medals. Sometimes the girl I rescue even makes a speech about how brave I am and kisses me in front of everybody. Then I go off to another special assignment. Now, though, we are pursued by a guard and as he gets closer, I can see that he is my older brother. He grabs me and starts unbuttoning my Army uniform and saying things about prossitudes, whatever they are, and dirty women, and sticking sharp things into their big chests until they hurt, and then he opens my uniform shirt and pushes a sharp ball point pen into my chest with one hand and grabs lower down with the other, and suddenly I'm sitting up in my hospital bed, trying not to scream or make any noise that will give it all away or tell anyone what they want to know: what I've been doing to cause this pain all the time. I lie still holding Teddy until it gets light out and I can sleep again.

The next morning, I get no breakfast because I'm going to have something like an operation and I'm going to be under anesthesia. The nurse says not to worry because no one's going to take anything out, they're just going to look around down there to see if there are germs. Of course there are germs in that place, but I wonder what else they can see if they look there. They can't prove anything, though, if I do not talk.

Then another nurse comes in to join the first, and Mommy comes in as well. She smiles at me and so do the nurses. The first nurse says, "Before we wheel you down to the operating room, we just have to give you a little shot to make you sleepy. It won't hurt at all."

I start to lose my nerve and say, "But I'm having anesthesia. That will make me sleepy. Why do I need a shot, too?"

The nurse speaks through her smile. "You have to get sleepy first. But we'll let you decide whether you want to get the shot in your arm or your backside."

Well, at least I get to pick the spot. That's good. That makes it less scary. I am thinking hard, trying to decide whether it's worth the extra pain of having it in the arm just so it's not done behind my back where I can't see what they're doing. Suddenly everyone moves at once, including my mother who grabs me and holds me down. The nurses push me down on the bed, pull up my hospital gown and stick the needle hard into my upper thigh. I am screaming and I can't stop. Even when they pull the needle out, I am still screaming until my throat becomes so hoarse, my voice sounds like a roar.

The nurse says disgustedly, "Look at your roommate. She doesn't make such a fuss over one little needle. She gets blood taken out of all her fingertips, several times a day, and she doesn't act like such a baby."

I look over at the girl sneering at me from the next bed. I hope she does get tortured by the Communists. I won't rescue her, that's for sure.

I continue roaring as the orderlies come up to take me to the operating room. One asks, "Well, are you sleepy yet?"

"I AM NOT SLEEPY! YOUR STUPID SHOT DID NOT MAKE ME SLEEPY! I DON'T CARE IF YOU GIVE ME A MILLION SHOTS, I AM NOT SLEEPY!"

As the orderlies roll me over onto the wheeled table and push me down the hall, I keep screaming, "I'M NOT SLEEPY!" Even as I try to sit up and can't quite make it, even as my head rolls around on my neck and the hallways and elevator spin, right until the mask is placed over my face, I keep screaming. I've never yelled so loud in my whole life.

The next thing I know about is the pain. It's in the same place as always, only a million times worse, and also, I want to throw up, only I hurt so bad down there, I'm afraid to move. I look around as well as I can to see if my brother has gotten into the room somehow, but I don't see him. The nurse was right; they couldn't have taken anything out, because how could it hurt so much if there was nothing left down there? But what did they do to me? Why would it hurt so much if all they did was look? Maybe everyone was so mad at my having to pee all the time that they made it so I could never pee again. Maybe they put something in me to block me up, the way my brother always threatened to, with cement or crayons or dirt.

I ask Mommy what they did, but all she says is that they looked around down there and now they were going to give me antibiotics and I would have to drink cranberry juice every day.

I lie there and think about my brother having people look at him down there and putting sharp things into him and blocking him up and him screaming from the pain.

But despite the punishment, I am brave and do not say anything or make a sound. I do not talk; I do not tell. I am a boy named Johnny. No, I am a man, a strong man named John and I do not tell; I do not tell; I do not tell.

Walking In

Jena

IT BEGAN WITH a door, a solid wooden door with an old-fashioned keyhole through which soft, yellow light was shining into a small, dark room. Drawn to the light, I reached for the doorknob and turned it, pulling back hard against the door's weight. An instant later, the door was slammed open by a huge male shape that rushed at me shouting, "NO!" in a voice so full of anger and hate that I knew he would kill me if he could get his hands on me. Sheer terror catapulted me awake. Sobbing and gasping for air I fumbled for the lamp by my bed. The small circle of light it produced showed me the reassuringly familiar walls of my room. I was alone and safe, or so I thought.

This dream was the first clue I had that I might have been sexually abused as a child. Until then, all I could remember were bits and pieces of my father's rages: chairs broken over my mother's head, knives flying across the kitchen, my own arm twisted until a tiny bone popped. The worst I managed to keep buried deep in my subconscious through all sorts of compulsive behavior. Everything I did, from academic work and competitive swimming to driving buses, I did with a feverish determination to prove I was the best, that I was important because I could produce straight A's, set meet records and manhandle a forty-foot bus around corners. I was convinced that if anyone ever suspected what an awful, guilt-ridden person lived behind my facade, they wouldn't want to have anything to do with me.

Eventually the performance standards I set for myself, which I was always raising, created an unbearable tension. My way of relieving the pressure was to go home, stuff myself to bursting with food, then vomit it all back up into the toilet. Then, to ease the guilt I felt for needing to do this, I would get out a cheap bottle of white wine or a six-pack of beer and drink myself into oblivion. I didn't realize that my insecurities and my need to prove myself stemmed from an old wounding that had left me doubting my right to be alive. I assumed that my problem was control, that I lacked the self-discipline to "get my shit together," as one friend was constantly urging me to do. It would take me until I was thirty-two to find the courage and professional help I needed to stop running long enough to look at what I so desperately didn't want to see.

At the time this first dream occurred, I had been sober three months, and only the support I got from the members of AA and my therapist, who correctly read the signs, kept me from drinking again. Other dreams and flashbacks soon followed: my father chasing me through the rooms of a huge house trying to rape me; standing beside a swimming pool and having a man come up behind me and rub his erect penis against me while my mother pulled down my pants and said, "Now just be a good girl and cooperate;" seductively flirting with my father to distract him from beating up my brother. The worst by far, however, was of a heavy male presence that would lean over my left shoulder at night, pressing his weight down on me so I could hardly breathe, fumbling at my crotch with probing fingers. So real were the sensations, so vivid was the sense that I knew this man and could do nothing to protect myself or prevent what was happening, that the dream began to follow me into my waking hours. At odd moments during the day, my shoulder would begin to ache, my vagina would burn and the smell of stale tobacco smoke mixed with beer and old sweat would wash over me. Other physical sensations also began to come back: hands at my throat, sharp pains in my pelvic area and a deep, constant, pulsing ache in my sacrum.

It's hard to describe how much these physical memories disturbed me. For years I'd worked with, trained and controlled my body. I knew down to a few hundredths of a second just how fast it could swim, exactly how much I could eat and still maintain my

The Incubus, 1989, 4′ × 3′, colored pencil, conte crayon, watercolors

A Glimpse of What Could Be,
1989, 3' × 4', pen and ink,
acrylics, colored pencil

size-nine figure, how to dress and act to keep people, especially
men, believing that I was a cute, young Southern California girl
with a sunny disposition. Now suddenly I felt out of control,
overwhelmed by sensations and emotions that were forcing me
back into a hell I didn't want to see. Out of desperation, to keep
from binging or drinking, I began to paint, buying huge 3 × 4-
foot sheets of charcoal paper, pinning them to my walls and slashing at them with my brushes. There was very little finesse or
technique involved in what first emerged. I didn't care what I
painted so much as I needed very badly to ease my body's discomfort. Long, red, wet gashes spilled across muddy spirals and
erupting sores. Splashes of gore, vaguely reminiscent of body
parts, screamed onto the paper. Then one day, after yet another

The Split, 1989, 3' × 4',
colored chalk, colored pencil,
watercolors, acrylics

night of what I've come to call the "Incubus" plaguing my sleep, I
felt a complete picture forming in my mind's eye.

The Incubus was born slowly. Once I realized what I was
painting, my body rebelled. Often I had to stop because of nausea
or because I felt I was about to be swallowed up by it, but always I
returned, like a sick animal that licks its wounds again and again.

Not long after I finished *The Incubus,* the dream stopped.
There was a blessed period of exhaustion and relief in which I was
finally able to sleep without nightmares. I thought I'd finally ex-
orcised my demon. Unfortunately, it was only the beginning.
What had begun as a slow, painful process of coaxing my mind to
release its memories quickly became a torrent. Possessed by my

need to get down what I was seeing, I'd paint until my shoulder cramped and I couldn't lift my arm, and my legs were swollen from standing in one place for hours. I quit one job and almost lost another when I simply forgot the time and failed to show up. I began to see everything and everybody in terms of color and shape, material for my brush, and I lay awake for hours at night watching the kaleidoscope of images play behind my eyelids. Eventually, ten paintings emerged. I have no way of judging them as works of art; I'm still too close to the process that produced them. And for once, it's enough to have done something entirely for myself. Friends and other survivors who see them are moved. I'm glad. If what I've painted can help speak the truth about incest, validate what survivors are experiencing and help prevent it from happening to others, then it's more than worth the panic I sometimes feel when they're shown, or the occasional revulsion on the face of someone who is shocked by what I've portrayed.

These days, I'm no longer painting. My healing process seems to be leading me instead to a quiet place where nothing but a willingness to listen is required, a place where I trust I will finally come to terms fully with what happened to me as a child and learn to love the woman I've become. It's a tenuous, frightening and infinitely hopeful place, but I know I'm coming home.

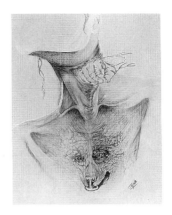

Voice, 1989, 2′ × 3′, colored pencil, acrylics, colored chalk

The Brightening Fire

Lynne Yamaguchi Fletcher

I DON'T HAVE SPECIFIC, concrete memories of being sexually abused as a child, but so certain am I that I was that being a survivor has become part of my identity. Even without the mental images, my body tells me that I was. And having been sexually abused by my parents as a child is the only explanation I've encountered that makes sense of my life as a whole. At the same time, however, I recognize that I may never remember: After some five years of exploring and processing, I realize that this near certainty may be the closest I ever come to knowing my past. Much of my healing has thus taken place, and continues to take place, in a void of sorts.

This is the context in which I wrote these poems: not remembering, wanting and trying to remember, and working to express and heal from pain that I could not attach to any specific incident.

I began my discovery and healing with the barest scrap of a memory, a flashback depicted in the poem "Again": One day I was crying, huddled against a wall, and when my lover came to comfort me, she suddenly became a not-quite-identifiable man in a T-shirt, who, I knew, with all the helpless terror of a three year old, was going to hurt me—again. Shortly after that flashback, I entered therapy—not for the first time: I had a long history of seeking help for chronic, unexplained depression. As I began exploring the ramifications of that scrap of memory, I quickly discovered that the profile of a person sexually abused as a child matched the facts of my life uncannily. I fit the pattern—gaps in memory, a history of self-destructiveness and sexual acting out, and so forth—to a tee.

I began attending a support group for AMACs—adults molested as children. There, week after week, I listened to the stories of other survivors. Some stories, some images, stuck with me; I kept witnessing them over and over in my head. To release them, I wrote about them, and to understand them, I wrote from a first-person point of view. "Father" is one such poem. I feel guilty about having written these poems; I worry that I've exploited other people's pain, though this was far from my intention. What was my intention? On the surface, it was to honor other people's suffering. Unconsciously, I think, I wanted to know what it felt like to remember such pain. Though I never confused other people's experiences with my own, in the beginning, in the absence of my own concrete memories, I borrowed others' to explore my own feelings.

Earlier, I had gotten to know someone who had been orally raped as an infant. Her story, too, came back to haunt me. How could anyone do such a thing to a tiny baby? I wanted to understand. But at the time, I found trying to imagine such primal terror from an infant's perspective unbearable. Instead, I wrote "Tulip, Sweet Tulip" from the perspective of the rapist.

This is a poem I have hidden, ashamed of having engaged in such an act of imagination, ashamed of the perverseness that my doing so must surely indicate. (Mustn't my belief that I was abused also be only a projection of my own perverseness?—after all, it was I who as a child had fantasized sexually torturing men. But where had those fantasies come from?) I also feel guilty for having given voice to a perpetrator when so many survivors have had their voices permanently silenced. What value could there possibly be in sharing such a piece?

Well, "Tulip, Sweet Tulip" is a superficial poem, but I discovered much in writing it. Unfortunately, I don't think the poem itself expresses what I have discovered I know, thanks to my parents, about the act of abuse: what it feels like to feel so unloved, so unlovable, so lonely, empty, ugly, and hurt that one could violate another being, even a child. I have been an emotionally abusive coparent. Under the wrong circumstances—had I stayed in an abusive relationship, had I not at last experienced the love and safety I needed to begin to let my repressed knowledge surface, to begin to heal—I could have become a perpetrator. How many other survivors could say the same? But we are not permitted to speak of this, except perhaps, if we are lucky, in the sanctum of individual counseling. How many other survivors know what I know?

Knowing this about myself has made going back, forgetting what I can't quite remember, an impossibility.

"Comet" represents a step further in my healing. This poem, like "Father" and "Tulip, Sweet Tulip" began with someone else's experience, but this time, merged with it is my own experience of having to clean the bathroom each week under the eye of a perfectionist. Its truth, its knowledge, comes much closer to home than "Father" or "Tulip, Sweet Tulip."

"Washing the Elephant" represents my "best guess," based on "random" facts and some details garnered through hypnosis, as to how my abuse might have happened. How accurate do I think this best guess is? The feelings are true, both the detached sense of bearing witness to the experience and the child's sick confusion: The circumstances are superficially but ultimately true. My father lacked the imagination to have made a game of any abuse. I don't, however, and the metaphor allowed me access to knowledge direct memory blocked.

Much later in my healing came "Dressing for Night." Here memory and expression joined at last in an act of articulation, not merely of imagination. "Dressing for Night" is all mine, and the power of that small claim is heightened by the circumstances that preceded it.

I wrote "Again," "Father," "Comet," "Tulip, Sweet Tulip" and "Washing the Elephant" while in graduate school, working toward an M.F.A. in creative writing through Warren Wilson College. The semester I wrote these poems, I was working with a teacher whose teaching style I found profoundly abusive. When I appealed, in tears, to the program director for help, I was sent back to try again. Good girl that I was, I did; I also unequivocally told the teacher how I felt about his style, and I continued to fight to be heard right up to the end of the semester. That I was able to continue to write under these circumstances, and to write these poems, astounds me and is testament to the power of the healing process I was then so newly engaged in. But by the end of the semester, relations between me and this teacher were such that I had to submit my work to the program's academic board (of which he, of course, was a member) to see if I would get credit for the semester. Well, the board gave me credit—and then took it away by requiring me to take a leave of absence and a fifth semester. The twist of the blade was that not only did his colleagues consider him blameless in the matter, they declared my response to have been personally "abusive" to him.

Looking back, and knowing what I now know about the phenomenon of denial, I'm not surprised by the board's verdict. At the time, though, it did me in. I felt as though I had been re-abused. This time, though, I had fought to defend myself, I had reported the abuse, and those whom I had expected to be my advocates lined up with my "perpetrator" against me.

I dropped out of the program and quit writing. I felt extinguished, dead, emptier than the page. I managed one poem, elegant, detached, elegiac, a year later; it felt like my last. I continued my healing. "Dressing for Night" came the next year, during an unusual day-long writing workshop that gave me a taste of the old fire. I wish that I could say that the flames took then, that the bitter wood betrayal left in me combusted in poems of heat and light... but nothing more came for a couple years, and real flames, not yet.

The path back to my art, that heartfire, has been a long one. I have been lucky. I have been blessed with opportunities that have kept me moving steadily back toward the light: as a member of the *For Crying Out Loud* newsletter collective, reading the always-moving work of other survivors and writing four times a year, in prose, specifically about healing from sexual abuse; having poems published in an anthology of Asian American women writers, and being invited to read at the Asian American Resource Workshop in Boston; having the opportunity, through my job, to put together a fun book about gay and lesbian culture; reading and selecting poems for the feminist monthly *Sojourner;* having the chance to write this essay and share these poems. This last act, writing this essay and sharing these poems, feels like a turning point. First, having these poems accepted for publication, given the context of their birth, is tremendously validating. Second, to write about my experience at Warren Wilson, I finally reread the letters I had written my teacher—something I had not been able to do before. The truth of what happened then is clear now. The flames lick my hands like a welcoming animal.

Again

The floor is cold.
The wall at which I plead
Denies me, whitely.
I want one thing: to be
Part of the plaster.

The man I cringe from
As you cross to comfort me was larger;
His squat arms cradled his paunch lightly,
Furred,
Willing to strike.
There is nowhere
That this three-, this thirty-year-old,
Can crawl to escape him.

Father

I held to the fragrance of cedar,
fingernails biting the closet walls at the end of
    my outstretched arms,
the pungent wood harsh against my cheek
either way I turned my head.
Behind me you checked the spread of my legs,
your right foot nudging mine a little farther.
I edged closer to the wood, away
from your heat.
Your thrust—
I was never ready—
seared my rear,
lifting me off my feet,
slamming me into the scent of cedar.
Enveloped, whole,
I vanished into the grain.
When you touched me again, softly,
I almost turned.

Comet_{TM}

Blue dust hovers as I sprinkle the tub.
I snort, kneeling naked on the grit
To scrub the thin white scum away.
My bleached ghost watches from the tile as I rinse.

You call this toilet clean? he asks.
One finger jabs and jabs, pointing. My sponge
Leaves a trail across the porcelain,
Smeared dust and rubber crumbs.

At night, I remember the tub's whiteness,
The gleam of a sharp face not my own.
Younger than I ever was,
She can forget his father weight,

Even as it crushes me.
Allowed to shower I cannot get clean.
The blue granules arc through darkness,
Pitting my skin as I scour, scour, scour.

Tulip, Sweet Tulip

The first time I saw that bud open
you were yawning in your mother's arms
as I bent to kiss her.
My hands prickled:
I'd shrugged off the ten-ness of your toes,
those impossibly animate arms,
the fingers that clutched and clung like monkeys';

but that open, floral hunger
dumbfounded me.
I never held you.
Evenings, home from the nursery, I'd watch
behind the paper
your mother feed you, watch your blind,
botanical thirst.
One night I visited your crib;
your lips worked even in sleep.
I touched them.
And jerked back from the sudden suction.
Then, flower, I gave you my finger again.

Your mouth haunted me.
Its shiny, wet noise followed me everywhere.
In the greenhouse, spading humus
or pruning the many-petaled roses,
I wondered,
would it be like a woman,
like winning,
like my hand.

Better than Mother,
sweeter heat.
Poppy, I cooed to your wailing,
your lovely, fluttering silk.
Poor tulip, torn tulip, sweet tulip.

Washing the Elephant

You first, he calls
over the sizzle of the shower.
The yellow bar foams between
my hands, cotton candy, surf
left hissing on the sand.
I rub and rub.
He bumps me lightly.
I reach up for the trunk,
blinking out a spray of water.
Soft as a gecko's throat,
the wrinkles slip away. Washing it
takes both hands.
Look, it's drinking the shower, he says.
I don't, but keep washing as
it fills and lifts, the way at the zoo
the baby elephant lifts its trunk
to its mother. He's supposed
to trumpet now, quietly,
but instead he sounds hurt, or
lonely. My arms are tired,
I let go, he grabs for my hands
but takes over instead.
He is washing too fast.
My stomach presses my hands.
From the corner of my eye,
I see the elephant spit up, a milky dribble.

Dressing for Night

You used to get me ready for bed.
I remember now; it came to me
As cold, a gust
Of Arctic that drove heat, heart, breath
From my chest and I could only
Laugh once
Before the shuddering shivering chattering contraction
Fisted me in grief.

My arms were stuck in my sleeves;
Because my back hurt, my lover
Was helping me dress for night.
As she pushed my head through the ring of cotton
The dark opened:
You took her place;
Fear filled me like wind
Fills the empty lighthouse.

Knowledge, not memory.
What the wind bore was witness:
To this: that your hands
In their act of fathering

Orphaned me.

Dripping the Polish

Laurie Williams

M Y NAME IS Laurie Williams. I am a natural blonde who was sexually abused first at age eight, then at eleven, at fourteen, sixteen and again at seventeen. At age twenty-one, after a four-year "liason," I married my abuser. When we met, I was seventeen, a senior in high school, and he was forty-two, my teacher. The photo of me as a blonde was taken in June of 1986, when I was twenty, exactly one year before we were married. That was the year I began doing art work again, after a three-year break. He told me I had no artistic ability; I believed him and stopped doing art work for three years, so when I began drawing again, it was in secret. At that time, my drawings were mostly of eyes, blue eyes, always crying. Or of a woman with torrents of blonde hair and blue eyes, crying. Or with hair and half a face, or only eyes on a page.

I moved to New York City in 1988 at age twenty-two and began divorce proceedings. I left behind my entire family and ex-husband/abuser who my family continues to advocate.

I began therapy immediately upon arriving and there discovered I had been sexually abused. I wanted to get far away from being blonde while I worked on changing many old patterns, so I colored my hair black. The photo of me with black hair was taken in December of 1989, one and a half years into therapy.

Since I was twelve, I have been obsessed with make-up. I had long false nails and would constantly and compulsively purchase make-up in an effort to improve my appearance. My goal was to look like a magazine centerfold.

After beginning therapy, my need to wear lots of make-up lessened considerably, and I was left with a huge box filled with all different types of make-up that I no longer used. Nail polish, lipstick, lip gloss, eyeshadow and blush.

After visiting the Museum of Modern Art, I was extremely intrigued by the works of Jackson Pollack. I would spend hours at the museum sitting in front of his work, sometimes crying. There was some strong connection. I decided I would like to try that form of expression—it seemed freeing. Not having enough

self photo, 1987

self photo, 1989

money to buy paint but wanting something with a paintlike consistency, I thought to try the nail polish. It worked perfectly and I opened up a new world for myself.

I began dripping the polish on the paper, then flinging it and smearing it with my fingers, and other paintbrushes. Soon after, I began incorporating all of the other make-up in the box.

It felt wonderful to be smearing, with my brushes and my fingers, and flinging—to be creating something beautiful with the make-up I had been using for so many years to cover myself up.

Then I bought some watercolors and realized they, too, had a free-flinging effect, and now I alternate between watercolor and make-up. The nail-polish works are very explosive and bursting with color: purple, pink, burgundy, orange, coral and magenta. Some of the first layers were started with lipstick, pinks, corals and oranges, with nail-polish bursts, like flowers, or dripped or flung over the top. Some have foundation or blush as a first layer, with lipstick and nail polish dripped and smeared to create second and third layers.

The watercolors similarly have a smeared first layer. Often I would stick my fingers in the paint and take them directly to the paper. Other times, I have taken brushes to make the first layer

Untitled, 1989, 14″ × 11″, watercolor

strokes and then dripped paint from the brush or flung it across the top. Once, I just put the paint on the page and added water to the paper.

The first time I took my work to therapy, my therapist asked me what the blue dot, the size of a period, was at the bottom of the page. I told her it was my signature—I didn't want my signature to ruin the work. She pointed out to me that over the year of my work, the signature had been getting steadily larger. I hadn't even noticed. Now I notice that my signature continues to grow larger. I feel it is part of the work, as I am part of the work, I am it, it is me.

There have been many times in the past three years that I have not known how I was going to make it through the night. I have been in such pain that I have wondered if it would be better to not be alive. At those times, I have turned to the paper and the nail polish or watercolor. Several times, my tears have been in the work, adding to the watercolors and afterward, I am able to sleep, I know I can make it to tomorrow. I keep most of my work on the walls of my apartment to show me who I am, where I have been and where I am going.

The Camera Doesn't Lie

Patti Levey

I AM ASLEEP AND *dreaming. In the dream I am asleep. I don't know where I am or how old I am. Suddenly, I feel afraid. The fear is so great it prevents me from being able to make a sound. I feel like I'm in a tunnel; all I can see is black. It is as if I have no body, only eyes. The feeling of fear is so intense that it seems like something tangible, an object with no form or substance. I know that I am about to remember something terrifying. My mind says, "NO," and a small voice from inside me manages to scream out, "Mom, Mom." I wake up immediately and find myself at home, in my own bed. I am thirty old years old and I am trying to remember what happened to me.*

For the past ten years, I have used self-portrait photography as an art form as well as a means of self-examination, discovery and healing. Besides being a photographer, I have a Masters Degree in Feminist Therapy and have been developing a technique and practice using self-portrait photography as a form of therapy with women.

It has only been in the past four years that I have begun to identify myself as a sexual abuse survivor. Up until then, my life had seemed to me like a puzzle for which I had many of the pieces, but I couldn't put them together because something crucial was missing. When I went to school to become a therapist and learned about incest and sexual abuse, all of a sudden, my whole life started to make sense. It was as if I'd put on 3-D glasses and could finally see the world with a new dimension. So far, the knowledge of my abuse has come to me in the form of dreams, body memories, chronic depression and fatigue, anxiety, compulsive behaviors and physical ailments. At present, I am still amnesiac about many of the details of the abuse. I am using photography as a means to evoke memory and to validate what I already believe to be true; my photographs are my memories.

I have always been a self-oriented, introspective person, so it seemed quite natural for me to take pictures of myself—to focus inward. At first, even though self-portrait photography was the most interesting and comfortable mode of expression for me and I

Right, *Bridal/Bridle Series: Three Blind Brides,* 1988, 11″ × 14″, black & white photo

felt compelled to do it, I still felt insecure about it. I felt I had to apologize for the need to focus on myself, the need to be self-directed instead of externally focused on the world around me. It seemed that what made me unique as a person and what made my photographs unique as works of art was also somehow devaluing, inappropriate and something to be ashamed of. To some extent, my feelings were validated by the art world and by the culture at-large that values photography as documentation, a reflection of the search for "objective truth" and "reality," as well as sensationalism. For the first two years as a photographer, living in New York City, I forced myself to carry my camera with me wherever I went. I would criticize myself obsessively for failing to capture the "perfect moment," because when I would see something or someone that I wanted to photograph, I would usually hesitate, freeze or somehow be unable to take the picture. I would mourn the loss of the photograph that had the potential for giving me a sense of self-esteem and also blame myself for sabotaging myself, for somehow being afraid to "succeed" or "grow up." Later on, I realized that my relationship to the camera in this aspect was a perfect metaphor for the double-bind that I and most other women find ourselves in, wanting to succeed in a male-dominated society that devalues them and what is associated with the female, including sensitivity, introspection and intuition, and then blames us for our own victimization and oppression. I believe that making self-portraits is as much a political as a personal act. It is as radical for a woman to take pictures of herself as it is for a woman to love herself in this culture.

Initially, my obsession with self-portraiture came from a need to reveal the most intimate and painful aspects of myself. I was reacting to the incredible system of denial in my family, the need to hide family problems, to preserve and protect the status quo, the family image, at any cost, even my sanity. Within this system, the camera was a tool for denial, a way to prove to ourselves and the world that nothing was wrong. Every important stage of my life from birth to early adulthood was documented by the camera. I was photographed at every birthday, holiday, vacation and family gathering looking beautiful, happy and perfect, but feeling angry and depressed. These images were then put into album after family album, becoming, ironically, my photographic history. In this context, the process of being photographed felt unpleasant and intrusive. It is no surprise that when I left home and began to express myself artistically, I used the camera to create my own photographic history, to reclaim my feelings, my body, my sense of personal power and my pain.

Considering my history, the camera is now the perfect tool for me to use in my process of healing from childhood sexual

abuse. The camera is no longer a tool for denial but a vehicle for uncovering and telling the truth. After all, "the camera doesn't lie!" (People do!) Generally speaking, photographs are considered indisputable evidence that something has occurred, that an event, such as a crime, has been committed. Photography is often used to document and chronicle change, such as occurs through healing and transformation. The process of creating photographs, exposing film and paper to light and transforming it. As I photograph myself, I expose myself and others to the truth, and in doing so, heal myself.

Self-portrait photography has always been a healing medium for me for many reasons. To begin with, it has been an incredible relief for me to be able to externalize what has been for so long internalized. The self-portraits have allowed me to get the pain out of my body where it has been contained and focused. Feelings such as anger, grief, shame, guilt and despair are less self-destructive, incapacitating and overwhelming to me when they are represented outside of myself in a visible, tangible and permanent form. My photographs are evidence of feelings and experiences that will not disappear, change or be forgotten; they can be accessed at any time or put away until I can deal with them. Because the photographs are one step removed from my body, they provide a safe place for me to express my feelings and have them responded to by others. In this sense, photography has allowed me to communicate nonverbally, which is especially healing since it is likely that my abuse occurred at an age when I was preverbal.

Besides being a tool for self-revelation and validation, self-portrait photography has always been the most satisfying, fascinating, intriguing form of creative expression for me because it most resembles the process of the unconscious. I work spontaneously and intuitively, often without a preconception of what I'm going to do. Since I am photographing myself, I cannot see my own image through the camera lens until it is revealed to me later, through the development of the negatives and prints, much like how what is unknown is revealed in dreaming. In this sense, the process of photographing myself is more a kinesthetic than a visual one. Once I have the camera positioned and focused, I *feel* where I am in the frame.

It has also been essential and empowering for me to be in control of the process of photographing myself. I always work alone, using a tripod, a 2¼ format camera, and a long cable release. I have intentionally included the cable release in my photographs rather than concealing it, because it functions as evidence that I am taking the picture of myself and that I am in control of how I am portraying myself. It is also a sort of metaphoric lifeline or umbilical cord connecting me to the camera, and consequently to the

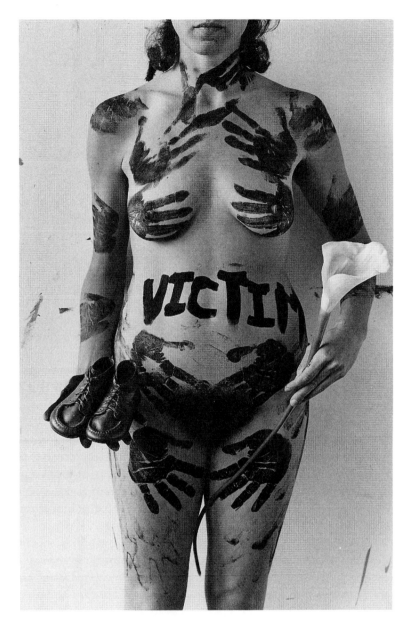

Victim, 1989, 8″ × 10″, black
& white photo

viewer and the outside world.

   Showing my self-portraits to others, whether on an individual basis or to groups, in classes, slide presentations, magazine
articles and public exhibitions, has been an integral part of the
healing process for me. My original need to photograph myself
was not only for self-expression and examination, but for others,
including family members, friends and the general public, who
needed to see and validate my pain. Yet exposing myself in the
way that I do, both physically and emotionally, has been, at
times, a painful experience. (I cried for three days after the open-

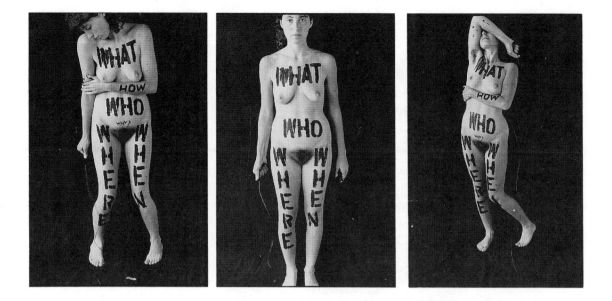

Who, What, Where, When, Why Series, 1989, 8″ × 10″, black & white photos

ing of my first show.) Although I can control how other people will respond to them, I realize that showing my work in public leaves me open to the possibility of being re-abused. My worse fear is not that I will be misunderstood or criticized, but that I might be seen as a sexual object and approached in that context. My need to expose myself and to be responded to in an supportive and nonthreatening way is a result of having been violated in the past. Fortunately, I have never felt threatened or retraumatized as a result of my work. For the most part, my experience of sharing my photographs with others has been overwhelmingly positive; I have received all kinds of useful and insightful feedback over the years, as well as encouragement and understanding.

I am standing in a large room with a high ceiling, white walls and a concrete floor. I am alone. The room is empty except for my belongings. I am naked. One whole side of the room is made up of windows looking out onto a small garden. Next to me is an open bottle of black tempera paint and dirty paintbrush lying on a paper towel. Square cardboard stencils of letters smeared with black paint are strewn across the floor, along with photographs of me as a child, and a pile of discarded clothes, sneakers and my watch and earrings. In my right hand I am holding the bulb at the end of my cable release cord that runs to my camera. My camera sits perched on top of my tripod, facing me. For a moment I sense the cold air around me, the smell of paint, the glow of the window light on my body. A thought passes through my mind: "Why am I here? Who did this to me?" I stare straight into the lens of the camera, concentrating on the position of my body. My arms fall limp at my sides and my right hand squeezes into a fist. I hear the familiar "click" of the shutter releasing itself. Before I have time to feel anything, I run down the hall to the bathroom, step into

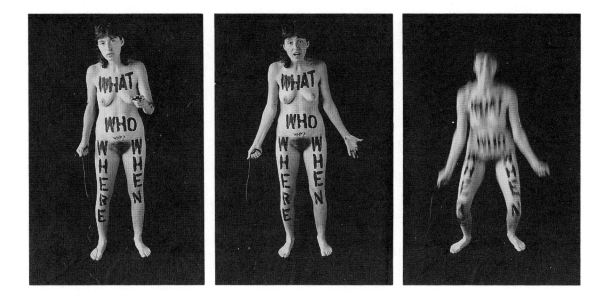

the cold metal shower stall and let the water wash the paint from my body. The paint runs down my arms and legs and disappears down the drain. Looking down at myself, I see that where the paint had been, the word "victim," pink and rash-like, is still visible on my skin, faint but legible.

I got the idea to paint words on my body from a friend—also a sexual abuse survivor and a therapist. She suggested that in my next photo session I ask myself/my body questions about my abuse. She thought that perhaps I would express the answers to the questions symbolically or unconsciously in the photographs, and I would learn more about the details of my abuse. After thinking about her suggestion, I went out and bought some paint, a paintbrush, a chalk board and chalk. I wanted to be able to write the questions and erase them. (The chalkboard also reminded me of childhood.) I wanted to create a series of photographs about sexual abuse that was different than any I had done in the past.

Up until then, my self-portraits had been metaphoric, dreamlike and surreal. Having been created with an audience in mind, they had also been aesthetically pleasing and technically proficient and complex. By using elaborate costumes and props as well as making multiple exposures in one photographic image, I was able to create a symbolic visual language with which I communicated quite effectively exactly how I felt as an adult survivor of childhood sexual abuse (angry, distraught, confused, isolated, wounded, incapacitated, out of control, dissociated from my body and the world around me, dead, ashamed) and how I felt in the process of healing and loving myself. This work, although powerful and healing, was somehow incomplete, in that I did not address

*Who, What, Where, When,
Why Series,* 1989, 8″ × 10″,
black & white photos

the abuse itself, only the *results* of the abuse.

My new series of self-portraits represents another stage of my healing process. It is not so much about the adult survivor as it is about the child victim. These images are not ethereal, dreamlike or symbolic, but concrete and direct. These images are less about the pain in my psyche and more about the memory in my body. By painting words on myself, I have, in essence, given my body a voice! Using words instead of symbols feels healing, in that it means breaking silence on a different level: giving the child inside of me the ability to speak for herself.

Although this new series of self-portraits has not evoked any "picture memory" of my abuse, it has given me some useful information about which parts of my body were molested and which parts are holding the secret. For instance, all of the words that I painted on myself that were statements I wrote on my belly, my solar plexus—my center of personal power. This is also an area in which I experience episodic and sometimes chronic pain and digestive problems, especially during periods of stress and *always* when I work on anything connected to sexual abuse. (My stomach hurt during the photo session as well.) In most of the photographs in this series, I have cut off my head/face, showing my body from the neck down, and in some I have focused on my torso, cropping out everything but my breasts, abdomen and upper thighs. In some of the photographs I put handprints in black paint on my arms, neck, chest, breast, abdomen and upper thighs. In another I stenciled the words "Who, What, Where, How and Why?" on my arms, legs, chest and abdomen. The "Why" was the last word I added, handwritten and smaller than the other words, painted directly above my pubic hair. (Perhaps that is the most difficult question for me to ask myself and to answer). During the process of photographing myself, I realized that I felt physically and emotionally dissociated from my body and the process I was engaged in. I found myself running back and forth from the studio to the bathroom, writing words on myself and washing them off in a sort of ritualized, yet obsessive manner. The same defense mechanisms that helped me to survive childhood sexual abuse—dissociation, compulsive behaviors and amnesia—are still operating to protect me, even in my quest for information, memory and truth. Ironically, I believe that it is as much my ability to dissociate from frightening experiences and feelings, as it is my blind faith in the creative process, that allows me to create these images and share them with others.

Although I did not create my most recent photographic series with an audience in mind, I did include these images in a group show in Mendicino, California, entitled "Art for Empowerment and Healing: A Show of Women's Work." The response to the show in general and to my work specifically was overwhelmingly positive. But by far the most moving feedback I received was from a young woman who thanked me for having the courage to create these images about sexual abuse. She had been raped when she was thirteen years old and she felt the photographs I took of myself with handprints on my body communicated exactly how she had felt afterwards, as if she still carried the imprint of the rapist's touch on her body.

In general, going public with my photographs while identifying myself as an incest survivor is a different experience than simply exhibiting my self-portraits as an artist. I feel more vulnerable on a personal level and a bit paranoid about the effects that my breaking silence might have on others, specifically family members and people who knew me as a child. Being amnesiac puts me in the awkward position of knowing the truth on some level, and doubting myself on another. I have the need to validate my experiences and feelings, but at the same time, I am afraid of hurting myself and the people I love by telling the truth.

In the future, I plan to continue using the camera in my search for memories. I would like to begin to work with someone I trust who could be present with me while I am photographing myself. I believe that having someone else present would help me to feel less isolated and more supported during this process and would prevent me from dissociating from my feelings in the moment. Ultimately, I hope that I will be able to reach greater insight into my abuse by becoming more conscious of what I am doing and feeling while I am working. I hope that the work I do continues to affect other sexual abuse survivors in a positive way, and that by developing my skills for self-healing I can become more effective as a healer, working with other women photo-therapeutically. I am also trying to accept the possibility that I may never recover complete memory of my abuse, that my dreams, body memories, feelings and of course, my photographs, may have to be enough. I don't have to remember in order to heal, but I do need to believe in myself. After all, "The Camera Doesn't Lie!"

Writing My Self
Into Existence

Roseann Lloyd

I STARTED WRITING POEMS and stories in grade school. I wanted to be a writer and write books like *Jo's Boys.* I wanted to have an active, happy family like the one in that book. My grandma read poems out loud to me, and she said I was talented. But I didn't have the slightest idea about how to become a writer. Various forces in my family—the way that incest pushes us into taking care of other people—and the culture of the sixties lead me to give up my thoughts of writing without even knowing I'd ever had them. I entered the practical occupations, marriage and English teaching. I did all the things this culture says you have to do to be a grown-up.

As a young woman, I was conscious that I'd been been sexually abused by my father, but I rationalized that it hadn't affected me. I was determined that it wouldn't affect me! I ignored the many indications that it was causing me problems and set out to look normal and have my perfect family life. I didn't write anything. I didn't talk about incest. Then in 1971, my brother died of a drug overdose, and in the extremity of grief, I started writing about his life and death, and eventually my own pain. During this time, some words in *Redbook* leaped off the page and changed my life—Masters & Johnson stated in their column that incest affects "all aspects of a person's life." For whatever reasons, these were the words that were the key to my willingness to ask for help, to say the word *incest* out loud to my friends.

In 1975, I went back to graduate school in Montana and worked on poems. I was on an adventure. To discover how they work. To find the ones I love. To see what's been done. How to find the magic.

There were many things I wanted to write about: childhood, U.S. culture, families, children, sexual abuse, the condition of women, the delights of the wilderness, friends, adult life. At the time that I tried to write about incest, there wasn't much written about it in poetry. But I had support from women in the women's movement, both friends and the spirit of the times. I didn't have many literary models for what I wanted to do. The poets I studied with in Montana, Tess Gallagher, Madeline DeFrees and Richard Hugo, never once questioned my subject matter. I understand this is not the case at other institutions. And it's not the attitude of many editors. I feel lucky that I was where I was when I started. I worked through the poetry workshop there to see how I could use the whole range of poetic forms to give voice to the experiences that were painful. I wanted to bring to words some sense of the emotional damage. As I've moved farther into my recovery, my objectives have gone through some changes, but the desire to name the pain continues to be present in my work.

It is difficult to write about incest. The sexual details of abuse may seem to be a turn-on to the reader. Yet some explicit details *have to* be used in the poems, because the denial of abuse is so strong in our culture. If a poem is vague, a reader may push the knowledge away, saying, "Oh, she misunderstood that kiss on the cheek." Denial thrives on diminishment. Detail is important, and the selection of a few powerful details is crucial. These details need to be connected to the feelings that are a result of the violation. Letting the feelings become evident to the reader is often just as difficult as selecting the details. The feelings include powerlessness, the loss of innocence and childhood, the terror, the lack of safety, fear, divided loyalties—all the stuff that happens inside of a child who is being abused, and the feeling lasting into adulthood—despair, addictions, isolation, the sense of not existing, being invisible.

As I've worked on my writing, aware of these issues, I've tried many approaches to writing about abuse. I decided I'd simply consider all the poetic forms of the Western traditions and those of indiginous people around the world as a treasure chest I could choose from. I experimented with many traditional forms, the power of chants and rhymes. Two of the poems included here, "Oh" and "Exorcism of *Nice*" came out of that work. I turned to metaphor when I started working on the poem "*Insect* Is an Anagram for *Incest*." My goal was to convey the terror of living in a house with an abuser. (Comparing the abuse to the feeling of being invaded by insects seems rather unfair to the Animal Queendom, but there it is anyway.) Using a metaphor goes more deeply into our consciousness than simply saying, "It was creepy." I wanted the metaphor to carry the depth of violation, in a fuller emotional way than the explicit description of actions. I don't think other people understand the experience if we—those of us writing about abuse—just say, "It was creepy, horrible." We need to find other ways to say this. Some poems start out at the level of "It was creepy," but then they need to become more developed to reach other people, as well as for the writer to reach new levels of understanding of what has happened. Poems that stay at the level of "It was creepy" are like a primal scream—it expresses pain, but not the dimensions and consequences of the pain. The primal scream is the first step, and then we move on to explore and express more about life. And even as I'm writing now about "conveying" something to other people, I need to say that I know that my first reader is me. I write to make my life real to me. I write my self into existence as I write my story. And that sense of existence and nonexistence is the theme of the last poem of mine included in this book. "Not Even a Shadow on the Sidewalk" uses the shadow metaphor, and stories weaving in and out of the metaphor. Lately I've been using a much more long-lined conversational language than I did in my earlier work, which to me feels like there's less distance between me and the voice in the poem.

In the process of writing about incest—an intellectual as well as an emotional process as you can see in the paragraph above—I was led back into therapy. Writing the poems opened up new levels of pain. I was overwhelmed by all the new feelings, memories, flashbacks, that came out of the writing, like a volcano. For a while, I had to stop writing and talk directly to another person about the abuse, free of the need to "shape the material." I needed to cry and express my anger and other primary feelings. I needed to make changes in my family life. My work with the first therapist hadn't gone deep enough. I mention this in this article about writing for two reasons. First of all, it is important for me to say that my writing is a wonderful and magical part of my life, but it doesn't provide me with all the answers. Some people say their computer is their best friend, but I haven't figured out how they get any satisfaction from hugging that monitor. Writing is sometimes a dead end. Secondly, it's important for me to say that I looked for a therapist several times before I found one who could actually walk with me on the journey I needed to walk. So my writing led me to therapy, and then that led me to other groups and back to writing again. What I learn in therapy often comes back to my writing in another form. I see my writing life and my "real life" as integral parts of each other. They are both real and interact with each other.

After working for over ten years on writing, I worked on putting together a manuscript of poetry. The writing about my childhood was central to the manuscript, but I didn't want my book to be only about incest. I wanted the book to show the full range of my life, aspects of me as a citizen, mother, teacher, etc., not only as a victim/survivor. I want my work to affirm the present lives that we have; many of us who were victims as children walk around looking like ordinary people. It's important for us and the culture to comprehend that ordinary people have been through extraordinary events and lived to talk about them. Twenty-five percent of all women have been abused before the age of eighteen—where are we?

That manuscript became my first book, *Tap Dancing for Big Mom,* published in 1986 by New Rivers Press. It's now in its second printing. The publisher, Bill Truesdale, has supported my work. By the time the book was published, I'd read many of the poems in public. I'm always keyed up at readings, but now I don't feel afraid of the fear—I see the fear and adrenaline now as a energy to use for clarity during the reading. I make changes as I go, in a sort of heightened awareness. There's an extra level of fear when I'm reading poems about incest because of all the myths around it, and the vulnerability. What I practice is the affirmation and knowledge that I'm not alone. Sometimes I'm shaky, but I take a slow breath and know that there will be someone else in the room who will connect with my work. This knowledge is always true.

When I first started writing, I thought my audience would be women. Being more public about my history, I've discovered that many men have also been been sexually abused as children. I think the next level of work about incest will be the men who were abused. I offer them support for the courage it will take for them to tell their stories, and to shed their tears.

In my work teaching writing, I've met many other people struggling to write about horrifying events. I like the fact that many of our images are similar, that I can see a pattern in the human reaction to abuse. The images are a connection. Getting the images on paper is one way to release the terror of the past. If we have common images in response to abuse, we can also find common images for the process of being healed.

When my book was published, I continued with my own poems, yet I felt released from the pressure to publish my own work for the time being. I co-translated a novel from Norwegian, *The House With the Blind Glass Windows,* by Herbjørg Wassmo, about a girl growing up in an abusive family, which was published by Seal Press. Then I worked on a book with another writer, Richard Solly, called *Journey Notes: Writing for Recovery and Spiritual Growth.* This is a book that may be used by people writing alone or in a group. And then I worked on editing a book with Deborah Keenan, another poet, published last year, *Looking for Home: Women Writing about Exile.* The poems in this book have a deep connection to my own work, and my struggle to break out of the exile imposed by abuse. Three collaborative books fast out seems to be saying something about my changing view of community! And a fourth is on the way. What seems to be happening with my work is that it's going in many directions at once but they weave together. I continue to write my own poems, and I'm working now on poems with longer lines, longer poems even than in *Tap Dancing for Big Mom*. I'm writing about friendships and community, working to find the images that can represent some of the trust and joy and safety that comes with recovery.

Exorcism of *Nice*

Mum's the word
Taciturn
Talk polite
Appropriate
Real nice
Talk polite
Short and sweet
Keep it down
Quiet down
Keep the lid on
Hold it down
Shut down
Shut up
Chin up
Bottle up
Drink up
Up tight
Tied up in knots
Tight-lipped
Hold tight
Tongue-tied
Hold your tongue
Hold still
Hold it back
Hold it in
Hold your cards close to your chest
Close-mouthed
Muzzled
Gagged
Garbled
Jammed up
All wrapped up
Tied up
Shut up
Zonked out
Tucked in
Caved in
Shut in
Locked in
Incoherent
Inarticulate
In a shell
Shell-shocked

Thunder–struck
Dumb–struck
Stupefied
Shut–down
Stunned

    Oh, Wicked Mother of the Kingdom of Silence
    I have obeyed you
    long enough.

OH

W.C. Fields, that fat old mother of Speak Your Mind, outrageous
even on death's bed:
> *When I think of all my money, I think of all the little orphans who*
> *could use some change, then, on the other hand, I say Fuck 'em*

It is reported that when women lay dying
90% murmur *OH*

When women lay beaten
it is said they cover their faces
and murmur *OH*

Opaque cream smooths
a new skin
      of the face
                 Trusty blue
mascara fastens eyes
to innocence
      The arch
to the brows
      alerts intelligence
And the sweet
      bright red
         holds
the mouth
      perpetually open
         in its
perpetual

OH

This mask is strong and real
like life
but more reliable   It will not tic
or flutter   It will not show
fear   nor any other
motion
    except for the mouth
       offering
          its cheery *OH*

     And the name of the mask is *Smile-pretty-now-never-mind*
     The name of the mask is *Suffer-in-silence, Carry-on*

The name of the smile is *Lookin' good*
The name of the mouth is *Sorrow*

OH   she said when he sucker-punched
her in the bar   *OH*   she said again
on the heating pad in bed   *OH*
she breathes into the world
Thin puffs of disbelief

Never enough air   for one clear sound
for YES for NO   for
LET ME THINK THAT OVER

    OH   the half-sigh   breath-that's-not-enough
      giving in
         even as it goes

    The name of this breath is *Scared-to-death*
    The name of death is *Suffer-in-silence-China-Doll*
    The name of the doll is *Little-Mother-of-Disbelief*
    The name of the doll is *Lost*
    The name of her smile is *Sorrow*

If you break a doll   it does not cry out
to the neighbors
Help me

If you take a doll to W.C. Fields movies
it mutters   *bad-mouth*   *trash*

If you wind a doll up
it sings:

      Victim once
      Victim twice
      I'd rather be beaten
      Than scared all my life

    The name of this song is *Raggedy Wife*
    The name of her dress is *Catch-my-breath*
    The name of her breath is *Dragged-out-death*
    The name of her death is *Porcelain Doll*
    The name of her smile is *Sorrow*

When it expires—that last
devoted *OH*—

it won't hurt at all   the practiced
half-breath
giving in
even as it goes

    But the name of Mother is *Lots-more-left*
    The name of Mother is *Curse-your-death*
    The name of Mother is *Spit-it-out*

The Fat Old Mother called *Love-yourself-enough*
    will give you
        breath enough
    to say what you need to say

Beginning with   *OH*
Say with full   slow breath
Say   *Mother I'm scared he hit me*
    Mother he touched me funny
        Mother don't turn your face away

For the name of Mother is *More-than-enough*
The name of Mother is *Slow-deep-breath*
The name of Mother is *Lots-more-left*

Her breath will carry you   beyond your sorrow
beyond your death

Your breath will give *Sorrow* a brand-new name:
    Sorrow your name was *Dog-at-my-throat*
    Sorrow your name was *Smile-pretty-now-never-mind*

    Oh Sorrow
        we will name you *Left-behind*

    Oh Sorrow
        when we finally name you

        we finally let you
            let us go

Insect Is an Anagram for *Incest*

1

hands spider their way
    under the covers   silky
secretions   spin out
       webs in all the bright
          and shadowed corners

    hands quiet as silverfish
burrow the night and day
      startle the leather-bound books
        sleeping in the attic

      glassy eyes twitch after footfalls
especially those that amble
       towards the wicker couch
      flowering in the basement
       hunch-back beetles
         peer out
           the fruit cellar
           the motionless blue jars

2

No room in the house is safe
Not any nook or cranny
Not the dusty closet under the eaves
cozy as summer woods
Not the cave under the bed
surrounded
by the spread's soft tassles
Not the cushioned window seat
on the second-story
landing   Not the bay window
with its paisley satin pillows
and one thousand peacock

eyes opening
to the neighboring fields

There are skitters everywhere
and footsteps   fingers   breath across
the back of the neck

The burrows under the snowball bushes
that lead to the cool dark
under the large and rambling porch
look lovely as grandmother's lap

Skitters   whispers   harsh
breath across
the back
of the neck

3

What can be done to rid the house of fear?
Scrub down the floors
Burn the curtains and drapes
Fumigate
Air the books on the sunny grass lawn
Sweep the ceilings with the rag-covered broom
Spread mothballs in the cupboards and eaves
FRESH PAINT   FRESH
PAIN   surely white
enamel allows nothing to hide

Cobwebs   spin   out
from the glistening corners   Eggs bubble
up from under the surface
sheen and the anagram tiles
face down
in their drawer   spell out
the insect names   over and over

4

Even though the bathroom tiles
have been scrubbed with Lysol
Even though the dishes are stacked in order
Even though the beds

are stripped and changed and the toys
sorted and put away

The Tinker Toys   standing at attention
in their cardboard tower
twist and flap their hands

The bride doll   locked in her train case
with the net and sequin trousseau
scratches at her face

The diamond blocks
arranged in their patterned box
perfect as the perfect pattern on the lid
grind chips of paint
off their wooden sides

And in the box that pictures maple trees and cloudless sky
the tiny men in red shirts
crackle their guns
like matchsticks struck
by curious children

In the drawer of the dining room buffet
the anagram tiles
click out
the secret letters   once again

5

My father's fingers   skip   spider feet
across my skin   my mother
was eaten alive   the paper on my desk crumbles
under the nub of the pen   and the child
in my home   hunches over   she
starts at every approach   outside
my window   the wet sheets
rise up from the line   billow
wild—monster crawdads
springing on the wind

Not Even a Shadow on the Sidewalk

for Susan C.

A woman on "Frontline" goes back to the house
where her father raped her—
she had to look at the bedroom again
to find what it was she was missing
There   she said   and the camera
did a close-up on the wall   *that gray wall*
that's where I went
when he came to my bed
That little child
is the part of me that's missing

I was jealous when I heard her talking
because I didn't go anywhere in particular
when my dad climbed on my bed
It's not that I can't remember where I went
I didn't go anywhere
I was just gone   like the people in Japan
blown away by the atom-bomb
Annihilated
There wasn't even a shadow left
on the sidewalk
to say   someone's missing

My symptoms developed   like the side-effects
of nuclear war—numb hands   missing hands
disconnected synapses
wheezing chest
damaged vision: staring at the white light
weak limbs
reamed out like the inside of a sewer pipe
aphasia   memory loss   splitting
headaches

Symptoms are a way to have feelings:
the body keeps on living
after annihilation
that is, something called "I"
kept living but never understood what people meant
when they talked about self-esteem
when they said incest victims had low self-esteem

I had lots of esteem
I always got good grades

first grade gold stars   Phi Beta Kappa
I was a good piano player   diligent
a good worker   good lay   good mom
I was no dummy
I could see the accomplishments
I had esteem
What did it have to do with me?

If the I   was a me, it didn't have a self
There was no scale on which to measure
low   medium   or high   self-esteem
There was no yardstick to measure   no shadow
on the sidewalk
someone   was missing

Some people call this condition *despair* and it was
Some people call it *abandonment* and it was that too
Some people call child abuse *murder of the soul*
I can see that is what
happened to me
All those labels make sense to my mind
but what it was as I experienced it
was simply
non-being

Drinking gave life to the ashes
of a self that wasn't there
When I was drinking I was there
I felt real
I could feel my hands
I could talk from the heart
I knew the me
who was drinking

Then I was secure being in the world
safe being inside my physical body
like the night in 1972 when four of us got drunk on Scotch
It was me and Mike and Jim and Mary
it had been raining and when it cleared up
we walked to the park to see
if we could see any stars—
we lay down on the grass and the trees
were that slippery wet green black and dripping on us and the
    grass was soaked
but we were laughing our heads off
we didn't care how wet it was

we had our winter jackets on even though it was spring
and we stayed there a long time   laying in that soggy grass
like four kids at a sleep-over   talking telling stories
feeling good together   liking the comraderie

When we got home   Mary went to bed with her coat on
The rest of us were too drunk to help her take it off
but that was O.K. too
I'd do the laundry in the morning
I had nothing better to do than wash muddy sheets
I loved being with them
I loved living like the night would never end

But in the morning it was back to nothing
Back to wondering what to do
with myself wondering
whether to make this choice
over any other   why this husband   or that lover
why   this job   no job   when would it be right to
go back to school   ready to leave for Canada
at the drop of a hat   etc. etc.
I did the laundry   cleaned
the bathroom   said   *Who cares*

it's all an illusion   all Maya

I got that word from reading Strindberg
and he got it from the Hindus
life is an illusion
life is the dream that's dreaming us   so what
does it matter what anyone does
That was my comfort
for nothingness
I was smart
I could do lots of things
I had time   all the time in the world

I thought this was sophisticated
I thought my drinking was sophisticated
After all   my favorite toast
was the skoal Bente and I used to say

Guttår min sjel   fukta din aska

which means in English *Here's to you my soul*
wet your ashes   I didn't feel the despair of

these words   I had not yet let
that terrible sense of abandonment sweep over me
I didn't know   something
was missing

I didn't know
that there wasn't even a shadow
on the sidewalk

to announce my missing name

Writing as an Act of Healing

Catherine Houser

B END YOUR KNEES. Ground yourself. Most of you are living from the neck up—get some of that energy down into
your feet—feel where you are on the earth, in the world."
I was surrounded by twenty other women, all writers, many
looking as bewildered as I felt—this was a writers' workshop, after all, not an exercise class, so why were we bending our knees,
breathing deeply, swaying back and forth and "getting in touch
with our bodies?" What did this have to do with writing?

Truth is, I had by that time had enough of my body. A week
earlier a doctor, an endocrinologist, having poked and prodded
his way across the full terrain of my neck, had pronounced,
"There's something terribly wrong here. We need to get in there
and see what's going on—I'm scheduling you for a biopsy." I
knew what that meant; I'd been there before, three years earlier,
in 1985, when they had first discovered, or shall I say first named,
the lumps in my neck. That was when the marble-sized lumps
crowding my trachea and pressing on my larynx, after having
been misdiagnosed by another doctor in 1979 as scar tissue from
an injury I'd had in a car accident, had been diagnosed as benign
thyroid tumors. Now, in the early fall of 1988, the tumors were
growing out of control. They had more than doubled in size and
were now dense, hard knots in my neck.

I'd seen enough doctors and studied enough about my condition in the three years I had lived with the label to know that when
these benign, dormant tumors begin to grow there is always the
threat that they've become malignant—cancerous. I knew by the
urgency in the doctor's voice that that was what I might be facing.
Never one to be a passive patient, I left the doctor's office with
my head spinning with ideas on how to deal with the worst-case
scenario—if the lumps were now cancerous. I knew from the out-
set that the simple solution was surgery—just have them removed, along with my thyroid gland, and I'd never have to
worry about them again. That had been an option even when they
were discovered to be benign in 1985. I thought then, and continue to believe now, that there was a reason for those lumps being in my neck—not that I had given myself the tumors but that I

had something to learn from this situation, and simply having them surgically removed was not the lesson.

Luckily, living near Boston, I found myself surrounded by both the most sophisticated of traditional medical options and the most untraditional of new-age practices. I began exploring both. Even before they performed the biopsy, I began seeing what's known as an energy field therapist. It was there, lying on her table as she directed energy through my body and at the tumors in my neck, that I had my first memories of being sexually abused as a child.

To appreciate this fully, one must have the full picture: I was thirty-two years old, a college professor and a writer who had explored what I had believed to be the full reality of my past in a 500-page novel I'd written when I was twenty-five. Furthermore, I had been through countless years of cognitive psychotherapy to deal with problems I had had as an adult as a result of my father's alcoholism and my brother's long-term drug addiction. I was fully aware of the possibility of my having been sexually abused as a child—I'd even explored that possibility briefly with a therapist I had seen years before and had come up empty—no memories. To add to what appeared to be a picture of nearly complete self-awareness, I had spent the previous two years supporting my partner in her own struggle to heal from the sexual abuse she'd survived as a child. I'd participated as a partner in group therapy sessions, I'd held her as she wept and raged through flashbacks, and I'd listened to her stories and those of others, checking them against my own reality and always coming up with the same answers—no memories of it ever happening to me.

So why here, why now? Therapists and survivors say that your subconscious never reveals more to you than you are able to handle at one time. Well, for the first time in my life I was in a safe place, 3,000 miles from those who had hurt me. That is how I came to understand the "why here, why now" questions that came up with the first memories. Others close to me over the years were asking, "But how can you be sure it happened? How do you know you didn't just conjure up those images from the stories you've heard or read?" As I tried to answer those questions, to deal with my friends' doubts, I began to understand for myself the powers of my body and mind and how those were being reflected in my writing.

Several months before the day my doctor poked at the bulging tumors in my neck and scheduled a biopsy, I had begun writing what was to be my second novel. It was a story that had been a long time coming; after nearly ten years of writing from my own personal experience—thinly veiled autobiography—I was determined to write a story that had nothing to do with me, that was pure, full-blown fiction. The idea had presented itself to me whole in May 1988 as I was giving a final in my freshman writing class. As my students struggled with their final exams, pieces of things I'd been thinking about for years melded in my head and I furiously fleshed out the characters and plot lines for my new novel. In brief, a baby born in the late 1950s is adopted by a childless Mormon couple who, in the name of God, ends up severely abusing her. At fourteen she gives birth to the adoptive father's child and flees to Hollywood, eventually becoming a rich and famous actress, dogged by her jealous, vengeful parents. One thing was for sure: This story was definitely not about me. I couldn't wait to get started on it. With the first words that I wrote, my life began to change. Scrawling Bruce Springsteen's words, "No retreat, baby, no surrender," as an epigraph at the top of a blank page, I set out on what I believed was going to be an expedition in fiction. What I found was truth more real than I could ever have imagined.

The process of self-realization began slowly. I found that after years of banging out stories on the computer I was retreating to pencil and paper. Not only that, I couldn't seem to write in cursive: Something in me was trying so hard to control what was coming out on those pages that I felt I had to print each word, slowly, deliberately. In the past I had been able to write five to ten pages a day; now, suddenly, working on this novel I could do at best about 200 words a day, sometimes not even that in a week. My writing process had changed completely. At the time, I didn't experience what I was writing about as threatening, only difficult, and I believed that was because for the first time in my work as a fiction writer I was "making it up" as I went along.

By the end of the summer, having done little else but work on the novel, I was tired and more than a little depressed. I no longer felt in control of either my own writing process or what I was actually writing—the novel had taken on a life of its own, moving in directions I had not entirely planned. As I sat in front of a half-filled page of pencil scribbles one day waiting for the next line to come, I absentmindedly moved my hand across my neck and found that the long-dormant tumors had suddenly, it seemed, grown into a hard, bulging mass. Initially more irritated at the inconvenience than scared about the possibilities, I made that appointment with the doctor to check things out. Over the next month pieces from a puzzle long scattered across my subconscious came falling into place.

In the space of a week, I was scheduled for a biopsy; had my first energetic healing session, during which I had my first conscious memories of being sexually abused; and ended up in that writers' workshop hoping to get away from my body and my memories for a few hours. But it was in that workshop that it all came together, that I understood how my writing, my truth, my health and my healing were all wrapped up together. My first conscious memories of the abuse were vague, elusive, difficult to put into words, yet they were the most real memories, most true feelings I had ever experienced—because they were visceral. More than remembering with my brain, I was reliving, refeeling the abuse in my body—the choking, the gagging, the hands wrapped around my wrists, the force of being held down. Though the words to describe this still elude me, I walked out of the healing session knowing like I had never known anything before; the certainty was both comforting and terrifying.

Two days later, still shell-shocked from all that was coming up, from all that feeling, I stood in that writers' workshop in Provincetown, Massachusetts, given by Rita Speicher and Margie Erhart, trying to "ground" and listening to a woman talk about writing as a bodily act, not just a mental one—and as an act of health, not just of angst. As one who had come from the Hemingway school of writing—hard drinking and hard living as the only way to write—I had to chuckle at the notion that writing could come any other way, much less through a healthy body engaged in standing, knees bent, and breathing deeply. Then, in a discussion about where writing comes from, Rita said, just matter-of-factly, that memory resides in the body and that it is memory that we draw on for our writing. As someone who had always thought of memory, along with virtually everything else, as a head thing, I shook my head, thinking, "No, that can't be right." Then, as I began thinking about my own work, the big pieces of the cosmic puzzle dropped into place: This was exactly what I had been living over the last several months. Body memories had surfaced first in an purely unconscious way in my writing about a sexually abused girl in my novel. With those memories—that is, with the threat of consciously remembering what had happened to me via the writing—the tumors began growing out of control, leading me to doctors and healers and ultimately to more body memories and the conscious memory of the truth of my own existence. I had, after all, been writing the truth, and I believe that that is what made this project so scary, so threatening that I had to try to control each letter that went on the page by sitting with my body tightly controlled, carefully moving a pencil, letter by letter, across the page.

The lumps were themselves a kind of body memory, a residue of the abuse. To me, it was not simply coincidence that I had these threatening tumors in my neck—I dream in metaphors, I write with metaphors, why shouldn't my body speak to me in metaphors? The tumors in my neck were first discovered when I was in graduate school, trying to find my voice as a writer—writing story after story about my family, about where I had come from. It made perfect sense to me that they began growing, becoming infinitely more threatening both physically, as they crowded my larynx, and psychologically, as their changes seemed to be linked to my writing the novel about the sexually abused girl.

As all of the connections I was making between truth and fiction, illness and health, and body and memory began to make sense, the tumors were diagnosed as cancerous. I set about righting the course I was on. Since the tumors were not life-threatening, I elected not to have surgery. Instead, I found the best doctors, healers and therapists I could and began working on all fronts to understand what my body was telling me and to do what I could to heal it. I started by changing my diet, radically, and began respecting my body as a source of information. At the same time, I began going to an incest survivors group, where, for the first time, I spoke my truth with my authentic voice. I began seeing a bodywork therapist who, through simple techniques of breathing and movement, helped me uncover more memories and helped me move to assimilate them.

Now, a year later, I am a survivor of both childhood sexual abuse and cancerous tumors that cradle my throat. My life has changed considerably as a result of what I have learned since, both about how to live in my body and about how to listen to what it has to tell me. I continue to write, to work on the novel that started me on this path. And, as always, what I could not say, I write.

from To Be Worth Diamonds
March 1956

Spring comes early in the Southwest and nowhere was it more evident than out at Evril's place. The irises, the first flowers of the new year, had already come and gone but neither Evril nor Sarah had noticed. Normally, Sarah snipped a selection of fresh flowers from the small gardens that encircled the house and kept them in a juice glass on the kitchen table. "A little bit of God's handiwork," she'd say every night at dinner just after the blessing. Gently, in an attempt at grace, she'd raise her meaty, work-reddened hand to just barely touch the tip of a petal, trying to draw Evril's attention to the blooms. He'd invariably reach past them to the macaroni-and-hamburger casserole.

Now the first flowers, the irises, lay dead and shriveled by the sun in the flower beds in front of the house. Blues gone gray, yellow tongues of light drowned out by the harsh sun, stalks of green beaten down by the winter monsoons. The flowers, once Sarah's pride, now lay lost among the weeds, while inside the clay brick house she looked after her new charge.

It had been a little more than a month now since Sarah had gotten her wish—a baby she and Evril could call their own. A month of screams in the night that would bolt Sarah upright out of dead sleep. A month of handwashing diapers and hanging them on the line out back. A month of tending to each of Rachel's needs and wants while Evril, in his customary way, stood back in the shadows and watched.

But Sarah was a hearty woman, and more than anything she wanted to show Evril that she was born to this kind of work—she wanted him to think of her as a good wife and mother. So, in the night when the infant's wail pierced the silent desert night, Sarah would slip out of the end of the wood-framed double bed she shared with Evril, and, tiptoeing barefoot across the cold concrete floor to Evril's side of the bed, she would pull the sheets up over his naked shoulders before creeping out of the room to tend to Rachel. Moving through the darkness, Sarah would find her way to the baby's room. Once inside she would close the door, holding the handle tightly so as not to let it slam shut, then she would stuff an old towel into the space between the bottom of the door and the floor. She never knew how long these 2 a.m. ordeals would go on, and she wanted, if at all possible, not to disturb Evril at all.

Once securely inside the little room, Sarah labored in the dark, by memory, to try to calm Rachel. It was a harsh room—concrete floors rolled with a single coat of brown enamel paint, surrounded by brick walls covered with a pseudo-stucco plaster swirled crazily across the bricks and covered in a pale pink paint. The baby's cries pinged off the concrete floor and echoed within the pink walls. The one narrow window in the room had offered Sarah the beacon of the slowly melting moon for the last several nights. But not tonight. Moonless nights in the desert offer their own kind of light, an otherworldly light. It is as if the stars conspire to direct their light straight down, focused on this one patch of dirt in the desert, all beyond, darkness. Everything is cast in white, the white light of millions of stars falling to earth with nothing to stop them—no streetlights, no house lights, no city lights. Evril used to say you could gut a cat and sew it back up again without a trace in the shadowless white light of a moonless night.

Cradling Rachel in the crook of an elbow, Sarah reached with the other hand for the lukewarm bottle she'd set on the dresser earlier in the evening. Her hand fell short of a firm grasp, though, and the bottle met the concrete floor with a loud crash, sending glass and milk to the four corners of the room.

"What the hell is going on in there?" Still full of sleep, Evril's voice sounded gravelly and distant.

"Nothing, honey, I just dropped the bottle. Nothing to worry about. I'll get another one. Go back to sleep." Sarah stood for a moment looking at the shattered glass, baby Rachel wailing in her ear, not knowing exactly what to do next. Finally, compelled by Rachel's squirming and crying, Sarah took a large, careful step over the broken glass, opened the door, and shot down the hall past their bedroom and into the kitchen. She held the baby close to her chest as she set the pan of water over the gas flame and retrieved a fresh bottle from the refrigerator. She then grabbed a rag, and as Rachel sucked on the terry cloth collar of Sarah's bathrobe, she returned to the baby's room. Tiptoeing through the broken glass, Sarah put the baby back in her crib, placated her with a pacifier and stuffed animals, and set about cleaning up the mess. Sarah worked fast and in an instant had the bulk of the broken bottle and spilled milk collected in the rag, but as she moved to pick it up splinters of glass tore through, piercing her fingers and palms. Again she rushed down the hall, this time dripping blood and milk, and as she reached the kitchen sink with the sodden pink bloody mess, Rachel let out a wail that vibrated the very foundation of the house.

"Shit. A man can't get a decent night's sleep around here." Evril was up and out of bed and storming down the hall toward the baby's room.

"Evril, honey, don't worry about it. I'll take care of it. Go back to sleep." Sarah ran cold water over her hands, frantically picking at the fine shards of glass embedded there. A feeling of failure welled up in her—her baby wailing away, her husband up in the middle of the night—she would never be a good mother or a good wife—and as a few last droplets of blood splattered against the white basin she figured Evril was thinking the same thing. The sudden hiss of the water boiling on the stove stole her attention from herself. Now the bottle was too hot. Sarah had turned off the faucet and was wrapping her left hand with a clean dishtowel when she was suddenly caught by the silence. How had Evril quieted the baby when she couldn't? Assuaging her waning motherly ego with the thought that the baby had probably cried herself to sleep, Sarah sat and cradled her aching hands while she waited for the bottle to cool.

But in the moonless light of Rachel's room, Evril stood at the edge of the crib, his hand resting on the baby's chest, the tip of his first finger covered by the petal-soft sucking lips of his baby daughter.

"Little desert rose," he cooed. Rachel squirmed under the increasing pressure of his finger against her mouth. With the baby's breath arrested, his own pulse quickened. Evril took comfort in both.

Creativity as the Way Out

Ayofemi Folayan

IT STARTED WHEN I was five years old: the process of forgetting, of drowning my feelings in a tide of numbness and fear. Each time the betrayal recurred, I retreated farther from myself, from my voice. I couldn't scream, because my grandmother and mother were asleep just walls away. So I learned to focus all my energy on a spot at the corner of the room, where the walls and ceiling meet. I sent all my anguish silently into that point, a supernova of agony and innocence that collapsed into a black hole only I knew about and had to forget.

I spent my time acting like a child. I no longer was a child, dragged forcibly into the experience of adults by the incest. So I watched how other children behaved, and acted like them. No wonder that later in life I perform as an actress, with such intensive preparation. My insides were hollow, as if they had been painfully carved out, like a pumpkin for Halloween. When I was eight years old I attempted suicide for the first time. A playmate who lived down the street had been fatally burned when a water heater exploded. I tried with my limited knowledge to replicate that event by pouring boiling water from a large Pyrex pot over my body.

While I was in the hospital, I discovered music. I was given a portable radio by one of the nurses, who tuned it to a classical music station. I did not immediately connect those healing sounds with the drudgery of practicing scales and counting meter that had been my daily relationship with the piano. I especially adored the piano concerti of Mozart and Rachmaninoff. As my imagination created images of huge concert halls and audiences cheering "Brava!" at my performances, I simultaneously generated a desire to live. After I was released from the hospital, I attacked the process of learning the piano with a vital urgency, determined to connect my efforts to the exhilarating experience the classical music on the radio had afforded me.

I lived in Boston, and in the summer open-air concerts were given by the Boston Pops Orchestra on the banks of the Charles River. I pleaded with my father to take me, which he did. I soaked up each note like a thirsty sponge, sitting on our blankets on the grass by the Esplanade, eating a picnic supper. There wasn't as much traffic then, so the music was the only sound filling up my hollowness on those muggy nights.

The summer I was twelve, I had set a personal goal to master the *Preludes* of Johann Sebastian Bach. I was thrilled that my abilities had progressed to the point where I could not only appreciate music but also create it. I contracted rheumatic fever in late August. Consumed by the intense fevers associated with that particular illness, I had no desire to practice. I lost touch with the very source of healing in my life. I had not consciously realized how effectively music served to restore my hollowed-out feelings.

During this time, I instinctively turned to sculpture as an alternative form of expression. While I did not have the energy required for rigorous daily piano practice, I could sit, first with clay, later with stone, and let my mind begin to explore potential shapes that called to be released. Once I had the image firmly fixed in my imagination, I could take tiny steps, chipping away at the clay or stone, until the vision was transferred to the physical sculpture. Since I was not able to go to museums, I read art books borrowed from the library to learn subtleties of technique. In the months while I was recovering, I got in touch with a different voice, one that visualized rather than heard the potential for beauty in my world.

It was still not a conscious process for me. I sort of stumbled into art forms that served me well, without any need to understand how they functioned, just as I managed to live without any conscious memory of the terror and betrayal that had been part of my life for nearly nine years. Looking back, I firmly believe that my survival was literally hinged to my tenuous connection with creative energy. In the present, I know that my process of recovery has been inextricably linked with creativity.

I crochet afghans. I am not a skilled artisan in this medium, but I am doggedly persistent. One single stitch at a time, the afghan emerges from a skein of yarn. It reminds me that my healing has come, one fragment of memory at a time, from the wells of my subconscious mind, where I have reconstructed and faced the terrors of my childhood. I thought I was insane, as elements of my experience surfaced like submarines, making brief appearances and then sinking again into the waters of the subconscious. I would suddenly be assaulted by a persistent odor or hear a particular sound, over and over, without knowing the context from which it originated. Fearing that I was "insane," I sought the help of a therapist, who recognized the patterns I was exhibiting. Over the next four years, using hypnosis, I was able to stitch together the meaningless fragments into a tapestry that revealed a horrifying reality of incest and abuse. Now I take those memories and gather them together in big piles, like rags that women have used for generations, to make a quilt of understanding and promise. Like the quilt, those bits of my experience will now protect and comfort me as I patch them into shapes and images that express my empowerment.

Though I no longer play the piano or sculpt, I create now with words. They bring me an endless supply of yarn and bits of cloth and thread that I can use in my newest endeavor. I am writing a parachute that will keep me aloft in those terrifying moments when the airplane climbs away and leaves me gasping as I plummet to the earth. My poems are a life preserver, that will buoy my spirit when the work feels too hard, like it will drown me, exhausted and clinging to the edge of my overturned craft. The process of writing supplements my life, like the vitamins and minerals I set alongside my plate each morning.

I came to writing with that same quiet desperation that has fueled the entire process of my recovery. In the midst of unraveling the tangled skein of memories that ultimately revealed my incest history, I attempted suicide, for what I hope is the last time. My therapist challenged me to find a reason to live. I was waiting to use the restroom in the hallway of Connexxus, a lesbian community center in Los Angeles. I overheard a teacher describing her syllabus for a creative writing workshop. Some wise voice inside me said, "That is what you need to do. That is where you will find your reason to live." That was January 27, 1986. I have written every day since.

When I touch the keys of a piano or pull a loop of yarn through a stitch in my afghan or put these words on the page, I feel an unbreakable bond with the universe. These atoms I am tossing into the immeasurable void where our galaxy floats makes my presence permanent. It doesn't matter what form my creative impulses take, they lead me forward in my life, like sunlight pulling the tips of the redwoods higher into the sky. I know there is a reason for me to heal, and more important, for me to live.

Anger Poems

1   Boils up
from that putrescence
in my stomach
where acids churn,
pushes up
through the raw flesh
of my esophagus
to my mouth.

I must spew it out
before caustic corrosive liquid
burns my tongue
sears the tender flesh
of my gums
or falls backward
to strangle and choke
in my throat.

2   A blackened corpse
sacrificed
on a charred and crumbling pyre

my body gutted
by the explosive flames
demolished in the scorching heat

tears burn hot on my cheeks
lava slithering
from twin weeping molten volcanos

my heart the ritual drum
tuned tight with fear
pulsing the rhythms of anger

3   Screams of anguish
echo inside
the cavernous cavity
of my bruised body
where pain drips
stalactites
from linings scarred
by the acid wash of my anger.

4   Like a tidal wave thrust
    from Asian storms
    it engulfs me
    forces me under its power
    erases the air
    with a watery swipe

    tsunami
    too near me
    it denies me
    then drowns me
    and drops me
    on scathing sand

    gasping
    I grab
    great lungfuls of air
    leap to the safety
    of rock
    where I cling and wait

5   Clouds
    like air-blown popcorn
    puffed into the sky
    turn dark

    the scorched and burned popcorn
    crackles and hisses
    with lightning
    belches great gassy bubbles
    of thunder
    and spits
    stinging needles of rain

6   Crashing into my head
    a piano's crescendo
    running raggedly across the keys
    the punch of mallet on tympani
    the jarring encounter of
    metallic cymbal with its twin

    plucked with vibrant intensity
    my soul emits a howling inhuman note
    echoing across the universe
    to land on a deafened ear.

First Flashback

There was an earthquake yesterday:
deep rumblings
of some ancient fault
encrusted tectonic plates collided
shifted and receded

the instant I remembered the incest
telephone wires snapped
communication silenced
gas mains ruptured
bursting spontaneously into flame

huge cracks in the foundation
splintered my life
pebbles of caulk hailed
glass freed from wooden bonds
smashed and shattered

rolling thundering heaving
the horizon at a tilt
level ground bulging
and buildings humbled
forced to their knees

there was an earthquake yesterday
6.1 on the Richter scale
damage estimates incomplete
only one casualty: my bruised innocence

The Art of Survival

Linda Ness

M<small>Y CHILDHOOD WAS</small> ruled by a drunken dictator who sexually abused me and my four sisters until each of us left home. Violent punishments were freely given for the smallest mistakes. In order to cope, Mom would go to the doctor to receive shock treatments and pills. For over ten years Dad's mistress lived in the same house, the so-called "live-in baby sitter."

There was no escape as a child... only fear and quickly learned survival skills. Crayons became my secret joy. I inhaled their waxy fragrance and brilliant colors. I dreamt that I'd find a brand new box of crayons under my pillow when I woke up. I didn't dare tell anyone, afraid that my only love would be taken away or used against me. With these crayons, I created happy clowns and nice, neat, little houses with flowers and birds. There was no pain in the colorful worlds of blue skies and smiling suns.

I ran away from home at sixteen. After several months of living by my wits, I was placed in a foster home and allowed to finish high school in another city. Again, art class was my source of pleasure and satisfaction. Images began escaping from my mind and finding expression. The resulting pictures usually were done so quickly that many art rules were forgotten, which gave an unusual and primitive look. I would laugh at the "weird" pictures. Part of me knew that there were many other things to "see" in these works if I would take the time to look.

After three months at a junior college, I ran away again. I hitchhiked to San Francisco and spent six months in the hippie drug scene. When that didn't work, I decided to get straight and get married to a man sixteen years older. The next three years were spent learning about positive thinking and attending intensive 12-step alcohol and drug meetings. However, my self-help therapy resulted in a suicide attempt followed by several weeks in a mental facility. The more I learned, the more lost I felt. I decided that maybe having a baby would make me happy and solve all my problems. But the baby died at birth from the complications of Down's Syndrome. I spent the next six months examining my

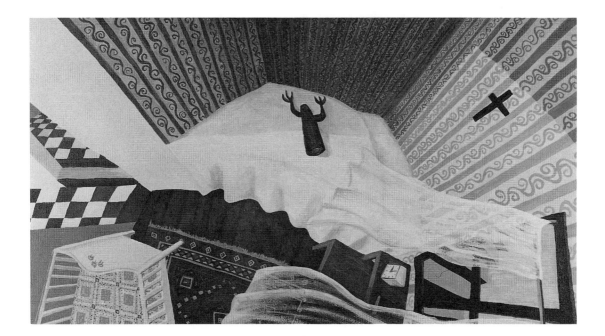

motives for having a child and being married. I began to recognize that although my husband was a nice man, he was old enough to be my father. So, at twenty-four years old, I asked for a divorce and decided never to have children.

Alone again, I became incredibly anxious as I noticed that there was no one around to blame for the way I felt. I became deeply snarled in a love triangle, playing the role of the mistress. It took nearly three years before I asked myself what I was doing. Was I repeating the dysfunction of my parents' lives? My life was an emotional roller coaster. I was either flying high or in the deepest depression. I was always angry and critical of everyone and anyone who got too close. Searching for anything to mask, numb or escape the intense inner emotional pain, I tried drugs and alcohol along with meaningless sexual affairs with men from work, bars or even self-help groups.

I was able to hide within my escapes for several years before I crashed. Spending several weeks under the blanket of my bed, I reviewed my life. My only memory of joy was of creating art. With renewed hope I ventured to the library for some art books. I loved the colorful photos of the Impressionists' paintings. The idea that light was color was very exciting. The little money I had was spent buying paints and canvases. The subject for the first painting was the corner window in the kitchen, where light streamed across a table to fill the room. Two weeks were spent trying to capture the light. But with the light constantly changing, I began to understand the challenge of the Impressionist

Out of Body, 1989, 28″ × 16″, acrylic on canvas

painters. With new insights, I explored the play of light and the subtle balance of colors and tones. I was thrilled with the result. There was real life here. There was excitement. It didn't hurt. I could now paint the world the way that I saw it. I had given life to a simple kitchen window.

The painting was done, but I couldn't stop. I wanted more. I needed to paint. That night I started another painting. For weeks I painted, gaining more confidence with each day. I was in love with this new world of painting and the wonder of capturing light. I could see the total picture in my mind. I created more realistic-style paintings, and little by little I was able to leave my house and face the world again.

Later that year, I returned to my parents' home for the first time in nine years and discovered that Dad was still sexually molesting my youngest sisters. Although I lived over 2,000 miles away, I offered them a place to escape to if they ever wanted to run away. They were on my doorstep within two weeks. But as the guardian of two teenagers, I was harsh and unrealistic, with lots of rules for their behavior. Was it any wonder that they compared me to Dad and his cruelty? They stayed just long enough to save money from their part-time jobs and graduate from high school. Then they moved into their own apartment. Soon after that, my inner pressures began to take their toll when I was hospitalized with acute colitis. The doctors did all the tests and declared that I was creating the toxic poisons that were eating away at my body. Their solution was for me to see a psychiatrist. But instead, I decided to quit my job and to be my own boss. I would reduce stress by making my own decisions and choices. I started my own graphic-art business. I made a commitment to take care of myself by eating healthier, exercising and learning to relax. I took a yoga class and learned to meditate and breathe. A ballet conditioning class helped me to appreciate and get in touch with my body. It took a while but for the first time positive changes were taking place in my life. I began to gain confidence in myself. While out dancing I even met an unusual man who showed me respect, love and how to have fun. Was I just imagining it or was life beginning to FEEL good? I was making positive choices in my life and it was beginning to show. My more figurative paintings were now beginning to reflect the softness of human curves.

We were married and within months I was pregnant. Because of the death of the first baby, a genetic test was needed to check the health of the child I now carried. Five paintings were completed during the three weeks I waited for the test results. The intensity of energy overflowed onto a canvas showing a huge pregnant belly and two enormous, filled breasts rising like a range of mountains to be climbed. With the birth of our beautiful, healthy daughter, there was so little extra time. I started simplifying the paintings to basic symbolic images.

That year brought not only the birth of my daughter, but the suicide of my only brother. Haunting images found their way onto two canvases. I remember that one of my sisters told me that I should burn both paintings. Was everyone going to deny his death as well as our abuse? If not his life, then his death could have some meaning by serving as a lesson. His intense energy had always found self-destructive or blocked channels. Trapped in his mind, lifelong nightmares became mixed with his daily life, resulting in bizarre actions. I began to understand that unless I wanted the same result in my life I would have to find a positive focus for my compulsive energy. It became apparant that the process of creating paintings was allowing my excess energy to be safely released onto the canvas.

The next crisis occurred when my daughter was a little over three years old. A friend was staying with us over the holidays. I found him lying with my daughter on her bed. My first reaction was to turn and ignore what I had seen. The next instant I had her in my arms and was carrying her to the other room. We talked about our "friend." Later, I told him to get out, that he was no longer welcome in our home. Although I was not able to put into words what I felt or feared, the man left without any need for explanation. I was grateful, but totally shaken. I was exploding with rage inside and desperately needing to find a sense of balance. The next day, I went to the office, sat down at the typewriter and poured out my pain through my fingers, to the keys and onto paper. This continued for the next eighteen months. I wrote down every detail that I could remember about my childhood and all the years of coping after I left home. For the first time, I was able to find and read books about incest. It was clear that for years I had

Retrograde Planets, 1988,
36″ × 20″, acrylic on canvas

been acting out old patterns from my parents and childhood. This explained why I had been so angry and bitter at the world, why I had spent so many years trying to escape. But even as I found answers, I found more questions. How could this happen? Why did the entire family keep this secret? Why had God allowed Dad to live and let my brother die?

With all these new ideas incubating in my mind, I received a large supply of acrylic paints from an artist who preferred oils. Then with some extra money from a large commercial art project, I got the materials together to make several large canvases. In between jobs, I started putting the images that had accumulated in my mind onto the canvas. The rules were gone. The paintings became a channel for the release of anger, fear, anxiety and pain. I was forced to see and take responsibility for my thoughts as I saw them reflected back to me on the canvas. The resulting paintings were quite intense, with sharp angles, electric colors and naked primitive beings. More images screamed to be released. Somehow I found the courage to let the images out onto a dozen more canvasses. Each painting seemed to demand attention and become more powerful. But when anyone would ask about my art, I would make some sort of joke and just say that they were weird. I really didn't know how to explain them or how to tell people that they were a result of childhood incest and its healing process.

In 1985, one of my paintings was selected for a local art exhibit. With the support of my husband and friends, I was encouraged to put together a public exhibit of my paintings. Invitations were sent and public notices for the opening night preview party were published.

I've always had a difficult time reading the reactions of viewers to my art. The first comment is that they love the colors and then there is a silence as the viewer begins to look a little closer. I often think that many people sense the meanings, but just like in real life, there is always a denial of the pain. The only viewers who have consistently been willing to talk are others who have come from abusive families. Sometimes, there is a sadness when no one is willing to acknowledge what they see or when no one is willing to look deeper than the surface colors. I wonder if I am being too subtle or too personal.

That year I completed twenty-eight paintings, had three more public showings and participated in two juried exhibits. The only problem was that I was so intent on the creation of the paintings that I was furious and frustrated when clients called for me to do a commercial art job. By September, my daughter entered first grade and I decided that I could no longer juggle everything. I dissolved the commercial business and moved my studio back into our home. This allowed me to paint full-time and to devote more

Right, *Bible Reading,* 1990, 22″ × 24″, acrylic on canvas

Unfinished Nightmare, 1988,
32″ × 36″, acrylic on canvas

attention to my family. Within the next two years, my fine art career continued with the sale of a few paintings and many public exhibits at alternative gallery spaces, as well as juried exhibits at two art museums, summer art festivals and the local arts commission gallery program.

Without the pressure of the business, I allowed myself to put more and more of the strange and haunting images of my mind on the canvas. However, the paintings were becoming quite disturbing, and I found that I was actually afraid to paint. I tried to intellectualize and logically understand, but I was afraid that the images would become even more painful. I stopped painting. I was panicked and had reached another point of crisis. Knowing that the basis of my fears lay in the childhood abuse, I called a sexual abuse hotline and joined a group for women survivors. For the first time, I felt I had a safe place to talk, be sad, scream, rage, cry, whatever. These women understood me and I understood them. With the support of the group, I began to face some of my fears and to let the little girl in me have a chance to cry and be angry. After months, I was able to finally finish the paintings and have a private showing. Other survivors attended and we discussed the symbolic meanings and the messages of truth so clear for us to see. It has taken me a long time to understand that many people are uncomfortable viewing my art because it shows the pain of truth. The fact that sexual abuse actually takes place within our society is hard for many to accept. Only recently have people been willing to even talk about it.

With the help of the group and the acceptance of my art, I have continued to learn and grow stronger. After reading *The Courage to Heal* by Ellen Bass and Laura Davis, everything fell into place. I understood that I was not to blame and I knew who was. The next time I talked with my parents on the phone, it was not the normal chitchat. The confrontation was long overdue. But my dad didn't want to hear it and hung up. I wrote a letter to all my sisters explaining that I no longer was going to live the lie that we had a normal or happy childhood. I also wrote in exact detail a confrontational letter to Dad and sent it registered mail. He returned a letter saying that he had been physically and sexually abused as a child and that he felt God had forgiven him. I must admit that I was surprised by his response. But four months later, during our next phone conversation, he commented that he thought Satan was behind all the lies that I was making up. I was stunned and screamed in return, "I don't believe this, are you trying to tell me that you didn't rape all five of your daughters?" Once again he calmly said that I was making it all up. I told him that he was as much a liar and hypocrite now as he was when I was a child. He hung up. Since that time, I've realized that he is not worth any more energy, and as far as I'm concerned he is dead and gone to hell. I refuse to continue to be abused by him and I refuse to abuse myself.

It is clear to me that creating art has become a substitute for violence and self-destruction in my life. It is teaching me to see the truth about my life. I've discovered that I must release the images or they will continue to haunt me and block my mind from other thoughts. Now when I have nightmares or a crisis in my life, I put the images on paper and later on canvas. I can stand back and "see" what has been bothering me. The paintings have been a witness to a lifelong process of healing. They are a gift that has saved my life. The energy has flowed through me reflecting a message of hope. We all have the power to change, to grow and to heal. I feel a responsibility to share my works with the public. I want the paintings to stop the eye and haunt the mind until there is a spark of understanding.

March to the Mother Sea: Healing Poems of Baby Girls Raped at Home

Judy Grahn

MARCH TO THE MOTHER SEA: *Healing Poems of Baby Girls* is a breakthrough project for me, in that it is the first time I have consciously used the word "healing" with regard to my work, though others often have described it as healing for them. And this is the first of my work composed for tape, not paper.

The set of fourteen poems, composed during the last two years of my four and a half years of therapy, is an expression of the recovery of memories of childhood incest and other mistreatment. This includes the finding, after long suppression, of my own baby voices again, a killing of the terrible crippling feelings that go with being secretly raped and controlled by a relative, and the replacement of those old feelings with the waters of the Mother Sea—a completely different set of feelings.

My healing has come about through the struggle to use the memories to recover from the consequent disability, characterized by symptoms as diverse as loss of hearing and verbal comprehension, inability to swim, fear of stability and material possessions and recurrent painful physical conditions and injuries including, for instance, fourteen bouts of strep throat.

Using art for healing is not a new idea to me, as I have done it all my writing life, with increasing consciousness that my own art, poetry, grounds me solidly in its aesthetic when I am disoriented, speaks for me in the world when I am otherwise mute, foretells my future, builds me a supportive community, affirms my collective history, makes money and other material advantage come my way, gives me a political and critical voice and provides me with a spirituality based in the female.

As a child, poetry was the single thing I "owned" in a household otherwise based in physical deprivation, lack of space or privacy, lack of a special place for me to be. My poetry lived in tiny notebooks with tiny pencils in a cigar box that I kept under my rollaway bed, when finally at the age of twelve my parents got around to providing a real bed for me. At seven o'clock each morning as I rolled my narrow metal bed into the closet, the cigar box was perched on top of it; my notebook and tiny pencil went into my Levi pockets along with my pocketknife and various found objects such as nails, bottle tops, interesting wood, animal bones and the like.

Poetry was valued by my sensitive, intelligent parents, so they gave me emotional support for doing it. Even more importantly, from my adolescent point of view, poetry gave me a way to get positive attention from peers and teachers who otherwise saw me as lower class, the child of a drunken fry cook. When my Girl Scout troop voluntarily performed my first long narrative poem, my eleven-year-old self felt I was part of the human world, a feeling I otherwise never had. Poetry could knit me to other people as my isolated and unhappy parents could not and I aimed my writing at the target: social knitting.

Once out as a single working woman and a lesbian in the huge, lonely urban environments of my young adulthood, I struggled to find the group context, the metaphors and subjects for my art that could once again allow me to use it to knit myself to a nurturing social fabric. Repeatedly I struggled and repeatedly succeeded, so that I have come to rely on poetry as sailors rely on ships.

Home-o, Home-o Mother

I cannot say that art alone heals me, though I certainly tried to do it that way. The art does help to group much of the distorted energy I received from every unhappy member of my family, and as the youngest child that was a heavy dose to try to absorb in one lifetime. But it has been the conscious journey of therapy, the true telling, the close examination of imagery and event, the modeling of feelings by my well-trained and sensitive lesbian-feminist therapist; and prodigious efforts on my own behalf—to complete every assignment, to go every week prepared, to take charge of my own course of treatment, and to take my art in with me—these allowed much more complete healing than unconscious art, left to its own devices, ever could. Conscious art, conscious spiritual rite and conscious healing, the coupling of consciousness and unconsciousness toward the end of healing in a female-centered psychological and spiritual context—that is what has worked for me.

I struggled equally hard to unravel myriad of the recurrent symptoms and physical disorders that have plagued me all my life. Under the specific details of each one I detected secret events of long ago. And as each physical metaphor for abuse has surfaced, the disorders have left me. To the extent that my conscious mind is able to carry the information and help me speak what is true for me, my body no longer needs to do this job. I now spend much less time in a state of secret illness, and I now think of my physical disorders as opportunities to attain another layer of information.

Everyone's incest experiences are highly individual and connected to all parts of a family dynamic. In my case, some of this dynamic has to do with class attitudes. My immediate family was the poor, addled, alcoholic and artful side of an extended family whose other members, as immigrant and first-generation Swedes with access to factory and railroad jobs, sent their children to college and middle- to upper-middle-class lives, and took pride in their ease of assimilation, as differentiated (in their eyes) from brown- and black-skinned folks—and from my folks.

My folks never could hold material possessions and orderly life together; at times my mother could not hold her grip on reality; at times my father or brother was taken to jail for drunkenness and disorderly conduct. Chasing pots of gold, my father gambled away his sweat-earned money. My mother is a schizophrenic who was not hospitalized because my dad distrusted all authority. We left her alone and she healed herself from periodic descents into depression and withdrawal. She considered herself "retarded" all her life, and so did her family.

That my financially successful, home-owning uncle raped me at the same time I wore his daughter's hand-me-down clothing, and that my aunt punished and mocked me, especially over my art, locked me early on into a class attitude that is bone deep. For me, the middle class was a dangerous place to be, and until recently I was psychologically unable to provide myself enough space, or at times even the simplest possessions, at times abandoning everything, even my life-saving poetry notebooks. I was compulsively driven to give away money, to "share" my grants and advances rather than use them for myself and my work. To my child self, poverty was safer than wealth, being nomadic safer than being "home."

The second piece on side one of *March to the Mother Sea* is my version of a child's voice singing: "My pretty pink dress is torn, and I'm scared to say why. My nose was bleeding all day long, I'm surely going to die... it's taking me the hardest way to find the earth my home."

Home, for the child, is safety, the nurturing enclosed place where extreme weather, strangers and dangers are kept away. Home is the enclosing place of warm family arms of concern, recognition and attention. Home, for the incest survivor caught in buried patterns, does not exist. For children used as sexual objects by their own relatives, home is the place of continual betrayal. In America, a million children a year run away from home, many of them because conditions on the street do not seem more hurtful to them than conditions under their family's roof. It isn't that the streets seem safe to them as that no place seems safe to them, and the only act that feels appropriate to protect themselves is the act of running.

Before I entered therapy at the age of forty-three, I would often, and to my own puzzlement, run to hide behind a bedroom door with my heart in my mouth whenever anyone approached the front door, *especially* if I knew or lived with the person.

In the fourth poem of *March to the Mother Sea,* my adult voice addresses my uncle and his threats to kill me if I told anyone what he did to me: "You built a safe house for your angry lust. Your house was never safe for me." Nor was any house safe for me.

In the sixth poem, ending side one, I pull a fish of truth from a river and am able to imagine getting to a safe place, a place with a fire and a frying pan where I can eat my truth and put my body down onto the great earth, getting well.

Later, during the winter of 1989, I composed the second side of the tape, eight pieces that gradually unveil the poetic line, "O Mother rock me, rock me down to the deep green sea where I can be with the jellyfish queens." The line is based in the psychological image of baby girls banding together to march into the Mother Sea, the very center of protection that is based in involvement, courage and keen observation. These qualities seem to me the opposite of the withdrawal, dissociated daydreaming, chronic anger and inability to involve ourselves in modern life that characterize the feeling-state of unhealed incest memories.

"Home-O, Home-O Mother," the baby girls sing and chortle as they immerse themselves in the depths of feeling and experience of the Mother Sea.

O Mother See, Hear and Speak

Before I could get to the Mother Sea, I had to get to the Mother who sees and hears what is happening.

One of the residues of my hazardous childhood was an inability to listen to my own voice on any kind of recording. I was so acutely self-conscious that I even had difficulty reading reviews of my work, inevitably seeking "negativity" in them and inventing it if it wasn't there. I expected authoritative judgment to be dismissive of me.

In 1975, Olivia Records made an album of my poetry—but I have never heard it. I have a collection of many tapes of my voice reading, made in broadcast stations and other places, to which I have never listened. Nor could I easily watch videos of myself or bear to be in front of TV cameras.

The threat, absorbed by my child's ears, never to tell the acts of rape and other abuse, on pain of death, coupled with my absolute need to use poetry and public speaking as my life's work, allowed me to talk about myself and my life only if I didn't hear what I was saying.

Obviously this interfered absolutely with my ability to work in modern electronic media, to expand my art in a modern context. More dangerous than the narrowing this did to my artistic career, was that in the late 1970s I began a heavy slide into a severe dysfunction that my mother has: psychosomatic deafness, or involuntary selective hearing. As of 1990 and her age of eighty-seven, she has never had a telephone and refuses a hearing aid. At least ninety percent of what is said in conversations goes over my mother's head, that is, she shuts it out. What follows from this is a general inability to focus on information, follow simple directions, drive, find her way around town, have conversations, remember what to buy at the store, etc. In short, "retardation," in the eyes of others and herself, and lack of participation in most social life.

As I approached forty, I began to notice the extent to which I had developed this disorder, how often I was pretending to listen to what I did not in fact hear. I was withdrawing into an internal and increasingly frightening world, losing the ability to drive or remember simple things. Through therapy and great conscious effort I have controlled this syndrome to a tolerable degree; though just as alcoholics recognize danger in any amount of alcohol, I recognize danger in any spacing out of conversations.

Speaking and hearing are so completely intertwined that as I have reached into my tumultuous subconscious to speak about myself and my early life, I have also become able to hear conversations in my present life.

March to the Mother Sea: Healing Poems of Baby Girls is an enormous step in this reclamation of my hearing, though "hearing" is not used as a metaphor anywhere in the poem. Instead the metaphor is "O Mother See," a pun on sea, since the poem is immersed in water imagery and is a hymn to O Mother Sea, the ocean of original creation, among other things. "O Mother See" is a clarion call, a message of direction I give to my subconscious and, by artistic extension, to the collective subconscious of all who hear my poem. The mother who sees and hears the truths of family life is much better able to protect her baby girls and boys from sexual abuse and battery. The mother/baby girl configuration within each adult woman has that protective function also. When it is missing or disrupted, the adult woman cannot take care of herself, though she may spend much time trying to care for others.

When the occasion arrived for the first half of the *Healing*

Poems to air as a Christmas program in 1988 on KPFA radio, hosted by poet Jack Foley, I knew I would at last be able to listen to my own work. For me, in addition to the thousands of acts of creating that went into making the tape, the act of listening to the tape itself became an act of healing.

By listening I don't mean the hundreds of run-throughs necessary to record and edit its complex sounds, I mean the act of public listening. The Christmas week night in 1988 of the airing of *Healing Poems for Baby Girls Raped in Christian Homes,* as I called my tape in that first context, I stayed home to listen to the program. I shivered in waves of excitement and a large dose of old buried terror. Women came to help me in my hearing; my lover Kris wrapped me in a special shawl and brought my ceremonial objects, an oval obsidian "truth-cutting" knife and my fox-headed wand. We lit candles and two friends sat quietly nearby. I huddled and fought the urge to leave the room.

My performance voice sounded surprisingly soft when it began to speak over the radio. When I made the recordings, the never-before-said words of secrets boomed out and reverberated from the walls, bringing the blood of shame to my cheeks. I thought that I was shouting. Later Jack would tell me that he and the radio engineer had never worked with softer velocities on a radio tape.

I wrapped the shawl closer as the sound of my Celtic drum began thumping. "Come on," I urged the radio, "boom that drum out." The sounds of the baby girls' voices I had played in chords on my sampling keyboard came up, and I urged them on. Then the music started for the fierce poem called "Killing Uncle Henry," which had filled me with nameless ancient fears when I first wrote it. "I'd like to kill you, Uncle Henry," the cool adult voice said, going on to tell Uncle Henry's secrets and the anger they arouse in me. I sat up straight and listened intently to the voice, the wonderful radio voice, defending me, protecting me, offering to strike back on my behalf. As I listened, oh so intently, I felt safe for the first time in my life; I could feel personal meaning in the word *safe.* To protect myself, to declare myself worthy of protection is to become my own mother, my own warrior parent, a mother who hears and sees what happens to her baby girl, and who takes action.

All The Way Down to the Deep Sea of Memory

As my four and a half years of therapy progressed, I worked hard to solve the riddle of knots that, among other things, caused me to panic in water.

Incest was not the only factor of my unusually violent childhood that took swimming away from me, though I'm sure it added a share of problems about exposing skin to strangers and undergoing the—to me, completely intolerable—teasing and eye-probing of boys.

In spite of my lifelong terror of water, I had tried a dozen times to learn to swim—with lessons, patient friends, physical education classes. Inevitably I panicked in the deep water, thrashed, went down, had to be fished out with a long pole, flunked, felt puzzled and ashamed at some mysterious personal defect.

Throughout my therapy, I dreamed of deep blue water, a huge lake or sea of it from which I was extremely remote. An ordinary, middle-class-appearing, white family rode on my dream lake, in a dream boat, a big white cabin cruiser, while I watched from a nearby cliff, alien, lonely, removed, eternally split from them. This existential feeling-position I took toward all of middle-class American life; I was a self-defined outcast.

As my memories surfaced over a two-year period, the blue lake in my dreams grew closer, until little pools of water began to lick my feet.

Apparently by the time adults in a family are sexually exploiting and harassing the children, a multitude of other problems also exist. As my secret memories surfaced in the course of therapy, I was appalled and astonished at the amount of violence hidden behind my mother's helpless, birdlike facade. Among other events, I remember her pushing my infant head under water, more than once, in moments of complete lost control and probable hallucination.

I prayed thanks then to whatever gods have allowed me to be childless, for I believe I might have repeated the hidden syndrome, which appears to run in my family's female line.

In struggling through my water panics in a swimming pool with my patient lover helping, I recovered images and sentences to bring the memories into further consciousness so that my body wouldn't have to be the sole expression of them. Meanwhile, I also composed very watery sounds for the brave baby girls on the second side of my tape. The baby girls go out onto the surface of the sea and then dive deep underneath. And this is the miraculous part—I am now able to swim in the deep end of the pool. I love swimming as much as I ever imagined I would, after all those disappointing times of trying; my swimming is like getting to live a big part of my life over again.

The sea wash of *March to the Mother Sea* is not one in which the baby girls wash the residue of incest off themselves, as they did that, not in an act of washing but in their transformation through killing Uncle Henry and through drumming and marching together in common understanding. They don't want to forget or put aside their experience, but to make use of it in their lives. Recovery, for me, means *recovering all of my self,* not transcending unwanted parts of my life; it means getting all the way into my life, using all its powers as creatively and horribly and joyfully and *really* as possible. So the sea wash is not an externalized cleaning away of parts of oneself not wanted; rather it is a taking of the Mother Sea into oneself, a joining with her forces; and allowing of the wordmusic to wash through one transformatively.

The Mother Sea is not only the external mother goddess of creation, the life-bearing and renewing waters of the earth; she is also the earth's menstruation, her ability to be visionary, and to see, to measure, outside herself. O Mother Sea is a calling for observant, conscious nurturing within oneself; a desire for creative interaction with nature; and agreement to enter the moil of life with truth that you will thrive.

By asking to be with—that is to conjoin, learn from, and take on as totem—the jellyfish queen, one is asking for reclamation of playfulness, selfness and self-protection. The jellyfish may look vulnerable but she is very self-sufficient and doesn't allow anyone to mishandle her. She stings like fire, and like the worldsnake has venom behind her sting.

The water of the Mother Sea completely pervades the pieces on the second side of my tape; we enter the water by listening, and the baby girls go very deep in their quest; the slow rhythm of waves takes over and our breathing slows as we take time to go within, to where the Mother Sea lives in us.

By the end of my therapy, I dreamed of putting my own boats in the water of a large lake. Admittedly these were three of the most ragtag boats you can imagine, one of them made of scrap wood and barely able to float, all of them just the merest frame of hull close to the water, all speeding along on the "mission" that propels me, while I struggle to gain some steering control. Not the beautiful put-together boats on usual lakes, but nevertheless, in the water, making the attempt.

I think of the tape as another kind of boat in the water, one over which I exerted an incredible amount of control in mastering some new and difficult technology (computer-based music, keyboard playing, home taping). The technology requires close attention to numerical detail and endless tinkering with paraphernalia such as cables, dials and plugs. By using such an exacting method, my conscious and unconscious creative minds are combined toward a single creative and healing end. This reminds me of the precision necessary for a healing sandpainting; the close attention that the healing artist, the family and the patient all bring to the art has everything to do with the success of the method.

Nurturing males? Some women are suspicious of the deep male-like voices on my tape as they sing with the baby girls on their march to the sea. These women perhaps didn't have the same experience I did, of coming to understand my father as the safest and in many ways the most feminist person in my family, and of my mother as sometimes dangerous, at least to her own infant baby girls.

Child rape is not perpetrated only by men, although most is, and mostly toward female children. The female child most represents free-flowing spontaneous vitality and emotion, qualities that are usually punished in males, causing them terrible unexpressed grief and longing. At the heart of the hidden grief in our patriarchal society lies a wounded female child for whom we are all responsible, and who carries burdens that belong to others. My responsibility as an adult survivor is not to act her out on anyone else's behalf but to hear her in myself and display this healing to others. To make a public display, not only of the wound but also of the healing.

Incest survivors have the capacity to remember everything, no matter how young we were when the assaults happened. Everyone in society needs to know that there are no secrets kept from children, nothing that happens to them that they don't keep somewhere in themselves. "One thing," the baby girls chant emphatically, "we all know. We know."

One or two women have reacted with disgust toward the baby girl voices from the high end of my vocal keyboard. "Chipmunks," they said dismissively. The voices of girl children are often mocked and derided in our society. We characteristically express stupidity, vacuousness and cowardice by using falsetto, feminized, little girl voices.

After hearing the high end of the keyboard I too was dismayed; people will dismiss this as trivial, I thought. Only after I had worked with the sounds for a while did I come to love them and to love the harmonies of the baby girls together as they chant the words of their poems.

After hearing my tape, my friend Adele Prandini expressed the longing we have to love baby girl voices. "We use these voices secretly, among lovers," she said. "And we love them, not just love them but crave them, need them, it's almost like we want to eat these voices when we hear them because they are so wonderful and so full of joy and life and vitality. No wonder kids sit for hours in front of cartoons. Those aren't animal voices they're hearing, it's *their* voices, little kid voices."

The second side of *March to the Mother Sea* is a long meditation, centered on the baby girls, going deep, deepest into the waters of life, blending with them. To ground the listener back in everyday life, it ends with a mantra that summarizes the whole that comes in recovering forbidden memories: "Everything/ about me/ is my own."

These words reclaim us from the theft that happens in rape and other forms of severe objectification. Perhaps the words apply to the inner feelings of rapists who are healing as well.

Voices of baby girls, young girls and grown women join together in this chant, over a chunky melody. "I love the piece," a friend in the music industry said after hearing it, "but it seems held back. I wish you would add an emphatic percussion, one made using some sound you feel really close to."

So I raided my kitchen, emerging with a big spoon and my favorite cast-iron skillet. This musical instrument, combined with my sampling keyboard and a signal processor to add a delay effect, lets me underscore my mantra with a percussion that one listener described as like an Amazon hammering the world out on her anvil.

Mothers who see and hear clearly take action. I have heard of women currently in jail or living underground rather than surrender their little daughters and sons to ex-fathers who were molesting and abusing them. These are real mothers, they are my mothers, and they are part of O Mother Sea.

The re-emerging goddess lives in a much larger world than the narrow one preoccupied with the endless wounds of colonization and the patriarchal obsession with penile rights and powers, coupled with disgust for the feminine and the childlike, that seems to be a root cause of child-rape in the first place.

O Mother Sea is calling on a great natural force infinitely larger than human society, calling on the waters of life as a metaphor of justice, involvement and large perception. The power of clear sensing and clear being belongs to the ocean, and when we call on this power of clarity, we call it into ourselves, into our basically water selves.

My uncle's theological system consisted of the innocent (female) child forever separated from the despoiling (male) adult, the good god and the bad anti-god locked in a combat in which my body was the battlefield. In myself I replace this theology with another: the all-encompassing goddess of waters, the Queen of Cups. She is the Slut of Sluts, and the Lover of Lovers. She is Prince William Sound before and after its oil spill, and the Sea of

Cortez poised pristinely just before development; she is the new waters off the industrial New Jersey coast and the older waters of the Red Sea. She is acid rain, and our tears. She is all the great oceans of the earth, and the smallest sexual dew trembling on our lips. Everything lives or dies in her, everything spews and dissolves into her, everything comes from her; everything comes to her and she comes to everything. Without her favor, we wither and die, for she fills and enables us. My uncle is within O Mother Sea, too, his own monsters clinging to his back. I push him away, out of me, so he has to make his own way through it.

The Mother Sea as home-o-mother is 180 degrees turned from my little victim self crouching between house walls desperately seeking security from terrors that live in my very psyche, and from which, until I am conscious of them, I am never safe. O Mother as the source of life and death is unimaginably vast and beyond judgment. She Is and She Is Not. In entering her completely we, as the baby girls and their deep-toned friends say so beautifully, "Beeeeee." They (and I) find beauty in embracing her completely.

O Mother Sea is home in the most all-encompassing and frightening chaotic way. She is home in the whole wise world. The world as home doesn't mean that I have learned to trust everyone—far from it. As jellyfish and all other creatures know, self-defense is part of life. But I have heard a voice, my own voice, defending me, so I can trust myself, more. I have killed the murderous patriarchal uncle who lived like a parasite within my vitality. I have owned overt female violence so that men don't have to act it on my behalf, nor do I have to blame them for every violent act. I have fished truths from my own rivers. With the baby girls I have entered the sea of simple delight, renewable life and social participation. Perhaps now I can make a home of the world.

Incest—"Show and Tell"

Bonnie Martinez

I HAD A HARD time writing about how my art has helped me in healing from my incest nightmare. As I wrote and rewrote and rewrote, I finally began to understand that part of the problem lay in the fact that I am not perfectly healed yet, and one of the residues of the incest is the feeling that I must be perfect about everything, including being healed. A paradox. And since I'm merely in the middle of the process, I couldn't possibly write a piece on healing incest through art.

And then something happened. In the middle of this writing process, I had another incest memory. It came out during a therapy session, but was incited by a New Year's Eve spent alone. So many of my memories seem to be connected to holidays. In this memory, I was five years old or thereabouts, and I remember standing on a staircase watching my parents and their friends laughing and partying. I was wearing a long, pink flannel nightgown with long sleeves and lace on the collar and cuffs. I was watching the party and wanting to be a part of the fun and apparent love. Then my father started to come up the stairs. He was drunk. (Actually, this is the first time I've had a memory of my father being drunk. Later in life he never drank.) He was laughing. His shirt was hanging out of his pants. He looked very handsome.

Next thing I remember, he had me upstairs somewhere, on my knees with my nightgown up around my waist, fucking me from behind. I knew about this. It wasn't the first time. Besides, my feelings were already bound in rock. I understood our relationship. I knew what I could expect. It had been solidly established. I was the good little soldier. I was getting attention. I was getting love and it felt good. And I was getting revenge on my mother for abandoning me to him in the first place. So many complex emotions!

A sign of my healing is that I was not totally dragged into the past and devastated by this memory to the point of self-abuse, as I have so often been before but was able to feel the experience, be furious, be vulnerable, ask for help and then begin to think about how I could put this into my art. A drawing, a painting. Put the memory down visually and it's on its way to being out of my system. It is part of the universe and not mine alone anymore to suffer with in silence. And an added attraction that time was the thought of revenge. As I become freer, the need to show the world becomes greater. I want to get back at them—dead though they are.

And therein lies a clue to how my art is part of the healing process. Concrete visualization. Solid visual, irrefutable screaming proof of the incest. No more silence. Clear pictures for everyone to see. No doubt about it having happened. The world will know my past, my pain, their evil, their guilt, all to my relief and healing.

This, then, was the second use of the art in my healing process—direct visualization and expression of the memories. During the past ten years of my life as an artist, the art has partly been a means for my subconscious to try to make contact with my conscious mind and feelings; for up until January 1988 at the age of forty-three, I had no conscious memory of the incest. I thought my childhood had been one that was happy, middle class and safe. Actually, I had very few memories of my earliest years—three or four to be exact.

In my early artwork, there were signs of the incest that I never really saw. Painful, powerful paintings that evoked anger and horror in others and myself, with names such as *The Scream, Virgin Sacrifice* and *Mourning the Two.* These all had hints of the great pain, fear and anger bottled up inside me, as well as clues to the origins of these feelings. During this time, I was in therapy and had been for years. As I approached the revelation of the incest, the drawings and paintings became more explicit, though still unacknowledged by my conscious self. Two prime examples of this are *The River Lethe* and *Corrected Nightmares,* which was an especially direct experience of the incest. My reaction at the time to the red penis-like object in the enormous hand that was attacking the child was that it couldn't be a penis because nothing like that had ever happened to me when I was a child. I had never been attacked by a penis. A year later I was to be proven wrong. I'm sure that all these images helped prepare me for the final realization of the terrible abuse that had been done to me as a child.

The next period in my art, which actually overlapped the *Corrected Nightmares* and *The River Lethe,* was a period of paintings of power places—Stonehenge-like organization of monuments, power places of the goddess. Over and over again places where safety and the goddess existed. A search to create safety in my life through my art. That the monuments can also be interpreted as phallic symbols I'm sure is relevant as well; but to me it was a pe-

Corrected Nightmare, 1987,
22″ × 30″, oil pastel, charcoal
on paper

riod of creating strong, powerful places in the world from which I
could draw strength. Of course, all of this was unconscious. All I
knew was that it felt right and good to paint and draw these
images in all sizes and mediums. This is only dealing with the
content of the work. Formal considerations such as color, composition, etc. were always a factor. The art was for art, not for the
healing of old wounds or for creating safe places in the world, or
so I thought.

The next period was roughly after the amnesia began to lift
and was characterized by experiences such as I described at the beginning of this piece. The art became the vehicle for visually exploring and expurgating the memories. Each memory I was able
to draw or paint was that much less a burden on my heart, mind
and soul. I was that much freer of it and the agony of the whole
experience. Some of the paintings are mythic in character and ex-

Father as Fetish Figure, or Din Din for Baby, 1988, 33″ × 55″, oil on linen

"To Bonnie, Merry Christmas, Love Uncle," 1989, 30″ × 72″, oil pastel on paper

plore the sense of my having been tainted by Evil incarnate, in the form of my father.

The paintings from this period are the largest I have ever done, as if the need to encompass the enormity of the experiences demanded as much space as I was capable of handling. I became totally involved with the subject matter, and all the love of painting for the joy of it—for the color, the texture—became secondary. The obsession was with freeing myself of the images that were haunting me. For those two years, painting had a totally different meaning for me; and so did vision.

A curious thing about the memories was that as I was actually seeing what was happening to me, and thinking about it later, I came to realize that the visual images had more actual clarity than I am capable of at my present age. At first, I couldn't figure it out. Then I realized that I was "seeing" what happened to me with the eyes of a child—undimmed by time and the need to not see. In that sense, it has been a wonderful experience of clarity. It doesn't make up for what happened in any way, but it has offered me a moment of beauty among all the ugliness.

Painting was documentary during this period, emotionally as well as visually, so that I wouldn't forget the original visceral reaction—the pain, the powerlessness, the betrayal, the experience of evil that came back so clearly. Though I hated remembering, I never wanted to forget again. Forty-three years of amnesia were enough. This journey and these memories have given me back my life—a life lost to me through the destructive and hateful treatment that created such fear and anger that I couldn't bear to remember. Now my life is my own, or at least the beginning of being my own.

The first painting I completed after my power place series is called *Family Portrait*. It shows me as a sexual object between my two parents, who have mask-like faces. We are near a power place and are all caught in a web. Then there are other paintings that came as a result of actual memories. One is called *Father as Fetish Figure, or Din Din for Baby,* which is from a memory of having my father's penis forced in my mouth for me to suck. Though this memory is from about the age of eighteen months, it is not the only memory of this kind. Nor was it the only time that this particular kind of abuse happened. This painting represents them all.

Another of the paintings is from a Christmas memory that concerns my uncle. Did he know about my father and me, or was he just another abuser? Or was I just so obviously a victim? At any rate, I had gotten sick and my uncle said he would take me upstairs and "make me feel better." Instead, he molested me. This piece is called *To Bonnie, Merry Christmas, Love Uncle.* It is a clear depiction of what happened. Perhaps it is the clearest of all the works from this period.

I also created a Family Album of small drawings using a dime store picture album. Since I had no real childhood album, I created one that tells the real childhood story of incest and abuse. I love this piece for the juxtaposition of the common picture album with the horror of the incest drawings. The album is so commonplace and is usually used for happy memories. Its use for incest drawings is meant to shock and sicken.

All this work has helped me in the process of separating myself from the experiences and the sense of complicity in the acts perpetrated on me. The current period of work is about integration and conscious healing. My paintings are finally about bringing my disparate sides together. They are beginning to be about beauty and joy. And, finally, so is my life.

Transitions in Layers

Vickie Sears

Journal Entry: October 5, 1989

IT IS A CLEAR, cold October morning. I am sitting on the floor next to an open window, looking out on the chestnut tree in front of the house. There's a strong breeze. Dry yellow-brown leaves clatter against themselves. Some race toward the ground. The broad leaves do not spin, but simply fall in plops. Rather like my thoughts this morning. I've been asked to write, especially as a sexual abuse survivor, about using creativity in the healing process. I cannot fathom what it means. Every thought deadens like the sepia leaves lying in the water-sogged grass.

Journal Entry: October 9, 1989

The use of the creative self in healing is what I, as a therapist, ask clients to exercise every day. It has to do with touching one's own inner resources. As a Native American, I believe our task in life is to walk in self-harmony. I assume that I, like the clients I see, am basically healthy, but am temporarily out-of-balance. I hold all the answers I need inside myself. I may need someone to help me see how I was hurt and to find my solution, but the truth of all healing is for me to use as much as myself as possible to re-gain my harmony.

Listening to myself allows me to draw on my creativity. Often I go toward my feelings by struggling through an intellectual period, staying in my head for varied lengths of time. Sometimes I can get to my feelings more quickly, deciding to paint a red swath across a piece of paper to show anger. Someone else might draw stick figures of their family, positioning themselves in the structure in the way they felt as a child. Some may just make sounds, unable to speak themselves, stretching their mouths into different shapes and sounds that they weren't allowed to do when a child. Other people might do something like jog and make each footfall a yell at someone who has hurt them, as a beginning way to learn how to have their feelings, whether sadness or anger or joy. Every one of these acts take courage and creativity—each is a personal statement.

Journal Entry: November 17, 1989

Thinking more about creativity and healing brought me to thoughts about art.

While creativity is integral to healing, it does not always get sung, read, danced or painted for the public eye. For some individuals, a part of their healing is the act of putting their life energies into turning creativity into a craft that will become their life work. I do not mean to imply that all artists are in a constant state of self-healing, although I think many are. Some artists turn the pain and joyful wonder of life into magnificence that can lend healing to others.

I cannot, for instance, read *Jane Eyre* without marveling at the woman's triumph. Then I remember the dismal early life of Charlotte Bronte and imagine how much better she must have felt, having written out her deprivations and anger/pain, after the public affirmation of her novel. I imagine it gave her a sense of empowered self-esteem and pride to speak and be heard in a way she could not be as a child.

The stretch of imagination is the creativity that brings healing. It does not have to become "public" art. We deserve to have ourselves, and anyone with whom we wish to share, as audience. We are enough.

Journal Entry: 1950

Somebody stole my secret diary and they read all the things and they laughed and told the other kids and so I ripped up lots of the book. I'm just going to hide things under the mattress and keep the very special things in my head.

Journal Entry: November 24, 1989

I have, from the time I could write, kept a journal. In 1950 I was nine years old. Don't add! I'm forty-eight now. When I was five I decided I wanted, among other professions, to be a writer. I wrote something almost every day. Sometimes it was a story. Sometimes a journal entry. I was living in an orphanage at the time and had to be careful that my writings were not found, so they would not bring punishment from staff or derision from the other children. Stories were destroyed regularly. Journal notes were written in couched terms. There is no name mentioned that refers to the staff person who found and violated my journal, but I remember.

When I wrote the 1950 entry, I didn't know that I would look back on it as self-revelatory or as writing fodder. I was only talking to myself so I would feel better. Today I see it as a beginning of "stuffing" my thoughts and feelings. I made a decision to neither talk nor trust. I stored my stories inside for a future, safer time. I know now that the words I wrote then had the power to wound the staff person who hurt me and make others laugh. The words were an invitation to generate feelings in others. Writing down the words brought me pain as well as release. I was a child without resources upon which I could count. The world was not a safe place. That's a lot of information for me to learn about myself. I can use it to change patterns and to know that the old reality does not have to run my present life, because there are people whom I can trust, and/or I can turn it into a poem, a drawing, a short story or a novel. I can decide to try to publish what I might produce or not. What is crucial is that I use the information to move past the incident. I explore its meanings, add the new awarenesses to know how I operate in the world, then I experience the feelings. It can be in any order. I just take advantage of all I've learned to heal myself.

Ultimately the act of having had my journal found and ridiculed has become part of my novel-in-progress, *One of Them Kids,* which is about two Native American children who are partially raised in an orphanage and foster homes. The notebook's destruction is a pivotal factor in Jodi Ann's creation of an imaginary playmate who defends her. I listened to myself, my inner children, when writing. The healing it brought came in being able to give my child-self power. Writing the memory down also made it more real for me—I validated my experience. I heard it. I transformed it while I wrote it, pushing it out of my body by the physical motion of writing. I cried in remembered pain. I laughed. I explored and know how the incident impacted my life in the long term, especially around trusting. I celebrate my being able to conjure a powerful imaginary playmate. I helped myself to survive.

Journal Entry: November 26, 1989

It is a wonderfully wet, cold day. I am sitting in a restaurant reading, waiting for a friend to join me for lunch. She is twenty minutes late, but I have a book and a lemon coke. I'm in a back booth enjoying the comings and leavings of people. The many hours I've spent in this cafe have brought a speaking acquaintanceship with many of the regular patrons. There is an amazing assortment of stories in this place. It always astounds me how easily we talk with people whom we think we'll never see again.

Kaye is now forty-five minutes late. My stomach is tumbling on itself. I order a bowl of soup. But my stomach does not quiet itself. There is a storm of minestrone buffeting me. I feel I will be sick. I tremble. I lean against the booth cushion, taking a deep breath. I say to myself, "I'm fine. I must be hypoglycemic." I eat a sandwich. The torment does not stop. I push the food away, saying, "O.K., I'll go inside to see if I can understand." I reach for my pen and journal.

Journal Entry: "Where the hell is she? An accident? An emergency? Why hasn't she called? Oh, sure. There'll be a message at home. Nuts. Who gives a damn. I don't care. I don't need her anyhow. I don't need nobody."

I stop writing. Re-read the lines. I think, "Oh yeah, Vickie. That's a nice clear adult voice. Right? Right." I say to myself, "Time to do what you suggest clients do."

I put down the pen, pulling in a long breath. I see myself slide down my throat going into my stomach. There is a small, familiar child riding a string bean that floats in a gurgle of soup. I ask her, "Why are you sitting in here?"

She answers, "I'm sitting on the steps of the place where Mommy left me and I don't know where she is and it's getting dark and I don't know when she's coming back for me."

"So," I tell me, "there it is again." The abandonment issue is a presence, needing to be dealt with again. Layer upon layer of pain eased by successive layers of healing done over years of time. Transitions in layers.

It seems to me that the quickest, most sharply felt pains are the unresolved stings of childhood striking my adult, bringing back the memories of wounded inner children. I have to hear this little part of myself, call her Kathy, to be able to nurture her as well as I would any living-outside-my-body child. Sometimes I do not want to acknowledge or attend to these hurt parts of myself, but I am their/my parent salving their wounds and healing them/me. I pick up my pen to draw.

Picture after picture is sketched. I draw me in a boat rowing toward Kathy. The string bean is by the boat. I extend my arms. Kathy is pulled into the boat. I let her cry, tears soaking my blouse. We rock. I make a balloon to write, "I'll never leave you Kathy. I'll always be with you. You can talk to me." Her balloon says, "Naw-uh." I write, "I know I have to earn your trust, but I want to." Her new balloon tells me, "Nope. I'll see. Maybe." Kathy tugs on an oar and we row together up the river that is our esophagus.

Since I can't make a triumphant yell in the restaurant, I do a soft whistle that draws slight attention.

Well, it took me less time than usual for my head-bound self to get to what I was feeling. Progress. It was also a shorter time for being able to talk with my child-self. Motion. I was able to hear the pain and move out of it faster. I can talk with Kaye now about her being late, as both adult and child, because I know both sets of feelings. Movement. Next time the abandonment fear arises, I'll understand even more quickly. Transition in layers.

Journal Entry: December 1, 1989

Drove to see Karen today. Had to pass St. Paul's Children's Home. As usual, my guts began to make guzzling noises at the hilltop that crests right in front of the damned house. Sometimes I can pass it with only stomach knots. Today the flashbacks came. The rape in the bathroom by the son of the couple who ran the place. The rape in the basement by him and another boy. The face of the foster-father as he watched his son feeling my breasts as he held me against the wall, never speaking as he passed by. My sense of powerlessness. His words slamming my brain: "All you squaw bitches like this, don't you? I seen it in the movies."

I had to stop the car. I halted right in front of the place.

I was fifteen when living there. Sexual abuse was not new to me. I was raped by a foster-father when I was seven and repeatedly abused by a woman staff member at the orphanage. Every foster home, except that of the only Native American home my brother and I ever went to, brought sexual or other physical abuse. I have worked on abuse memories for years, but what happened at St. Paul's has only been done partially. A story I call "Thinking on This," which appears in my collection, *Simple Songs,* speaks to one incident that happened there, but there is more I've barely dealt with.

I call my fifteen-year-old self Dana. Sitting in the car I asked, "What do you want to do here, Dana?"

"Run. Burn the place down, then run!"

"But Dana, it's someone's home now. We can't raze it."

"I don't know. I don't know."

Sweat fell over my lip. I had trouble getting air. I clasped my hands together to quiet myself, asking, "What will give us the most control over these recurring flashbacks?"

A long time elapsed. Rain began to thrum. Finally I said, "Let's go in the house. We don't need it to haunt us any longer, Dana."

There was a scream inside. "He'll grab me!"

I said, "It's not the same time, Dana, and I won't let anyone hurt you."

Dana grew quiet. I sucked in enough air to cross the street, walk up the stairs and wait until a woman answered the door. It was all forever. I explained that I had lived there when it was St. Paul's, asking if she would mind if I looked around. Surprisingly, she held no hesitation. She told me that at least one person a year came for the same reason. She said I could begin wherever I wanted.

As I ascended the stairs, the sounds in the house were drowned out by those of my childhood. Elvis Presley was groaning about the Heartbreak Hotel above the whirr of a blender and the cacophony of children's voices of all ages, arguing about whose turn it was to do which chore. There were urgent whispers of, "No, please don't. I don't want to." There was the silence of Darlene, a five year old, laying under a grunting fourteen-year-old foster brother.

I entered the bathroom with the cupboard out of which one of my offenders had popped after I had undressed for my bath. The floor had tiles now instead of cold, grey linoleum. I watched Dana struggle under the boy. She scrubbed herself to a magenta color afterward. My skin rosened on me, burning its memory. I saw Dana brush-brush-brush her teeth to wash away the thick salt of cum. I said, "It's O.K. to cry now, Dana. No one's here but you and I." And we did.

Dana and I wandered in the house allowing the movie of events to be replayed. Some memories were handled. Some were stacked for a later time. New memories arose that wanted attention.

Ready to leave, I stepped into the kitchen to thank the woman for her generosity. She said, "Most all the ones who visit say the house don't seem so big now. Way they act, it must of been some kind of awful. Is that right?"

I answered, "Yes ma'am. It was some kind of awful."

Descending the stairs under my own power, I knew I would never have to walk up them again. I recalled a 1950 journal entry I happened on when I first started to work on the creativity/healing piece. I had written, "People pass you around like a shared candy bar that nobody really wants or likes."

From my parked car, I looked at the house. It was smaller. It was muted as a vaseline-covered camera lens that hides the age-lines on actors' faces. There were memories waiting for me to work with, but they too were softened.

When I got home, I chopped kindling and thought about the rapes. I made lots of noise that my puppy, Tsa•la•gi, thought were play for her. Dana threw kindling onto the porch. Now I'm writing here to remind myself that I have done a brave deed this day. I retrieved some of my power. I diminished the monster house. I say no one will ever hurt Dana that way again.

Journal Entry: January 19, 1990

Time has not lain easily with me since going to St. Paul's. Cobwebs are not always easily struck down. They often leave a dark residue on walls, requiring repeated cleaning, just as does a wounded spirit. I have sung and drummed songs of prayer to excise the shame in my history of sexual abuse and foster homes. I have gone to the forest to scream anger and howl a crying. I have spun in dance to whirl the memories' spells out from my finger tips. I have written stories as the Creator-of-All-Good-Things has told me I should. I have used my spirit, body and mind for healing. I have begun, again-again-again... layer over layer, seeing them grow thinner as I retrieve and reweave the memories into shapes made of my power, returning them to myself as gifts.

Ultimately every person on a healing journey must decide what it means to be healed. My journey toward that state is an active creativity in which I try to use all of myself that will allow me to nurture myself. I must attend to each child within me to repair the damage done to them. That may mean a birthday party for my seven year old who never had one, or a trip to the zoo for Kathy who never saw an elephant. Each child's needs must be addressed according to their age and developmental stage. I must reparent my inner children, accepting that I am my own parent. I teach them to say "No" and "Yes" and to know/ask for their needs. I constantly remind them that they are not to blame for the abuse they have experienced—they are good and wonderful.

To be healed, for me, is to continue to move toward a time when I will not have flashbacks or nightmares or feel overwhelmed by my past or the people who abused me. It is to have a strong sense of my elemental goodness, so that I don't have to always hold anger. I do not necessarily have to forgive the offenders, I just don't have the energy to make rancor a constant in my life. A healing is where I will have the strength in a year or five or twenty to say, "Oh yes, here's my abandonment issue again. How will I deal with this layer now?" I want to have power to deal easily with the old trauma, using my full creativity. Healed means, for me, to own my power and share all facets of me with whomever I choose.

Epilogue: January 21, 1990

I have written this essay in a circle, in the same way in which my mind so often works. I started with my head-controlled self, looking for answers. As I wandered, I stumbled into my feelings. From there, I could go to the real place where understanding comes. Once there, I could unite my body, mind and spirit. While my spiritual self believes I cannot separate those three parts of myself, the truth is that there has been enough damage done to my system via the sexual, physical and emotional abuse that I am always striving toward an internal unity. What I realize is that whether we begin our journey of self-understanding with our feelings or our minds, it is all a personal experience and our "right" path.

In my tribe, as in many others, songs are ways of healing. I have sung here a song. I have made here a circle that is singing. We have made a circle.

Emily

The two chapters following are from a work-in-progress entitled *One of Them Kids*. These chapters relate to Jodi Ann's creation, at the age of six years, of a powerful imaginary playmate who will be a protector and confidant.

Chapter 16

Emily is so tall her ears reach to the top of the door. She's got chocolate fur that is so fat my hand can't be seen up to my wrist. She's all soft an' lets me smooch my face in her tummy. Her nose hairs ain't brown though. They are white. Some of the hairs in her ears are white too but mostly she's brown like me and very very tough. Her nose whiskers ain't soft like her ear ones. They wiggle up an' down when her nose bounces. Her nose gets all bouncy when she smells stuff. She can wrinkle it up like a raisin when her heart is going fast, like when she's been running. That's just like mine does only it's a faster thump thumping, all heard on the bone that is a "v" in her chest. Sometimes she's just sitting still an' something makes her heart start going an' her feets start running. She gots giant back ones. They bang on the ground then. Emily lets me stand on her feet so I can hug her tummy. If I stretch real long with my arms, I can tickle inside her ears. She don't like that so much an' flops them flat then thunks her front feet on my shoulders. Sometimes she pats my face just like Grandmother used to do a long time ago. When she does that she looks right at me with her giant brown eyes so I get feeling all soft inside. Not scared like sometimes. My eyes are black. Emily gots a sorta yellow around her brown circle. I guess rabbit eyes are just different than people ones. Both Emily's eyes work too. I got a funny one that don't go the same way the other one does. Emily says it's O.K. though.

Emily don't never get scared even when her heart is going fast like mine does when I hear Ichobhad's shoes coming. Emily just tells me how to go away inside my head.

Emily can punch out anybody here an' she don't need no spoonknife either. She does it all with her giant feet. She don't never use her big teeth though 'cause she says it hurts too much an' told me not to do it no more either. I bet Emily could knock even old Ichobhad right on her bottom an' punch her eyes out if she wanted.

One time I seen her take Ichobhad's glasses right off her face an' throw them on the ground, jumping them to smithereens. Ichobhad didn't do nothing either except pick pieces out of the dirt. Emily jumped right over her without never saying nothing. She just smiled a big tooth smile an' come over by me to munch some grass like nothing never happened.

One other time, when everbody was to supper, Ichobhad was being her mean self, so Emily got up behind her an' put her ears behind Ichobhad's very own ears. I started to laugh, only Ichobhad gave me her hard look so I put my hand over my mouth to squish down the laugh.

It's pretty tight in the locker where Emily lives, only she says she likes it in there 'cause it's easy in the nighttime to come crawl in bed with me. Emily is the bestest an' most funny an' tough friend I got an' she comes help me whenever I want.

Chapter 18

I'm pretty short an' very skinny an' fast when I run, but being fast ain't no good when there is a gang of kids waiting to pounce on you. I get into lots of fights even if they gots a rule here not to fight. I have to help Billie Jim too 'cause he is littler an' gets beat on lots. Him an' me just get whoomped on lots 'cause we're brown so I don't want to be brown sometimes, only Emily says she don't want to never be nothing except brown an' reminds me that my Grandfather said that brown is a good color, like the earth. Being brown is O.K. with Emily.

One time after Rachel an' Yvonne an' Mary Teresa beat up on me, I went up to the rainroom an' was looking down out the window crying, just a little bit see, when I seen the three of them was sitting over by the social work building right by the sidewalk. I was thinking on how I could jump on them from a tree to get them back when I seen Emily was strolling down the sidewalk. She stopped next to them an' asks, "How come you beat Jodi up?"

Mary Teresa yells back, "Because she's an ugly squaw brat!"

Emily don't let nobody say nothing else 'cause she jumps

over to them an' puts her arms around all three of them, bangs their heads together an' squeezes them so tight they start turning blue. She drops them down takes a big gulp of air and starts slapping Mary Teresa's face back an' forth between her hands like it was a ping pong ball. When Rachel an' Yvonne start to run away, Emily stomps a foot over one of each of theirs an' they can't move nowheres. Then she slaps both of their faces too. When she is done with that Emily squats down, pulling each of them over her knees an' gives them all spankings. She tell them they have to come apologize for beatin' on me an' saying I was ugly.

I was just a whole smile all the time this was happening.

Emily went on her way, skipping down the sidewalk, leaving the three of them laying in the grass rubbling their spanked butts.

Emily is my bestest pal, next to Billie Jim an' the neatest rabbit in the whole world.

Clay Voices

Sherrin Loyd

FIVE YEARS AGO, I was uneasy with discussions of abuse. I feared it was a remote possibility that I had been "sort of" abused. I joined a group for lesbians over forty dealing with childhood sexual abuse, making it abundantly clear to the women in this group that I was not sure if I belonged. I was warmly welcomed and told to stay. That first night I heard horror stories. I knew I was not like these women and decided I would not come back. But I did.

When asked to share my story the second week, all I could remember was when I was very little walking with Mom and Dad across the short bridge in front of Grandma's house. There had been a storm and the water rushing under the bridge was loud and brown. Dad was holding my hand and asked me to look at the water. When I said no, he picked me up and with one hand held me out over the water. I cried and screamed for him to bring me back. He laughed.

I also told the group that I used to get into trouble in my family if I did not fight back. One time my brother chased me holding a snail in each hand. I ran and locked myself in the bathroom. I got in trouble because I did not stand up to my brother and tell him to leave me alone. Yes, "get in trouble" meant "spanked" and yes, "spanked" meant with a belt. Although I knew I had been spanked, a fact verified by my siblings, I still had no memory of it. My only concrete memories were of my brother being hit. The group encouraged me to return.

After three years with this group of women and one memory, I began to trust I had been sexually abused as a child. The one memory came on a Saturday during the third year of therapy, when I went to a wrecking yard to see if I could find a car seat to replace the broken one in my car. I took a friend with me. I did not know why, but this seemed like a dangerous task. We got out of the car and walked into the wrecking yard. I felt nauseated by the smell and stood still, clearly seeing in my mind's eye what looked like the photograph of a hand. A large, old man's hand. And I suddenly and clearly knew that hand had been inside of me.

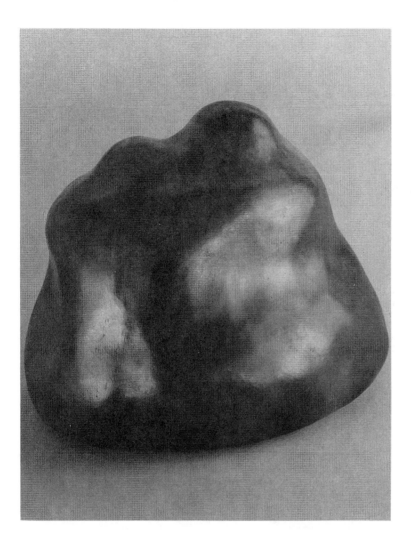

Unknown Territory 7,
1989, sculpture

Ted, a cousin who lived with us, used to smell of car grease. I recently found out from my family that he shared my bedroom with me from the time I was six until I was nine years old. My parents asked him to leave after the police brought him home drunk one night.

In 1989, I attended a conference at the Ben Lomond Quaker Center near Santa Cruz where, on the first evening, two women handed out small bags of clay. I laughed and said, "No thanks." She said, "Just hold it." And so I did. Absently, I started squishing the clay around in the bag (I detest getting my hands dirty). Every so often, I would peel down the plastic and see if anything had evolved. A couple of hours later when I peeked again, I saw a mean, dirty old man. At that point, I abandoned the plastic and started to flesh him out. Amazingly, without any thought, by the time I had finished, the piece had been transformed into a fat god-

Top left, *Unknown Territory 3,* 1989, sculpture

Top right, *Unknown Territory 4,* 1989, sculpture

Right, *Unknown Territory 6,* 1989, sculpture

dess whose mouth was wide open, heralding the way of the others to follow.

This is how I work with clay. I pull or slice a piece of clay off and wedge it. I let the clay absorb everything that is in my mind. Then I start slapping the clay into a ball. Sometimes before it forms into a ball, I see a part of the piece it is to become. Sometimes I will start with a butt, or maybe I see the nose. Often, I have no idea when I sit down what I am going to make. I just keep handling the clay. If nothing emerges, I make a ball. Then I continue squeezing it, changing its shape slightly, until I see something begin to emerge. Sometimes, nothing comes forth.

That is what my clay work has been about. Transforming what has been ugly into something now beautiful. It allows me to stand back and look at what I have been holding inside. As I began sculpting one of my most recent pieces, I was crying, knowing that this sculpture of two people would be about rape. Then, slowly, I began to see one woman holding another. By the time I had finished the piece, I saw that this was a sculpture of me holding and nurturing myself. Through the clay I am healing myself.

Just as importantly, I am doing this work in the presence of other women. I take my pieces with me to both group and individual therapy. I simply share them. It is enough. These women see who I am and that is a very great thing.

I began sculpting at the age of forty-three, before I had specific memories. A friend said to me, "Your hands remember." She was right. My hands do remember. As I make each piece, I remember and experience the emotion reflected in the piece. But once it is done, I feel wonderful. I feel better than wonderful. I feel heard and seen. Many of my early pieces were of screaming women. Then I made the sculpture of me nurturing myself, and I thought perhaps I was done with screaming. But the next piece was yet another screaming woman. I plan to scream for a long time to come.

Unknown Territory 5,
1989, sculpture

Pieces of the Map:
A Survivor, Healing

Joanne Barrie Lynn

Like all healing journeys, mine is idiosyncratic, eccentric, unique as a scar. I am using the art of poetry as a primary healing tool, wrestling with the manuscript of a book of poems, trying to fathom what it takes to heal from incest. It's difficult to be objective—I'm in the middle of it, with at least as many memories yet to unfold as what I've already remembered.

Nearly five years ago, just before my thirty-eighth birthday, I had my first memory of incest at my mother's hands. That memory began a slow healing that has picked up speed in the last two years, triggering the first serious writing I've done.

Poetry, though, is my second art. From age five I studied ballet intensively until age fifteen, when my mother canceled all my dance classes. Writing poetry helps me find again that joy and spiritual balance. Every poem is a dance through my mind and another path to healing.

As I heal, I find extraordinary teachers. One of them is Pink, a split-off part of me, my eight-year-old self, who holds my rage and my playfulness. She left me during a time of unbearable terror and reappeared in my life last summer, in a flurry of ponytails and pink skirts. She is becoming as much at home in my adult body as I am with her daredevil energy. She is delightfully embarrassing. We like each other a great deal, though I think she's arrogant and short-sighted, and she loathes my caution. She wants me to write about her, but not yet. She hasn't danced enough.

The most extraordinary learning I've found as I heal is to value myself as a woman. My betrayal from infancy by my mother and other women, coupled with my nurturing father, taught me to trust only men, take only men seriously. Until a few years ago, I saw the value of my femaleness mainly in attracting and nurturing men. I tried to write like a man.

Women—poets, artists, musicians, old and new friends, lesbians, and a sprinkling of witches—have been my teachers. I am amazed at the respect and deep regard I find among women. I'm delighted with the power of my writing, when I write like a woman.

This is an intimate healing, and difficult to share. Writing about it clears up some of my confusion, the "fog of war" that surrounds any trauma, global or personal, and shows me the pragmatic functions of poetry in my healing:

to unlock memories: Memories are sometimes hard to retrieve, but occasionally they write themselves in a poem, straight out, with no rewriting. Such a gift staggers me.

to reframe: Nearly two years ago, I put my mother out of my life. "Menorah" wiped out all my guilt by showing me the obscenity of contact with a rapist. *Of course* I'll never see her again.

to work through problems: "Maggots" was the result of intensive discussions with several artists using their art as a healing tool, as we stumbled through painful, sometimes horrifying memories that we couldn't shut down. Writing such a poem forces me to see that "why?" and "why me?" are no longer important questions. In my life, incest is. Poetry helps me focus on what needs to be done about it.

to reclaim what the rapists stole from me: Rape steals so much. Rape stole my physical health, my memory, my sexual passion, my courage, my kindness, the fine edge of my intellectual acuity, my art, my education, my playfulness, my rage, my time, my place in the world. Every poem reclaims a piece of my loss; every word reclaims my voice.

to give the terrible relief of telling: Every poem is a healing ritual. In "My Mother's Friends" the time of writing was short—less than a day—but the mental and emotional preparation dragged on for several unpleasant months. I had to relive scores of rapes before I could believe it. I was always afraid, always tired. My family suffered.

It was three or four months before the layers and layers of detail finally convinced me it was a memory, not some bizarre fantasy. I raged and grieved for a few weeks, and from that chaos came the healing ritual of this poem. Every time someone hears it or reads it, I'm healed deeper.

It's frightening to write this. I sweat. I cry. I light candles, listening to the rain. I find places of safety.

My formal style of writing is one such place of safety. Because I grew up immersed in ballet and classical music, formality in my art is second nature to me, and very safe. From that place, the details of my wounding become less and less important. They are signposts to health, acknowledging how far there is to go; reminders of my strength, of what I've already survived.

What poetry requires of me is simple:

the intention to heal: the basic, moment by moment choice, at every level, for life. Once I began to write seriously, I realized that if I stop, I die, either by accident or by illness. If I continue to write, I can be whole.

love: deep connections, fervent and tender, with myself and with others. This is treacherous ground, whether or not sex is involved, since anyone raped by a parent is betrayed to the point of utter confusion. Learning love again, from a place of my own adult power, is the deepest healing. Sometimes a poem teaches me that I love someone; sometimes I can express that love only in a sacred formal way, like a poem.

going public: an extension of love, since no one heals in a vacuum, and the ultimate rejection of the rapist. Reading my poetry in public is terrifying, but every reading brings me a deluge of new poems and memories. Other women tell me my work triggers their own memories and their art. We enrich each other and make the world safer for all of us.

delight: playfulness, a sense of humor. Like ballet, poetry is fun, an absorbing puzzle. I'm learning to celebrate every moment of joy, however small, as a lifeline.

But nothing, neither love nor art, can take away the pain. Healing costs. I've lost my mother, not to death, but to her own disgrace. I've lost respect for my long-dead father, who should have known more. I've lost old family friends and most of my birth family. I've lost the certainty, shaky as it always was, of what I am and where I belong. I've lost, and my family has lost, our relatively peaceful life to the maelstrom that accompanies any healing. All this in addition to what the rapists stole from me.

Is it worth it? I'm learning to live in the present. I look ahead, sometimes with dread, to the memories I might still need to relive, and remind myself that anticipation can be keener than reality. I look back at some moment of healing and say "I couldn't do it again," and there is always someone who loves me enough to say "You don't have to." I'm learning to ask for such comfort.

I'm learning I can't exist alone. Starting with my chosen family, and extending to my friends and the larger community, I need the support and love I find there. I like solitude and such a need seems a high risk, but again, I'm learning to choose between life or death.

I'm learning to love myself. I'm learning that women can be trusted, that I'm more than a second-class man. I'm learning I can take risks, make mistakes. I can look foolish and not die of it.

It's worth it. There is a place inside me that no rapist ever touched. It grows as I nurture it, and every year the touch of rapists in my body diminishes. Even my cells are all replaced every seven years.

It's frightening to heal, but I can't stop any more. I'm writing for my life, and every poem is a piece of my journey's map. Though the patterns of wounding and healing are as clear to the reader as highways to a pilot, I have to slog through the debris, not knowing if any given path will end in illumination, or a cliff in the dark.

And very occasionally, when I miss the light and step off that cliff, I catch myself dancing, anyway.

My Mother's Friends

were old, smelled
of stale silk
violet toilette water
One by one they didn't care
how ugly grey I saw them

or how my breath stopped
when my party dress came off
their knobby fingers
scourging
all my private places

Dressed again
I drank cups and cups
of hot sweet tea
my mother's wealthy friends
paying us off in smiles and cakes

and further invitations

Menorah

for Maurice Sendak's "Dear Mili"

I come to his work unexpectant
    in the dark of the year
   knowing enough of Holocaust to see
    the tower of Auschwitz
       dwarfing the skeletal children
and fall in fear with him
   layer
     under layer

In this terror I lose myself
  following light
    whatever it ignites
  following labyrinthine roots of trees
    like bones
   clear as a Mozart cantata
candescent as truth

I am ill with Christian forbearance
    for a mother clever enough
   to have left scars that can't be seen
My escape from her debauchery
    enrages her
   She slavers for my return
to the tomb of what it was
      to be her child
       tattooed
    with the invisible numbers
    of her fingerprints

  She is not absolved
I light my first Menorah
    in honour of the artist who knows
   the children of Auschwitz
do not return to comfort the guards

Maggots

for Kim Newall

They are insatiable, memories
    Touch one
  they swarm to the bloodheat
        maggots on a wound
What unspeakable lust
      laid those eggs
          that feast when they hatch
    on putrescence?
  Yet their fat appetite
      eats away the rot
cleanses the wound for healing

Let the flesh creep awhile
Or walk wounded forever

Taking the Private Public

Clarissa T. Sligh

January 8, 1982
I entered the bathroom and locked the door. The mirror over the bathroom
sink reflected the agony and despair in my face.

LTHOUGH I WAS gainfully employed as a financial analyst, I envied the courage and determination of the artist
whose reception I had just been to. It reminded me of a
dream that I had given up on. Now the pain of that loss made me
feel bad about myself. Looking in the mirror, I promised myself
that I would sketch a self-portrait every day for a year, no matter
where I was or what I was doing.

Without realizing it, the decision to set aside daily drawing
time was the beginning of a search for myself. During the nine
months that I sketched, many questions began to surface. In an effort to give them some form, I began to make quick sketches of
family members from snapshots. Each time I pulled out the family album, however, heavy walls of fog blanked my mind, making me feel sleepy and exhausted. At that time, I did not know it,
but that wall of resistance would become a wall of terror that I
would have to push against in order to do creative work.

Now as I looked at the snapshots, they seemed to have no relationship to the reality of my childhood. In typical home outdoor
shots, everyone is smiling at the camera in the backyard, on the
front steps, in front of the car, in their Sunday best.

Now as I looked at the snapshots, they reminded me of how
our bonds of affection had been laced with barbs of conflict and
violence. In an effort to work through the vague and uneasy rec-
ollections, I began to write and rewrite memories while shooting,
reprinting and collaging the old photographs. While trying to focus on pleasant memories, forgotten childhood experiences—
many of which were frightening and taboo—began to re-emerge.
The writings took on a life of their own. The snapshots sucked
me into the frame and transported me to another time and place.

As I worked, I grappled with the shadows of anger, confusion
and guilt which hovered over me. I did not know it, but I was to

SHE DIDN'T KNOW WHO SHE WAS, BUT SHE KNEW SHE WASN'T WHO YOU ALL SAID SHE WAS. SHE DIDN'T KNOW WHO SHE WAS, BUT SHE KNEW SHE WASN'T WHO YOU ALL SAID SHE WAS. SHE DIDN'T KNOW WHO SHE WAS, BUT SHE KNEW SHE WASN'T WHO YOU ALL SAID SHE WAS. SHE DIDN'T KNOW WHO SHE WAS, BUT SHE KNEW SHE WASN'T WHO YOU ALL SAID SHE WAS. SHE DIDN'T KNOW WHO SHE WAS, BUT SHE KNEW SHE WASN'T WHO YOU ALL SAID SHE WAS. SHE DIDN'T KNOW WHO SHE WAS, BUT SHE KNEW SHE WASN'T WHO YOU ALL SAID SHE WAS. SHE DIDN'T KNOW WHO SHE WAS, BUT SHE KNEW SHE WASN'T WHO YOU ALL SAID SHE WAS. SHE DIDN'T KNOW WHO SHE WAS, BUT SHE KNEW SHE WASN'T WHO YOU ALL SAID SHE WAS. SHE DIDN'T KNOW WHO SHE WAS, BUT SHE KNEW SHE WASN'T WHO YOU ALL SAID SHE WAS. SHE DIDN'T KNOW WHO SHE WAS, BUT SHE KNEW SHE WASN'T WHO YOU ALL SAID SHE WAS. SHE DIDN'T KNOW WHO SHE WAS, BUT SHE KNEW SHE WASN'T WHO YOU ALL SAID SHE WAS. SHE DIDN'T KNOW WHO SHE WAS, BUT SHE KNEW SHE WASN'T WHO YOU ALL SAID SHE WAS. SHE DIDN'T KNOW WHO SHE WAS, BUT SHE KNEW SHE WASN'T WHO YOU ALL SAID SHE WAS. SHE DIDN'T KNOW WHO SHE WAS, BUT SHE KNEW SHE WASN'T WHO YOU ALL SAID SHE WAS. SHE DIDN'T KNOW WHO SHE WAS, BUT SHE KNEW SHE WASN'T WHO YOU ALL SAID SHE WAS. SHE DIDN'T KNOW WHO SHE WAS, BUT SHE KNEW SHE WASN'T WHO YOU ALL SAID SHE WAS. SHE DIDN'T KNOW WHO SHE WAS, BUT SHE KNEW SHE WASN'T WHO YOU ALL SAID. SHE DIDN'T KNOW WHO SHE WAS, BUT SHE KNEW SHE WASN'T WHO YOU ALL SAID SHE WAS. SHE DIDN'T KNOW WHO SHE WAS, BUT SHE KNEW SHE WASN'T WHO YOU ALL SAID SHE WAS. SHE DIDN'T KNOW WHO SHE WAS, BUT SHE KNEW SHE WASN'T WHO YOU ALL SAID SHE WAS. SHE DIDN'T KNOW WHO SHE WAS, BUT SHE KNEW SHE WASN'T WHO YOU ALL SAID SHE WAS. SHE DIDN'T KNOW WHO SHE WAS, BUT SHE KNEW SHE WASN'T WHO YOU ALL SAID SHE WAS. SHE DIDN'T KNOW WHO SHE WAS, BUT SHE KNEW SHE WASN'T WHO YOU ALL SAID. SHE DIDN'T KNOW WHO SHE WAS, BUT SHE KNEW SHE WASN'T WHO YOU ALL SAID SHE WAS.
SHE DIDN'T KNOW WHO SHE WAS, BUT SHE KNEW SHE WASN'T WHO YOU ALL SAID S

HE WAS. SHE DIDN'T KNOW WHO SHE WAS, BUT SHE KNEW SHE WASN'T WHO YOU ALL SAID SHE WAS. SHE DIDN'T KNOW WHO SHE WAS, BUT SHE KNEW SHE WASN'T WHO YOU ALL SAID SHE WAS. SHE DIDN'T KNOW WHO SHE WAS, BUT SHE KNEW SHE WASN'T WHO YOU ALL SAID SHE WAS, BUT SHE KNEW SHE WASN'T WHO YOU ALL SAID SHE WAS. SHE DIDN'T KNOW WHO SHE WAS, BUT SHE KNEW SHE WASN'T WHO YOU ALL SAID SHE WAS. SHE DIDN'T KNOW WHO SHE WAS, BUT SHE KNEW SHE WASN'T WHO YOU ALL SAID SHE WAS. SHE DIDN'T KNOW WHO SHE WAS, BUT SHE KNEW SHE WASN'T WHO YOU ALL SAID SHE WAS. SHE DIDN'T KNOW WHO SHE WAS, BUT SHE KNEW SHE WASN'T WHO YOU ALL SAID SHE WAS. SHE DIDN'T KNOW WHO SHE WAS, BUT SHE KNEW SHE WASN'T WHO YOU ALL SAID SHE WAS. SHE DIDN'T KNOW WHO SHE WAS, BUT SHE KNEW SHE WASN'T WHO YOU ALL SAID. SHE DIDN'T KNOW WHO SHE WAS, BUT SHE KNEW SHE WASN'T WHO YOU ALL SAID SHE WAS. SHE DIDN'T KNOW WHO SHE WAS, BUT SHE KNEW SHE WASN'T WHO YOU ALL SAID SHE WAS. SHE DIDN'T KNOW WHO SHE WAS, BUT SHE KNEW SHE WASN'T WHO YOU ALL SAID SHE WAS. SHE DIDN'T KNOW WHO SHE WAS, BUT SHE KNEW SHE WASN'T WHO YOU ALL SAID SHE WAS. SHE DIDN'T KNOW WHO SHE WAS, BUT SHE KNEW SHE WASN'T WHO YOU ALL SAID SHE WAS.

SHE DIDN'T KNOW WHO SHE WAS, BUT SHE KNEW SHE WASN'T WHO YOU ALL SAID SHE WAS. S

HE DIDN'T KNOW WHO SHE WAS, BUT SHE KNEW SHE WASN'T WHO YOU ALL SAID SHE WAS. SHE DID

N'T KNOW WHO SHE WAS, BUT SHE KNEW SHE WASN'T WHO YOU ALL SAID SHE WAS. SHE DIDN'T K

NOW WHO SHE WAS, BUT SHE KNEW SHE WASN'T WHO YOU ALL SAID SHE WAS. SHE DIDN'T KNOW W

HO SHE WAS, BUT SHE KNEW SHE WASN'T WHO YOU ALL SHE WAS. SHE DIDN'T KNOW WHO SHE WAS.

SHE DIDN'T KNOW WHO SHE WAS

148   CLARISSA T. SLIGH

begin a passage through the "shadow areas" of my life. And I did not want to make the trip.

April 27, 1984
Funny, I never had all the contact printing problems I am having now. The dark brown and beige overtones are dirty-looking. The image quality is good, but the chemical looks a sickly dark, dull brown.

The photographs are printed on a heavy etching paper coated with Van Dyke brown light-sensitive chemicals. They are newly framed memory pictures from my distant past. It is clear that they are reconstructions. Still, I felt guarded about showing them. Embarrassment and guilt about "betraying family secrets" made me feel like I was being "bad."

Could the viewers be nonjudgmental? Would they think my experiences had been tough only because I had been poor and Black? I wanted them to recognize that the particular and peculiar experiences of this girl should be part of the landscape of children's stories. I wanted them to understand that there were other lives outside of their personal experiences.

May 18, 1984
New York City. The time for the opening reception has come. I am terrified, but I know I am supposed to act like I am cool. I gulp down two glasses of wine in a frantic effort to relax myself. Several people asked me if they were true stories. When I answered yes, one person responded, "How sad!"

Perhaps it's odd, but I had never considered those hard times as sad times. In the semi-rural area where we lived, we had also had lots of fun.

A young couple thanked me for sharing the stories. "They make us feel less alone about our own lives," they said.

I sighed with relief that at least one other person could understand.

Several others began to tell me stories they had kept secret all their lives. I was not prepared to become their confidante. I felt uneasy. I did not know what to say. This was in the early eighties. This was when people did not talk about incest. If it happened to you, it was something to forget.

In 1987, I was finally able to show my work to my family. Their responses ranged from silence, to curiosity, to denial and anger. The best part of it was having some of my siblings share similar experiences with me.

Left, *Who She Was*, 1987, 22″ × 30″, photo-collage

Reframing the Past, 1988,
1988, 24″ × 24″, photo-
collage

Wonderful Uncle, 1988,
11″ × 14″, photo–collage

September 30, 1989
Now as I go back to bring the past into the present, and take the private
public, I see that many of the things that seemed so terrible back then were
not as hard as having to bear them in isolation. That secrecy became a big
part of the way that I could feel bad about myself.

Much later, I began to understand how shame and embarrassment and fear of being avoided and becoming isolated keeps us
quiet and apart. Once we internalize these oppressions, public hatred, disgrace and ridicule become tools used to keep us in our
place.

Today, I just assume people have seen my work and that it is
a big part of the reason that they want to get to know me. I no
longer avoid people who have negative responses. Since I feel that
I don't have as much to hide, I am not as terrified. It is easier for
me to see the ways in which they might have become re-
stimulated.

It is hard work to cut away illusions about our lives. All the
behavior patterns that I learned in order to survive way back then
are still trying to make me behave. Often when I open my mouth
to speak about the past, I feel like I am going to be slapped down
by the big, invisible hand of God.

Each time I actually manage to speak, I get another glimpse
into how I gave up my real self and my awareness of my bril-
liance, my beauty, my power, and the right to expect that everyone would want to love and connect with me.

As I make visible, understand, forgive and heal the pain and
hurt that I got just because I was me, I become more able to relax
and reclaim pride and joy in who I am. I regain my power and
freedom as the healing occurs.

Womon Throwing Off Rage

Katherine F.H. Heart

THE ACT OF painting helps me to capture raw feelings as they emerge from unconscious to conscious awareness. I have discovered aspects of my abuse and keys to healing encoded in the symbolic language of painting. As the creative process evolves, words as well as images emerge out of my unconscious.

My paintings often take a number of months to complete because of the amount of energy and emotion that needs to come through. *Womon Throwing Off Rage* is a good example. This painting began out of the only dream I've ever had in which I experienced my own death. I was consumed in expressing all of the energies evoked by the dream for over four months.

The setting for the dream was at the ocean, where I had run away from a group of people who would not accept my anger. I ran along the shore into an approaching storm. The charged air went through me and an enormous rage rolled up my spine. At the height of the powerful release, a lightening bolt struck me. Later, the leader of the group found and cradled my charred body as my spirit watched safely from a distance.

Experiencing the interconnection between bodily (internal) elements and nature's (external) elements helped me to break through a long isolation. When I awakened from the dream, I was immediately compelled to begin painting. I began with broad strokes, making horizontal layers of pale gray watercolor wash over the expanse of a large illustration board. The Rorschach-like pattern of the wash became a vague structure in which to project my inner feeling-image. (This method allows me to be with the initial watery stage of my creative process and the emergence of new awareness.)

After I'd outlined my internally felt/seen body, I wanted to work the detail in a different medium. Colored pencil represents safety to me, stemming from lengthy periods of elaborate drawing with colored pencils as a child. I spent many childhood hours completely absorbed in the pleasurable sensation of creating fine, subtle shadings of new colors, without thinking about Dad abusing me or worrying about my younger siblings. The pressure exerted through the pencil was a special outlet for my right hand, which was at other times forced to masturbate my father's penis. I feel a satisfying sense of being in ·control of emotional exposure through my choices of texture, hue depth and level of transparency when using colored pencils. I experiment with risk-taking through blending colors in semi-unpredictable layers.

In *Womon Throwing Off Rage,* I used the highly sharpened point of the black pencil to make flowing incisions separating the foreground and background layers of ocean. This was an important representation of my growing ability to separate past victimization (background) from the depthful richness of the present healing process (foreground), also described by less flat, multi-dimensional coloring schemes in the lower part of the painting closest to the viewer.

Making incisions into the illustration board was hard work, physically painful for my hand, and at the same time satisfying. In adolescence and early adulthood, obsessive athletic training and cutting my arms were the only ways that I'd found to express my wounds. Since completing the painting in 1985, the training compulsion moderated and I have had only one brief incident of self-cutting.

With the visual images for the painting came words about the meaning and source of the energy which moved through me. While working with colored pencil in the painting, I often saw and heard words drifting into awareness through an internal fog and felt compelled to write this stream-of-consciousness in a journal next to my easel. A prose poem gradually congealed and found its own structure. The poem further differentiates shades of meaning from the raw energy of the painting. Writing while painting forged new visceral connections. As colorful images and feeling words flowed excitedly and gracefully from painting to poem and back, I felt a profound meeting of rage and ecstasy.

The watery edge where the conscious and unconscious intermingles is completely open and free-feeling, and it is frightening not knowing what is waiting there to emerge. The fear of being overwhelmed by rage was channeled into a gentle, slower process that allowed me to remain in control. The long painting-poem allowed a fuller integration of feelings and meanings than would have been possible with briefer, explosive techniques.

The stoic, secret anger of my childhood would not let me forget that Dad made me masturbate him on almost a weekly basis from the age of six to fourteen. In being so used, much of my sense of self as a woman was lost or damaged. Writing and drawing allowed re-membering—literally putting dismembered parts back into a whole sense of self. The concrete form of the product bears witness and is an historical record that frees me of the psychic burden of keeping everything in memory.

When his penis assaulted my mouth, my capacity to form words and speak them was severely damaged. This most common form of sexual child abuse left no physical evidence to make others suspicious. He caused a silencing of my feelings and spirit. Attempting to speak feelings brought shame and humiliation for many years. My healing process would have been incomplete without finding safe, natural means of being with the feelings and learning the words, and then finding expressive forums.

I have an undeniable drive to express the full impact of my experiences and to have this understood by the public, especially men. On a number of occasions my readings have moved men to tears. My motivation isn't to hurt others, but to help them connect with the feeling of victimization. Making my work public and participating in speak-outs has helped me to complete the healing cycle by getting the damage out of my body, psyche and spirit and giving it back to the individual and collective perpetrators. Public action also mirrors and empowers my private struggle to break through denial in my family.

The obstacles I face as a womon artist are less within myself than in the public's continuing denial and protection of the perpetrator, especially when he is head of the family. I have learned that being sexually abused as a girl, being raped and living under the constant threat of assault as an adult woman is and has been commonplace, and is the most effective insidious method of patriarchal control over the lives and spirits of women. Despite the inroads made in public awareness, invisibility and silence about sexual assault continues to permeate this culture. It is in the interests of the patriarchy to keep the feminine bound up and wounded, unable to come into full creative power.

Alongside those who deny and don't want to see or hear about the issue are people who are deeply open to it. When I speak to groups and exhibit my paintings, many people express a hunger for the spiritual richness and nurturance that is clearly visible. My role as a politically conscious womon artist is to bring the psychic experience of sexual assault and the creative resources of the healing process out of the underground and into public/collective consciousness. As a survivor, I can't do less than speak out and insist that my reality be seen and heard. And as an artist, I can't do less than use my freed creative passion to envision a world without violence.

Utilizing visual art and writing has helped to create a healthy adult identity that reflects my true inner life as a womon. As a child, I did not have the freedom, power or language to commu-

Womon Throwing Off Rage,
1986, 29″ × 33½″ painting

nicate the pain. At the core of the incest wound was my broken heart, cut by parental abuse, distorted by misunderstanding and isolated through silencing.

In becoming aware of the symbolic language of womyn-identification, I realized that I had uncovered the unique creative vision and voice I had sought for many years. I moved from an abstract identification with the dream-figure to embrace my core identity. *Womon Throwing Off Rage* mirrors my truthful fury and primordial beauty from deep below the shame of abuse. The creative process evoked the empowering resources of an ancient and whole feminine collective consciousness. With art as my witness and ally, I have re-created and claimed the original self that my father's abuse and patriarchal conditioning had caused me to lose. Creative expression healed my body and revitalized my spirit and, in the process, my incest wound was transformed into a creative wellspring.

Womon Throwing Off Rage

Hair flying wild smudging
the air electric   her breasts
fling fireballs without the
aid of hands

After twelve hours in her hair I dress
the body with transparent gold pencil
a crimson boulder takes the steep canyon
trail up each vertebrae leaving bloody
prints and scarlet splashes   layers of
sloshed and caked tissue her chin
lifts in the ecstasy of release

Clear bedrock formations
emerge   hot stone is
catapulted from a gilded volcano
she rages with the elements
of rapture   molten cleansing
relieves her of a
long held burden

There are obscuring mists   sucking
marshes   subterranean violent storms
primordial dangers   in the inner
world of the abused woman
if she can retain a glimpse of self
while identifying with our
sisters-of-the-raging-elements
she can claim primitive powers
we must go there   mad   unguided

Eighty percent of my body is water
what would be more natural than to swim
far out from shore   secret myself into an ebb
of wave   swirl to a dervish spouting water
at drunken boatmen   or to dive   deep
learning a new language   among families
who do not judge but watch me grow gills
olden ways to breathe

Iron   zinc   magnesium   sodium   coalesce
in bones and muscles   threatening to rupture
fountains of magma setting everyone ablaze

our role is to remind them that there exists
a greater force   than hu-man ego

What is on the other side of rage?
it's not a matter of getting over rage
or raging   then not raging
don't ever give up the capacity to rage
rage is the source of daily passions
the energy to begin and sustain
the readiness to become angry in a moment
could save your life in a late night garage

Rage is the place I am immediately taken
during newslash atrocities   acts of
torture   wife beating   molestation
a murky myriad of oppressions
across the   road   nation   world

I begin to dance in the rage
crux of energy amidst a void I whirl out
carrying fresh light on my heels
on tips of scarves   on silver edges
of a timeworn gown   at a stop
in the stillness   gathered around
is laugh   and   play   pure spark
joy filled again.

A Disturbance in the Surface of Things

Nancy Redwine

I HAVE BEEN A writer since I was twelve. I was never going to write about incest.

I know the story of the women in Delphi who knew what they knew from what they breathed. And of the Pythia, who hung over a chasm in the earth from which a vapor rose.

I know the stories of many women. I know innumerable stories of rape, torture and molestation. I know stories of irretrievable childhoods and families silent for generations. I know my mother's story. I know my lover's story. I know my friends' stories. I know the stories of women I have only met once. I know the stories of women I have never met.

I know these stories word for word. Breath for breath. I know these stories with the inside of my body. I know these stories from the ground I walk on. I know these stories from living in my mother's body. I know these stories from what I breathe.

I tell the story of what my body has experienced at the hands of others. I tell the story of my body, which is her body and your body and the body that we all are. What happened to me happened to you, and to her and to my mother and my cousin and the woman who walks past me on her way to work. What happened to me is happening to the ground I walk upon and to the air I breathe.

The Pythia inhaled that which had been contained, that which was being released from the recesses of the earth. The sites chosen for temples were places where there were disturbances in the surface of things.

My voice rises from a chasm. A voice of nauseous gases and noxious odors. A voice that makes me sick with knowing. A voice that makes me dizzy and confused. A voice that makes me aware of the pain in my body. A voice that tells truths in a tongue that I can speak but cannot always understand. A voice that rises from all that has been buried and compressed under the ground I walk upon.

I am telling that which was never meant to be told. I am telling the truth that was called a lie. I am telling that which imbedded itself into my body in a way that was about not telling. How I learned to smile when I don't feel like smiling is about not telling. How I learned to laugh when I am not amused is about not telling. How I learned to carry my body is about not telling. How my feet grow in on themselves is about not telling. How I learned to not breathe is about not telling.

The telling tears at my body. Old fissures re-open painfully and allow me to see into the graves of memory. That which has been hidden rises in clouds of steam, which simultaneously confuse my mind and open my mouth to something that has been foreign to me. My own tongue. My own language. My body.

The Pythia would become intoxicated by the spirit of the deity rising from the earth, and she would speak what became known to her. She would shake and gesture wildly.

As a child, I practiced not breathing. I believed that if I didn't breathe I wouldn't feel. I would be as good as dead. As a child, I was suffocated by a body much larger than mine. I was gagged with a cloth. I was choked by a penis in my throat, drowned by semen. A hand pinched my mouth to stifle my cries.

In my life, breathing is an act of rebellion. I practice every day. What I know, I know because I breathe.

I lean into the warming wood of my desk with one of my feet up near my vulva and the other on the floor. My chin and cheek alternate resting against my bent knee. Flat river rocks rattle with the movement of my hand across the page. My other hand holds the edge of paper, bears witness to the writing. My face sinks deep into itself. My shoulder rocks itself tight and then loose. I am aware of my belly against my thigh. I am telling. I am telling what I know with my body. I enter, and all manner of my breathing changes. I am breathing through my eyes, through the soles of my feet, through the palms of my hands, my ears, my point of contact with the chair.

I was never going to write about incest.

The Pythia did not speak in the tongue of her culture. She did not speak in the tongue of her father. She spoke in the tongue of that which rose from what had split open the surface.

Five years ago, I started writing a story about breasts and what happens when a woman named Enid leaves her bra in the dressing room at Mervyn's. She learns a new way of walking. Her center of gravity changes. Her body speaks to her.

I thought I was writing a short story, but the more I knew

about Enid, the more I knew about myself, and so I let her tell me the story. She quickly took me into her childhood and into her imagination, where she was creating a culture made up of fierce and smart women. She took me into her family, where her relationships with her mother and her father opened up in my face. Awareness opened in my belly.

One morning, about three months into the writing, I woke to the knowledge that Enid was being raped by her father. I stayed in bed for two days, trying to keep my eyes closed.

In reference to the Pythia's voice, it is said that she did not speak in ordinary tones, but shouted or cried.

It's not about me, I told myself. I remember everything that happened to me. This is Enid's story. I am making it up. I am in control. I am a fiction writer. I will not write autobiography.

Enid's story is the vast field of my body: a landscape I traverse and investigate. Across this terrain there are openings through which I enter; sometimes climbing, sometimes falling into levels of my experience that are simultaneous with Enid's experience, with your experience, with our experience. There are openings from which rise dizzying yet clarifying visions illuminating the viscera that connect and carry me through this finding. There are layers and layers of cells in my body, and each cell has a story. Each has a voice, if I am willing to listen that closely.

My feet will tell what they know if my face will hold itself against the ground. My mouth will speak itself if my wrists will lay quietly against my inner thighs. My breastbone will only speak to the deepest crease in my palm.

I am crying out loud. I am telling. I am telling you because you probably already know something, and in the telling I know more and in the listening/reading you know more. And for a few moments, we know something so clearly that we want to know more. We want to know what it feels like to live in our wrists, to be alive in the arch of your foot, in Enid's third intercostal space, in my jaw bone, in her eye sockets.

I am reconstructing my voice. I find pieces of it everywhere. My voice is a whistle, a whine, a scream, the shiver of leaves, the thud of a deer hit by a car, the hiss of an avalanche, the boxed voice of a doll turned upside-down, a gale of laughter, a quiet cough at the back of my throat.

The voice that says, shut up, is the voice that tied the gag in my mouth. The voice that says, you are making this up, is the voice that shoved fingers into me, the voice that lay on top of me, stealing my breath, my dreams, my smell. The voice that says, you are a liar, is the voice that covered my mouth to muffle my words. The voice that said, tell me you love me, tell me how much you want me to be doing this, is the voice that said, I will hurt you until you tell me the truth that I want to hear.

I speak in the voices of the women Enid created. The women who want everything to be different and who struggle, argue, despair, play practical jokes and drink a lot of coffee down by the river that used to run underground.

I speak in the voices of insects, flies and cockroaches, as manifestations of the women in Enid's culture. As teachers in their experience of being those who are exterminated. Pests as Enid is a pest, as I am a pest. Noisy and irritating in my father's house. Crushed beneath his shiny shoes. Reborn in multitude.

I speak in the voice of Lydia, a woman with her own memories looking at her own pain in the face of Enid, who she sees on the bus. Lydia who tries to run away. Lydia who finds herself in the company of fierce and smart women. Lydia, who sees and cannot look away, cannot save anyone and has heard too many of these kinds of stories.

I speak in the voice of the doll on my bed. In the voice of the monster who lived in my mother's room. In the voice of the little girl who could destroy the world with what she kept held in her fist. I speak in the voice of my childhood sexual fantasies. In the voice of the imaginary horse I rode everywhere when I was nine. In the voice of the wild naked woman who watched me from the woods beside the freeway throughout my early twenties. I speak in the voice of my memory that was buried under the floor of my room. In the voice of the rapist who tells me all my memories are lies. In the voice of terror that tells me everyone raped me all the time without end, without beginning, that even now the air rapes me, hands cover my body. I speak in the voice of the woman who is ten feet tall, has blood dripping from her mouth, razor-sharp fingernails and a stick with nails poking out the end of it walking up the rhododendron-lined path to my father's house.

The women present at the inhalation translate the words of the Pythia and often reproduce them in verse. It was commonly believed that the Pythia answered not only out of her own consciousness, but in the voice of the vapor. The voice of the earth. The voice of the chasm.

I am writing my own story through the voices of many. Memory is a story of many layers, times, truths and voices; of past and present living in the same body at the same time. My story is a memory of Enid's story telling itself to the memory of my body. In the telling I am taken to a level of presence in the world that I cannot occupy without my memories. A place that we cannot occupy without my body.

I am a Liar

This is the name my mother calls me. It is the name of my smile. It is the name of the movements I make with my body. I will not tell you my real name. It could hurt you. My real name slices toward the outside. The name my mother calls me slices toward the inside, where the blood does not show, where the blood is not yours and coagulates in a thick bog that smells and attracts insects.

I was named Liar as a family tradition. I am named after my ancestors who were all liars. I lie. I lie down. I lie down and do not get up. I lie down underneath the rotting bodies of my ancestors, who were all blind and whose eyes weep into my hair.

I am a good liar. I make up everything. I make up this house. I make up this happy childhood. I make up this loving mother. I make up this protecting father. I make up this soft white body. I make up this image I see in the mirror.

She named me Liar to protect me. To protect those around me from my real name. She named me Liar to protect the family. To protect the church. She named me Liar to protect herself.

My real name is whispering itself into my ear at night. My real name is leaving dead animals on my front porch. My real name is eating through the varnish on the family hope chest. My real name is calling my father in the middle of the night with death threats. My real name is bending the cross on the front lawn of the church into a pitchfork. My real name is scrawling itself in red ink across the pages of the family Bible. My real name is squeezing cracks into the supporting beams of this house. My real name has tracked me down. My real name is not going to keep you safe any more. My real name scrawls itself across the land in fire.

Quake. Be afraid. I am a girl.

That Night a Voice

breaks through the evening news on the radio. A voice echoing from radiators, from battery-powered animals, from Suzy Homemaker ovens, from irons all over the city. A voice calling out names. Come sister, cousin, girlfriend. Do not be afraid. Fear is an anger held inside of your clenched fist. Open your fingers and let it walk. They crawl, they totter, they stomp through the streets. Sparks fly up from the flints their bodies are becoming.

There is no talking. They walk around in a circle. They walk up main streets and down side streets. They go forwards and they turn around and go back. You wouldn't know they were there except that your electrical appliances have gone on the blink. They are agitated by something in the air. The blender goes on and on at its highest speed. The television broadcasts a bright pulsing light. The radio blares a station you've never heard before, drumming a cadence that turns your skin red. You can't take that nap you thought you'd take.

Cars are being driven in a wide circle around them. Curtains are being pulled closed. Birds pull themselves into flocks, even birds that never flock together, and swoop low. Flies perch still on the lips of garbage cans, their jaws still, their heads nodding slightly. Cockroaches come up from the foundations of the city.

Girls are taking the streets, pissed like you've never seen little girls be pissed. They shiver with the anger that has flooded every household in the city like an invisible explosive gas. They carry no signs. They carry no weapons. Their hands are open and empty and much bigger than they'd ever imagined.

Enid is all shook up. She doesn't even know how she got out the door. She is hiding behind a shrub in the front yard. Lydia is hiding in a bar where the pinball machines are shivering and shooting one ball after another, webbing the glass into tiny splinters. The beer sign is flashing a pulse faster than her heart can beat. Lloyd is at a small table, trying to concentrate on the book of Revelations. His eyes are dilating wildly and his drink shivers a blinding amber light. Men rub their eyes in confusion. Nobody notices the man in the back booth having a heart attack.

I Come to Your House in the Body of an Eight Year Old

I am at your door and you let me in without question. I have been walking. My feet are bloody and bare. You invite me to sit, thinking me a guest. I bare my teeth in impatience. Blood outlines each tooth.

You know who I am. You look toward the door I entered, afraid that I am not alone. Afraid that there may be more of me out there ready to knock. To knock down your door. You know why I am here. I knock the plate of cookies from your hand.

I come to your house in the body of an eight year old. I have been making my way back here for years. I am here to destroy the world as you have known it. I am here to make room for myself in this house of your memory.

I stand in your living room. With my long fingernails, I pick scabs from my scalp. I bite your cat. I eat your goldfish. I spit at your family portraits. I leap on your furniture. I shred the covers on your bed.

The sounds that shoot across my tongue make your skin contract and your bones curl themselves into some sort of cage. The pipes under your house groan and strain. I move toward you, down low on my haunches. A retching begins deep in your throat.

I am your oldest nightmare.

I am your body.

I return to you in the body of an eight year old. It pleases me to see you so afraid.

I lay on the floor at your feet. I tear my clothing away so you can see my broken skin shimmering. Your hands open and close. Your arms cross and uncross your chest. Your knees buckle and lock.

I am moving back into your memory. My mouth weeps of blood and saliva. My vagina oozes and cries out in sharp, short beats. My skin is a bruise the color of oil on clean, cold water. My face shines with mucus. I look into your face. I have come home to live with you.

You thought I would be easy to hold. You remember me as an empty house. You remember me as a plastic doll. You have remembered me smiling. You have remembered me silent.

Dare you touch me. I am spiny and razor-boned. I am hot sand between your toes. I am pebbles into your knees as you scurry away from me. My vagina is a knife slashing at itself with each step. My eyes are dry and hard as blocks of salt. My mouth is raw and burnt from all that I have tried to say through these trampled lips. I am not what you remember.

I come to your house in the body of an eight year old. I rise from your feet. My fingers are a series of explosions. My heart is beginning to peel from this exposure. You take me into your arms. You are slashed. You are pierced. You are beaten by my heart. Blood runs from your ears, from your mouth. It coagulates into a blanket that holds us. The whole house rocks us.

Drawing with the Power of the Earth

Debby Earthdaughter

MY MEMORIES STARTED in a flood of flashbacks triggered by urinary tract surgery. I was overwhelmed by the flashbacks that ran through my mind like a movie, over and over with new variations. I hoped I could clear my mind of the repetition if I drew and wrote what I was remembering. And this did work to a large extent. I have stacks and stacks of drawings and writing from the early memories—image after image. I have always written and drawn, but this work had a new urgency to it. I felt that if I couldn't write, draw, talk about it I would break apart. My painting gave me focus during the worst of the memories when I thought killing myself would be better than more memories. I resolved to do whatever I needed to do just to make it through each day. I was in graduate school at the time and would get up and go to school, but come home early in the afternoon and paint and paint.

Purification is a painting from that time. I was calling on the powers of my body to cleanse myself of the effects of the abuse. I would bleed out my abusers with the cleansing power of my strong woman's body; my fists are clenched from the karate class I was taking. I called on the powers of earth, water, air, fire and moon. My connection to nature was one of the biggest things that kept me going as a kid, and I needed to re-establish the depth of that connection to heal from the incest. My focus was on painting, writing, doing healing rituals, walking outdoors and speaking with other incest survivors.

I showed several paintings at a winter coffeehouse show of incest/rape/battery survivor artwork at the Women's Center in Cambridge. This was shortly after I confronted my uncle and grandmother by letter. I felt a five year old's fear then, because my uncle had said he would kill me if I ever told. I just wanted to stay in the house. But I summoned the courage to go show my work. I felt strong doing it—that I was not ashamed to say this is what happened, it was awful, but I will not be its victim.

That spring term I took an amazing feminist ethics course with Mary Daly that helped me understand the oppression of women and of the earth as one big system. It gave me a way of thinking to challenge that system, to say, "There is a better way to live and I will be part of making that happen." When Boston College denied a full professorship to Mary Daly, I joined protests of feminist students. I had decided I wanted to leave graduate school and work at a food co-op to support myself and have my mind for my art and writing. To walk through the halls of Boston College ululating with other amazons was my saying, I don't care what you think anymore, I don't need academic approval, I am strong and good in myself. I dove into feminist literature and read and read and read. I painted less then but went through a great transformation in thinking.

Late that spring, I showed artwork in the art area at the "Looking Up" gathering in Maine. Again, I was frightened to do it, but afterwards felt so strong. I was preparing then to confront my uncle and grandmother in person, so it made me feel stronger to show my art and see the art of other women. I felt the power flowing through us and our decision to perceive things clearly, feel the great pain and transform that pain into energy to make change.

Throughout, it has been vital for me to draw on the power of earth. I started a witches' circle that first winter with a few friends, and that circle has given me a lot of strength. Before my confrontation, I made a power jacket for myself. It is turquoise for the color of communication, and has a goddess snake and animals for each of the four directions. In a ritual with the circle, I charged that jacket, as well as myself with power. My uncle and grandmother ended up backing out of the confrontation and that was a big letdown, but the strength I gained from my preparation in meditation, ritual, doing karate, painting, writing, making the jacket, and calling on women to support me was very powerful. I thought less about incest in the summer. I needed to lighten up a bit and have more fun. It was good for me.

I entered artwork in the "Spirit of Survival" conference art show at Boston University and doing that set a lot in motion. I knew my grandmother and uncle had abused me because I had clear memories from age five. I had had a nagging feeling of abuse by my mother also, but no clear memories. (Although I knew always on some level; early on there was my mother entangled with my grandmother in *Purification*.) A few weeks before the "Spirit of Survival" conference I started having more preverbal body memories and got angrier and angrier. I trusted the feeling that it was my mother who had abused me because that was my gut level feeling all along and it got stronger. A week before the conference, I did the *Yo Baby* drawing while drawing with my

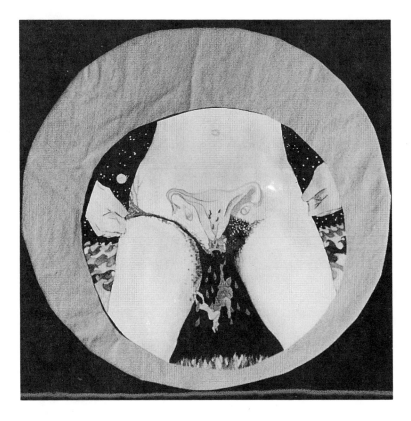

Purification, 1988, watercolor

housemate, who is also an incest survivor artist. At first I didn't even want to show it to her; I felt ashamed. But I showed it to her and she felt it was very powerful. I couldn't stop thinking about it and wrote a confrontation letter to my mother. I sent a photocopy of the drawing to show how I felt. I hadn't done that before. But I knew she couldn't get me now; my ability to make that drawing, to face it, showed my power, not my vulnerability. I put that in the mail and went to the "Spirit of Survival" show with my old paintings that I had shown before and this one new one.

I was afraid because there would be a big crowd of women and men. But I had enough time to meet and talk with the other artists to feel O.K. And seeing other women's art always makes me feel so up—here we are these strong women who aren't being held back by what happened to us, instead we are publicly speaking out. I saw very powerful artwork there, and it was good to connect with the other artists, women I knew locally and women who asked about my art.

That started me on a roll of new painting. *Yo Baby* was important for me to do because I made connections between the incest and other abuse. Yo is the postal abbreviation for Youngstown, Ohio, where I'm from. "Yo baby" was what friends of

Yo Baby, 1989, crayon

mine in college would say sometimes when they saw my mail from YO OH. This drawing sets the abuse where it happened. The central image is the abuse by my mother. She is hurting me. But there is more. My father's fist is coming down on her head; he beat her a lot. She later got the courage to leave him after he shot her. Through the window, you can see the steel mill where my father worked—at this time Youngstown was Steel City, USA. The greyness from the mill hangs over everything and seeps in through the window. I want to say that the abuse that happened to me wasn't isolated. The physical abuse in my family was directly connected to the structural violence of class. Owners of the steel mill exploited my father and so many other workers; he worked in dangerous conditions with no say in what went on while they made a profit off his labor. Instead of getting angry at the owners and losing his job, he beat my mother and drank. Like most women beaten by men, she probably felt less and less able to leave as the abuse continued. She had few job skills to use to support herself and a baby. For me, this drawing said that the abuse in my family wasn't random isolated violence. I don't think any violence, any domination, any exploitation is random—it's all part of a system of oppression whether it is physical violence or the violence of a system that has a handful of wealthy white men getting rich by controlling and exploiting everyone else. I think every action that breaks the chains of domination and submission is part of taking the foundation out from under patriarchy. When we refuse to be further abused in any way, we are no longer the slaves of patriarchy. A hierarchy can't exist without slaves.

I began to challenge classism I experienced in my life. It was so much like confronting incest. We have these myths that everything is O.K—America is classless, there's no incest, no wife beating, etc. When I began dealing with the incest, I unleashed a great deal of power in myself because there was no longer this place in my mind that I was always skirting away from. Thoughts and images could just flow. Something similar happened when I started to talk about class as related to incest and other patriarchal abuses. I began talking about class, even if it made middle- and owning-class people nervous. I wouldn't sacrifice myself to their comfort, anymore than I would to my abusers. I had friends who said to me it was O.K. to be angry. That my anger about incest, classism and other violence was real anger from real abuse.

I am becoming what Mary Daly calls a Fury—"a Wild woman who flies with the wings of Righteous Rage." I have felt so connected to all that loves life—to the trees, to the animals in my neighborhood, to the woman inside us who is fierce and not tamed. When I have been afraid of people, still the very trees have said to me to be strong and take action—paint, write, speak out. It is only a small minority of life on earth that wants patriarchy to stay in place. Alone I may feel small. With the force of all life on my side I feel very powerful.

Powerful and protected by the power of earth. That is what *I*

I Sleep Protected, 1989, watercolor

Womonshapes, 1989, fabric

Sleep Protected is about. While I am vulnerable, sleeping, I call on these animals to protect me, to give me good dreams. They are my protectors and guides.

I also did a drawing called *The Good Mother* in bright pink pencil (not shown). I had been unhappy with the shades of pinks and purples and turquoises from sets. I *needed* these colors and had finally bought a bunch of single pencils that I loved. That bright pink was so soft and warm and alive to me, and the picture of that woman taking care of that baby just flowed out. I drew a mother who would protect me, who could be strong enough to flee bad situations rather than take things out on me. The abuse by my mother has been the hardest to face. If your mother does not love and nurture you, who will? This drawing has helped me remember how I have mothered myself and been mothered by others. She has been a source of much comfort hanging above my bed.

Rather than wait until I try new materials and techniques to get just what I want, I would like to show *Womonshapes* now in their roughness. These quilted pieces are full of life, of the curves of hip and breast and yoni. Full of the flow we feel monthly through our moontime, full of the spiral of life we are part of. In each hand-sewn stitch I have said to myself that my body is good, alive, not ruined by the incest, but is still a good woman's body, full of life and love. They are a way of saying I love my Self. They are a triumph that I have defied the brainwashing of the patriarchy that says women are bad, are for abusing, must be contained.

Even though I experienced awful abuse, I have been able to cling to life and draw on the power of life. I am alive and strong, a woman, a lesbian, a feminist, an artist, a writer. Alive!

Reference

1. Mary Daly and Jane Caputi, *Webster's First New Intergalactic Wickedary of the English Language* (Boston: Beacon Press, 1987), p. 126.

Wording It

Cheryl Marie Wade

I WISH THE WORDS were my father's hands. I would fold them and lay them on the page. If they began to take off, agitated, moving in directions I despise, I could cage them with brackets and set them aside, stop them in their tracks with one mighty period. I could make them small and delicate by creating them in lower case. If they refused to obey my commands, I could simply chop them off, send them hurling powerless into the void with a push of the delete button.

Sometimes I pretend the words are my father's hands. I fold them and lay them on the page. I admire their power and strength. It gives me great joy to make them stay within the boundaries of my page. I love them for their beauty and mystery, the surprises they reveal. I fear them because I cannot always control them. Sometimes they take me on journeys I am not ready for. Sometimes I must protect myself from them by hiding. Some people call this writer's block.

I know the words are not my father's hands. Words never betrayed me. They never violated me. They never lied to me or made me ashamed. They never caused me to drown myself in sleeping pills or alcohol. They never caused me to fear love or to hate my body. They never caused me to doubt my sanity. They never taught me to distrust or lie, distrust and lie.

Sometimes I resent words because they did not come to my rescue. As much as I love them, they should've rescued me. Where was "no" when I needed her? Where was "help"? And "heal"? She's here for a day, making what I assume are promises; then before I can hold her firmly to my breast, she's heading down the road.

But unlike what I offer my father or his ghost, I forgive all the words. In the past five years, they've worked very hard to make it up to me. They introduced me to buried feelings. They were there with me when I confronted my mother and brother. They helped me articulate the truth to relatives and friends, shrinks and other strangers. They constantly challenge me to reach, reach, reach. For deeper truth and understanding. For self-respect. For self-love.

The first word I loved with passion was the word Cheryl. As far back as I can remember, which is preschool, I fought for the word Cheryl because I loved her. When someone tried to mess with Cheryl by turning her into Cherie or Cher, I said, *"It's Cheryl."*

Grown-ups thought it was "cute" that I insisted my word be respected. I simply thought it was necessary. I believe now that this claiming was my first survival tactic. I held onto my name as if my life depended on it. Because my life depended on it.

I believe I understood early on that people will use words to lie, even to the point of telling you you are someone you know you are not. Cheryl is a strong word. It is important to defend words, to protect them. It is my job to make sure my words are never turned into lies.

The first time I submitted a piece about incest for publication, I used a pseudonym: Julienna Andrews. Or maybe it was Alexandria Surette. Something as distant from Cheryl Wade as I could get, yet connected. Andrews was my grandmother's married name. Surette was her maiden name.

The minute I mailed it, I regretted the pseudonym. Partly out of ego. I thought it was powerful piece, and I wanted to claim it. I knew if it were printed, I would make them put my real name on it. My full name: Cheryl Marie Wade. That is when I added my middle name to my work. As a tribute to my grandmother, Marie Evangeline, as a way of feeling close to her spirit. Also, it was a way of noting a change in me.

When I do my job well, I bring words together and give them a form that makes my meaning of them accessible to you. When I write about being an incest victim or survivor, I can spend weeks, even months on my words, so important is it to me to make sure I'm not pushing them in directions that are comfortable but dishonest. I spent so much of my life pushing words in directions that were more comfortable than honest: yes i love you i don't care yes i love you i don't care i don't care i don't care.

It has taken me a long time to do this piece. The first day of work on this essay brought the retrieval of a memory. I had to stop writing for awhile, I was so angry. I didn't want to remember that I tried to kill myself at least twice before I was eight years old. As painful as that is to know, it is also a validation. Yes, the incest was happening. Yes, I knew it. And, yes, I tried to tell.

The first poems I wrote about being an incest survivor came out in a fury. I had just been through what the shrinks refer to as a "psychotic break" (I say one person's psychotic break is another's revelation). I had a hard time trusting the poems; they had been too spontaneous. Besides, I love revising, and I resented that they didn't respond well to my suggestions.

My first poem, "Shards," went through over fifteen revisions in a two-year period. I wanted it to tell everything, to change the world, to be the best poem ever written about being an incest survivor, and I wanted it to heal me:

> I did as I was told
> (I am good girl)
> but in my panic to obey
> I bit too hard
> this glass lie
>
> now shards are everywhere
> and the secret bleeds from me

That is the original version of the poem. It is a little piece about a small part of my experience. That is all it was willing or capable of being. When I finally realized that, I felt fine about leaving it alone. And by then, I knew there would be other poems, so the fear of not saying everything stopped controlling my relationship with it.

During this same period, I wrote many other pieces filled with rage and sorrow. The prevailing theme was "the stolen." I wanted people to understand that calling myself a survivor is an expedient thing to do. Sometimes it just feels like one more label designed to "neaten" the reality. To rein in the chaos with a word. And sometimes it works. I am grateful when it does, when I can say the word survivor and feel empowered. But too often the word seems hollow, like those trivializing euphemisms for disability—differently abled, physically challenged, handicapable. Such complex realities are not held in one word or two.

I wrote "Shards" and the first draft of many many incest poems right after my "incest coming out party" at a Women's Voices Workshop in 1985. It was there I discovered women were speaking out about this reality. Woman after woman said: "My writing is fueled by my need to heal from incest." And for the first time I felt community with women, and I understood how very not alone I am. And then I heard myself say: "Being an incest survivor fuels my writing." It was such a simple truth. Suddenly I knew it. I had always known it.

Memory, or lack of it, is a big issue with every survivor I know. I am no exception. "Santa Cruz Memory" is really more of a supposition than a poem about an actual event. My family really did take a trip to Santa Cruz when I was a little girl, and there are bits of memory in the poem that are true, but... I want people to understand what it's like to be caught up in the process of trying to reconstruct your life from fragments. I used Santa Cruz because there is the childhood memory, but more importantly, the Women's Voices Workshop was in Santa Cruz. It is a magical place to me because it is where, at the age of thirty-seven, I had my "revelation" (one person's revelation is another's psychotic break). It is where I began the conscious act of healing.

I have read "Santa Cruz Memory" in public, and I definitely think of it as a piece to be read aloud. The audience response is one of held breath. Sometimes when I read it, the pace becomes so fast as the poem progresses that I lose my breath. I don't always want to read this piece. I have to be feeling strong and secure to want to read it. It's as if I'm saying as I read: remember remember remember.

I know. But I don't remember.

When I first began writing about being a survivor, I joined a disabled women's writing group led by Naja Sorella. I met Naja through WRY CRIPS Disabled Women's Reader's Theater, a group I worked with for four years. She was the first person I ever heard try to make a connection between her childhood abuse and her disability, which is environmental illness, an immune system disorder. Her work inspired me to make my own connections.

It has been an extraordinarily difficult connection to make. I have started several poems, trying to explore the idea that changes in my body from rheumatoid arthritis have a deeper context, but I've created nothing that illuminates enough, yet:

> bones of my child hands
> dried to the frail of a sparrow's wing
> working to reveal the secret
> of his hands
> that soothed and ruined
> innocent graceful bone
> to gnarled stub twisted
> working struggling to reveal the secret
> of the sureness of his hands
> as they loved and ruined
> my sweet girl hands died
> giving birth to truth
> of a father's gentle murderous hands.

That's the idea, but presented too simplistically. Also, my gnarly hands are very very alive, so... I'm not sure why it's so hard. I imagine it has to do with how invalidated this view is. Am I just trying to blame my father for my disability? If I really believe this, will I hate him even more? Will I feel even more sorrow, more loss?

And yet, making this connection has changed my view of myself. I feel great strength is the heart of this viewpoint. Not blame. Not self-pity. Not loss even. To write this poem, to state the connection, albeit imperfectly, is to say: What a powerful thing my disability is! It's as if my body had no ability to lie, and even though I was powerless to stop the abuse or to speak out about it, my body insisted on trying to tell the truth. That's how I choose to look at it. It breaks my heart.

"Pierced Ears" is my most deliberate attempt to write a poem about healing. I've included it for that reason, and because I've been told it's effective. What I like best about "Pierced Ears" is how good it feels to express my connectedness to women, past, present and future. I have often called on the spirit of my grandmother to guide me, to protect me. I feel her presence always:

> you live, gramma, in dreams and memories
> where you walk with the sureness of age
> and hold a promise   earth and body are one
> you are a silvery spirit   my furious phantom
>   in your loving palms cactus flowers bloom
>   in your eyes a story never told
>   and your laugh   the full life of an ordinary woman
> i hold you in my heart where you are
> swirling   swirling
> and i embrace the breeze from your full skirt
> of magic   sorrow   and blue iris

My women friends are a treasure in my life. My closest friend, Diane Hugs, a woman severely disabled with MS, is a ritual abuse survivor, an incredible writer and one of the funniest people I know. We share bone-crunching pain and outrageous, healing laughter. She knew I was a survivor long before I would admit it. Her abuse was so severe and so sustained that I can still barely hear it. I am outraged that she had to endure so much, that she has been hurt so profoundly.

We challenge each other as writers. We are from such different backgrounds, take such different approaches. We don't always work well together. We try always to be mindful of each other's boundaries but make mistakes. We forgive. She loves and encourages me; I love and encourage her. This must be what it's like to have a sister. If this isn't what it's like, it should be.

"Listen" is a piece inspired by my friend Amy Gup's reading of a poem she wrote about how painful it is to not be listened to, how hard it is to get people to listen, really listen. Watching her push through her shyness before an audience and reach us all with her power as a writer, as a woman, moved me deeply. For hours after the reading, all I could hear, roaring through my mind and heart was that word "listen."

Listen is a word that resonates for me as a survivor. I think it holds inside it the word "notice." I can barely stand to think about all the times someone could've noticed, and didn't. This piece is a testament of all those years before I told the truth. And a tribute to all the memories still stuck in my throat. I hope it is a call to my own thunder and lightning.

I love performing my work. From the first time I wrote a piece about incest, I wanted everyone in the world to hear it. Well, except my father's family. But I don't think about them when I'm in front of an audience. All I'm thinking is: I'm in control here. I have a great deal of confidence in my ability to reach people with my work through live performance. Far more confidence than with the written word. I think that has to do with the fact that I have no formal literary training. Being disabled and a woman, I was not exactly encouraged to pursue a career in writing.

The first time I performed a piece about incest in public, I had many women come up to me and tell me how brave I was. Once I had written the truth, it never occurred to me that I shouldn't go public or that not everyone does. Bravery implies taking action that you know to be dangerous, risking your own well-being to help others. I am not being brave when I perform my work. I am just doing what is natural for me to do. If it didn't feel good, I wouldn't do it.

When I perform, I am as far from being a victim as I can get: I'm The Woman With Juice.

"Here" is a piece I performed many times with WRY CRIPS. When I performed it in the context of the disability group, the audience assumption and the feeling I had while performing was that it is a poem about surviving being disabled in a physicalist society, with all the horrors that implies. And, of course, it is about that. But when I read it recently at a women's poetry reading along with many of my incest survivor pieces, as well as disability poems, it seemed much fuller and richer. As if I were reading it for the first time.

An important part of healing is being able to say "I am" and know what that means, or at least have some sense of what that means. I've written a number of pieces that are an assertion of I am. "Here" is the most complete. Every part of this poem reflects my identity. From the strange, disjointed rhythms to the sensuality, to the jokes and the sorrow. I always feel empowered when I read this poem aloud, and I am still stunned that I was able to write it. It surprises and delights me that I was willing to reveal so much in one piece.

The first time I performed "Here" was to an audience of 350 people. There I was, movin' along, singin' a song, feeling about as good as I think it's possible to feel in this body, in this lifetime. When I came to the line, "I can picture Springsteen's thighs anytime anywhere," this enormous roar of laughter rose up and embraced me. It felt like it would never stop, although it really must've lasted no longer than a minute.

I know the laughter was partly a release for the audience's tension and because the line comes out of left field, taking people by surprise. But it was also an affirmation, an appreciation of survivor humor. If there is anything better than laughter, I haven't found it. It's definitely one of my top three pleasures, right up there with dark chocolate and having that itch I can't reach scratched.

"Here" is a performance piece. My gnarly body and radiance are parts of this poem lost to the page. My quirky gestures and voice inflections are parts of this poem lost to the page. Or maybe not. I can't tell. All I know is that when I perform it, this poem can bring the house down, and I know for a moment that there is not a woman alive who is stronger, more beautiful, more whole than I am.

Listen

the last day of innocence
she learned
to let only the easy surface of words
slip through
learned to hold
the breath and thunder   of syllables
in her throat
father's whisper of love
love in her mouth
she learned:
make noise   no one hears

words trap behind her teeth
if she could speak
perhaps she would say
listen
listen to the storm in my throat

Santa Cruz Memory

I think I was four when the family went to Santa Cruz
Mother says there's not much to remember
It was a dull trip
She's not a woman who ever remembers much
I remember my father sunburned so badly
we could peel the skin from his back in large hunks
I remember my father's skin
I believe I was four when the family made that trip to Santa Cruz
Mother says there's not much to remember
She's not a woman who wants to remember much
I can see my brother seated on a huge inner tube
the tumble of waves
They say he almost drowned
That is the story the family always tells
I think it was me
I remember my father's skin
the ocean of pink thigh
I am the one who really drowned
on the family trip to Santa Cruz
when I was four
or five
or two
Mother says what's the difference
There's not much to remember
It was a dull drip
I remember my father's skin
wave after wave after wave
Mother won't remember
I was the one
I remember my father's skin
and Santa Cruz

Pierced Ears

My left ear I pierced
to say   no
because I had not strength
to form the word.
Through the hole in my left ear
I placed the gold band
of my father's betrayal.

   My right ear I pierced
   to say I am a woman:
   I belong to all the piercings of all
   women of all ages.
   I pierced my right ear
   to link arms
   with that first dark woman
   who shoved a sliver of bone through her nose
   to claim   to reclaim.
   In my right ear
   I wear the silver loop
   of my survival.

Here

There is a woman here
middle-aged   in her prime
with long legs
and a short fuse
A woman who loves to write
poems
and dance
I have rhythm in the marrow
laughter, too
I love to laugh and laugh

There is a woman here
who has scars
visible and otherwise
more than you'd want to know
more than I want to count
A woman who believes
in magic
I long for magic
I love stones
before they're polished
I can picture Springsteen's thighs
anytime   anywhere

There is a woman here
with a stiff back
and incredible flexibility
who tells lies for protection
the truth for survival
who sits in a chair on wheels
and hauls sacks of self-doubt
as if she were a stevedore
A woman who survives to dream
dreams

I braid my hair in my dreams

I have electric hair
and need to be loved
soft soft lips
and hate to be loved
eyes shadowed by memory
and want to be loved

full round hips
and I'm afraid to be loved
I love so easily

There is a woman here
full of colors
A survivor
who survives to be
a woman
here

Drawing Me On: A Portrait of Healing

Janvier Rollande

On The Threshold,
1983, 22" × 16¼", pencil

FOR YEARS I drew my small daughter... alone, half-dressed, sad, vulnerable. I was drawing my own inner child, over and over... seeing the same image in variation... alone, abandoned, resigned... small, sad, deeply sad. I drew my mother... alone, defended, cold, fading away, not present, not seeing. These images compelled me. I felt their quiet presence, like dead people inside me... seen, but without words. I couldn't title them for many years. The pencil spoke my feelings... the feelings of a small child, whispered in the softest greys, emerging like ghosts from somewhere within the pristine paper, apart from me, a part of me... my own personal haunting... of sadness, always sadness... a stained and heavy shroud enveloping my consciousness.

For years I couldn't feel. I was a quiet child, reserved, withdrawn. I was a silenced child and an adult with no voice. I didn't speak. I didn't write. I didn't draw. I was afraid of my voice, afraid to listen to my heart, fearful of its ragged beat. But, as a child, I was drawn to the sounds of others. I read books about happy families and copied the illustrations. In these hours, I was transported beyond my world and into another... a world I later discovered was also mine... a world of calm and harmony, of gentleness and beauty... all within... evoked by the rhythm of my pencil in quiet concentration. Alone with myself, I could begin to feel myself, to feel my presence, my life. And I was safe.

In time, I heard the sound of my own voice... a powerful whisper, a light breath. The birth of my daughter woke me from the coma of a lifeless marriage. Her need of me, her utter dependency and trust, her vociferous demand for the care of her life led me to the slow and painful awakening of my own needs, buried long ago with force and neglect. I tested the silence of my self with a therapist. I began to draw what I felt... not always understanding, but always feeling... nameless feelings given form, made visible... levels of feeling... the adult and the child speaking simultaneously, their voices clashing and blending... fear and sadness and anger... terror and grief and rage... and shame...

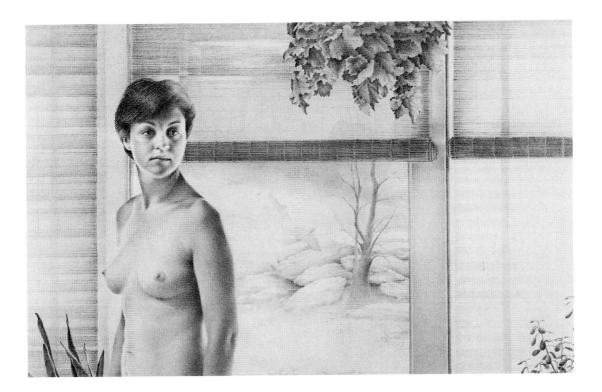

muffled sounds deep inside, growing louder only as I grew toward healing.

I first approached the wailing with caution, obliquely... looking at my small daughter, seeing her innocence, her vulnerability, and feeling the sadness of my lost child... looking at my mother, seeing her distance, her coldness, her anger, and feeling my grief at not having. Looking at myself and seeing myself, and feeling a direct response for myself, has been more difficult. I drew few self-portraits. *In Her Garden* was one of the first... a portrait of my inner landscape... barren of life, desolate, an after-death where the silence is palpable and ravens circle and search for carrion... the ravens of my childhood... their harsh voices crack the stillness... I look over my shoulder, eyes moving toward the square of light, but turning inward. I long for those open spaces where new life can find root... the wide, deep spaces of my dreams.

It's there that my next self-portrait was born: *I Was a Child*... an image that came to me in the night, where most fears come alive... the small child in her underwear separate from her family, and a soft, external voice: "I'm sorry that you had to feel this pain; that you must feel it again now. But if you want to heal, you must look at this image." This image of the child abandoned, the child submissive and broken, the child with limp arms, weary and

In Her Garden (self portrait inspired by Martha Mayer Erlebacher), 1986, 26″ × 22″, pencil

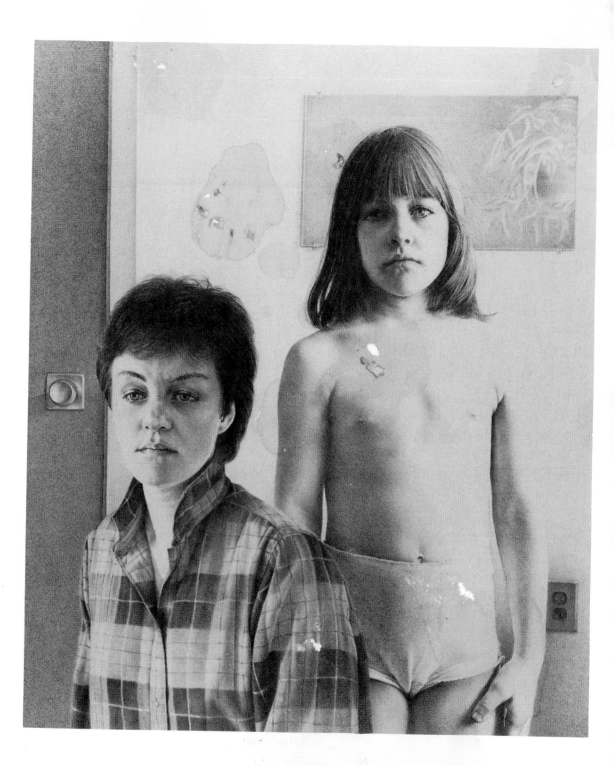

dispirited. In this image, I have lived... the adult and the child... in one small space... two presences, large and powerful... two voices, separate and one.

This drawing was the opening of a door, a careful stepping toward a more conscious healing. The child has been seen. Her cries have been heard. Her experience has been named. Incest. It shouldn't have happened. The child was not to blame. The adult can reach out now to embrace her child, to rock her gently, to calm her screams, her fears, her sense of dying. The perspective shifts. The child no longer looms large, but snuggles safely within the adult, serene, comfortable, cared for.

My foothold on this planet has often felt precarious. Invisible and silent, I could so easily fall between the cracks. As my drawings are seen and recognized by others whose truth is the same, I feel more grounded, aware of the substance that gives me weight. My truth not only speaks of grief and isolation and pain, but also of grace and beauty. My drawings have led me to my heart, to the acceptance of my self, to the opening of life within me. At times, they have touched the untouched places in others and moved them to feel. "I don't usually like this sort of thing," one abstract expressionist once confessed "' it there's something about these... " Something.. quiet weeping of the ravaged child. It is the ten_ _ ie adult healing. It is the gentle strength

Left, *I Was a Child,* 1987, 13″ × 14½″, pencil

Right, *Mother and Child,* 1985, 26″ × 22″, pencil

There are drawings that wait for me as my heart opens wider to let them in. Heroic drawings of black and white and infinite subtleties of grey. Layers of color, speaking of darkness, of light, of transitional shadow. In voices rich and full and varied, they confide my secrets and declare my truth. They sing my song with courage and dignity... my song that is about beauty and life... that is about me.

Pieces of the Night Sky:
My Body's Legacy

Judy Bierman

WELCOME TO THE night sky. It is a place neither public nor private, where the shapes we see reflect our choice of focus, where we must first and foremost acknowledge the power of perspective. It is not a neutral sky. Here the moon weeps often and the stars itch. Birds eat each other's shadows; the sounds come paper-thin, myriad and trembling. It is a sky without expectation, pieced with longing and never complete.

I have come here often. For twenty-some-odd-years. When it was not safe to touch the earth. When I could not survive any intimation of boundaries or any human contact. I have flown with my ears pinched by the cold and with salt curling down the inside of my wings—I have flown here in all seasons. Many times I have come to forget, painting pictures with my mind's flights, places I would make my own if I could. And in the same breaths (unaware) I have come here to remember, in the only safe way possible.

Through two decades of hiding from my healing, two decades of complete amnesia, I made reference to my experience of incest over and over in poetry and songs. Though I never understood my own words, I never resisted the need to attach them to paper, to make them audible and tangible. And I never doubted that they were profoundly (I could say, unspeakably) mine. They gave me no particular direction, offered very little hope. I did not share them with anyone. But I treasured them. And they always did, and still do, speak the truth to me.

Two years ago, I ceased to ignore this truth. I began to have conscious, physical memory traces of violation and rape by my father. These memories continue to increase in frequency and intensity. I believe, in fact, that I have only touched their surface. And now my journeys into the night sky have become intentional. I have come to lean on my writing and music in a new way: to accept their leadership in the process of healing. It's as if each piece of my work is a brush stroke in a picture still too large for me to discern, perhaps still unframed, but certainly with its own rhythm, design and necessary information. My role as a writer has been increasingly one of giving permission to my many and various voices to speak in whatever way they choose: acknowledging the immensity of the sky and the darkness of the journey; accepting the notion that clarity comes only when I give up the need to be anywhere in particular (time or space) in my healing. It is an act of suspending judgment.

Giving voice to all parts of myself—allowing the sounds and images to flow without critical intervention—is the hardest and most fruitful part of my recovery. Without my writing, I would have no means of coming to terms with what happened to me, precisely because the *form* allows me the time and space to learn to believe a new scenario. Believing my own story is very difficult. For the most part my memories have been kinesthetic—my body reliving rape and its aftermath, my body re-enacting the abuse. I rarely have any "pictures" at all during these experiences, and more often than not I walk away from them feeling crazy, unwilling to believe I have been the victim of anything more than a set of bizarre, albeit violent sexual fantasies. I feel ashamed and inadequate.

Who experienced this abuse? Who is remembering? Some sixteen months ago, frustrated in my efforts to pull memories back to the surface, more and more aware of the contradiction involved (there was good reason to forget), I took note of a suggestion that it might be easier to "remember" being young if I re-experienced the physical awkwardness of writing as a child by switching hands. When I put the pen in my left hand I was astonished to discover a whole being there—a child—with very strong feelings and vivid memories, confused, angry, lost, ashamed, needy, and very, very young. She speaks with a different cadence than my right hand. She has made me aware of a complete vertical split in my body, head to toe. It seems she has been in hiding for thirty some odd years of my life, trying to meet her emotional needs indirectly and for the most part ineffectively.

But she is no longer shy with a pen. Over and over in her writing she substantiates my body's memories. She has been waiting to tell her story, waiting patiently in the dark of me for someone to pay attention. I am now beginning to understand just how much she is in fact directing the memory process. Her descriptions offer a landscape for my body's motions and emotions. Over time I hope I will choose to walk that landscape—to believe her, to believe myself, to integrate her pictures of my forgotten life with my own feelings. In the meantime her words stand free and clear. They will never disappear. They are stars in the night sky with a shape and presence of their own. They are clearly visible should I choose to look at them. They are all pieces of my life, however I decide to treat them.

My inner child is one of five internal voices I have identified so far. Some sit on my body's left side, some on my right. I record conversations among them when it feels pertinent, helpful or simply unavoidable, and these conversations teach me a great deal about the thickness of the work I've taken on. My child's voice was the first to emerge. She is the loudest, the most prolific and by far the most developed; by now she is confident of an audience. In time perhaps my other voices will share this confidence. A healing voice sits by my right ear. She does not write, though she sings at times, and will only make her presence known in a climate (internal) of relative safety. I have an adult public voice in my right hand (she is composing this essay). And in each of my hands I carry a protective voice—one extremely self-critical, one extremely angry.

Who exactly is recovering? What are all these voices put together? Where do "I" fit in all of this? I have no answers outside of the landscape of my work. And so I am beginning to ascertain a responsibility to be very direct with my words, to listen as closely and as fully as I can and to record what I hear with precision, though without judgment. I am learning to respect the needs of all my voices, even when they disagree (which they usually do), even when my discomfort growns intolerable. Many times I find myself impatient. I tire of the confusion. I struggle to move through the world in an adult's body with a three year old's perspective battling an abundance of critical static. I cannot explain myself to myself, let alone to friends who would like to be helpful. And so I return again and again to words—to the play of light and shadow against the surface of my skin—trying to know my movements as shapes in the wind, night sky noises, each with a place, a history, and a reason for being. Externalizing my voices in this way continually widens the sky and offers additional space/time to recover.

Writing is my body's effort to re-integrate itself. The three poems included here exemplify this integration; though all were written by my right hand, each speaks to a different aspect of my recovery. There are many aspects to this journey, and these days my writing takes many forms. In all of them, I consecrate my inner child's return. I record her memories in detail, in the present tense. I struggle with the process of remembering, of being outside time, concurrently young and old, here and there. I argue with my disbelief. I give my child permission to hope. And I attempt time and again to portray the legacies of abuse in my life in their full dimensions; a young child's desolation, fear, rage, shame, confusion and grief. Each is a constellation I can visit and ask others to visit with me. My work seeks an audience: my child speaks, desperate to be heard and to belong, to find her way back.

All creative work is fundamentally integrative—an expression of what was not taken from me. It is an expression of my self. For a survivor of incest, this self is not easy to come by. I still do not have a good understanding of where my father ended and I began—physically, emotionally, at times even spiritually. I am easily confused by boundary issues. I take responsibility for what was done to me. I feel ashamed. I try to disappear. But I have no doubts that my writing and music are of my self, and they sit in the world as evidence of my right to be here. At times they have taken on the quality of grass growing through the cracks in the pavement—the refusal to stay quiet made manifest.

I have always been jealous of those who take their creative work "seriously," who know they have something to say, people for whom silence is not a central issue. All my life I have wanted "to be an artist." Slowly I am coming to realize that this is most simply a desire to be in the world again, to belong, to dismantle my protective habits, to find my own heart and to speak from it without fear.

Once again I must ask myself to suspend judgment. For at this point in time my heart is very young, and all my child's dealings with the world, her writing included, reflect this. Her images are dense and mix the modalities of the senses:

> the wanting creaks its door open
> ripe with fruit
> unmanageable...

She does not create without a specific audience in mind, usually my therapist (the first person she risked contacting on her return). She has little patience for self-correction, little interest in the world outside her immediate needs:

> ... hands like ripe cherries
> spilling out the door, unaccustomed
> to permission
> i have waited for you a long time
>   i would love to have you safe
> i long to let the fruit take its course
> know it is neither beginning nor end
> hold a hand that will not take me away
> hold a hand that does not turn hard and wanting
> hold your hand.
> i long to hold your hand...

She is always in search of an echo—a validation of her voice that can offer some limits. More often than not she is angry. And as yet she is not old enough to engage in her craft consciously—to "practice" or to see a long project through to completion. Her energy is frenetic, moving around the corners of the room, eager to touch, fearful to stay. This is a very different presence in the world than I am accustomed to presenting. But I struggle to accept it at face value. In addition to writing and music, I have recently begun to allow my younger self to paint and to draw, activities always taboo to my "non-artistic" adult selves, knowing she has much to say in her own fashion.

I find I must continually resist the temptation to criticize her inexperience, her rage, her loud insistence on directing my life. It is difficult to stay faithful to the task, confident that a child allowed simply to express herself will naturally grown up. At times I have hopes of re-parenting myself long enough and well enough to make some real "adult" choices for my life in the years to come, if I am lucky and the world is willing. We will have to wait and see about this. It is enough of a challenge now to accept my confusion, shame and anger, and to remember their origins. Often I would rather not believe them.

Thankfully, one consequence of speaking my true story is to discover that others *do* believe it. These days if I risk engagement, I usually find someone is listening. I no longer need to be alone; it is now a choice I make, and a painful one either way. The very act of going public validates my inner child's voice *and* terrifies all the parts of me that have been committed to secrecy for so long. It crosses old and sacred boundaries. It is a step outside the realm of survival into a new world with different rules built on a fundamentally different premise, one of acceptance and trust.

I am wary of this world. I find myself hesitant to take it on. The risks feel extreme and the rewards iffy at best. And so I straddle two worlds, no longer willing to accept my exile, but without the skills to make a home for myself. I feel extremely awkward. I don't want to be apart; I don't yet know how to connect. And it's clear I will have to learn this from others. For two years I have been meeting with three other women artists recovering from incest—sharing our stories, exploring this new world together through writing, drawing and talking. Their support in this process has been an invaluable piece of my healing. To be public at all with the experience of incest is to demand a safe space. I am beginning to believe this is possible to do. It will be a long process.

In truth I do not relish the task of healing. Believing myself is believing a new harsh and painful picture of my life. I am an adult with a young child's emotional skills, as yet unable to stay with my own feelings, to contain them, to share them directly. The risk of stepping into the world, safe as it may now be, often overwhelms me. I would like nothing better than to forgo the night sky, to put my feet back on the ground and wait until daylight when the road is clearly marked. But the fact is I have yet to find my own feet, and my art these days belongs to the dark of me, to that which has been hidden and has survived intact. So be it. I thank the stars for their insistence. I thank the moon for her grace. I thank the sky for offering me a safe passage home.

i didn't have a mommy
i had a hand instead.
it rubbed my tummy
under my clothes down low
it squeezed my thigh
it traced the outline of my ear

i didn't have a mommy
i was a last frontier for someone else.
he explored me
eager to plant a flag somewhere.
he caressed me. he loved me with
the smile of first possession
he held me open and mined
my inner reaches
he built a fence around the outskirts
to keep everybody else at bay
to mark his territory.
and i loved him.

but i wish i had a mommy.
sometimes when i'm standing at the fence
the deer come to eat from my hand—
we are watchful together.
sometimes i dream of flying
but i am of the earth—
it is the earth growing
inside of me now
she is my greatest comfort
she teaches the art of self-reliance
very slowly.
she teaches the tree, the soil
    to be   without having
    to have   without needing
    to rest between changes
and to honor each other.   she knows
i will soon be with myself
irrespective of fences.

Remembering

It was just an hour.
Where were you that hour?
Where were you?
I was in bed.
I was in bed with someone I thought I loved.
But we don't talk about it.
Were you in bed, too?
Don't talk about it.
I was being pulled open.
Leg by leg, arm by arm. Mouth, too.
Open, open to someone else.
We keep that private. That's not common knowledge.
Where were you?
My body was pulled apart so I could take him in.
My back arched high.
I was doing back bends like I've never been able
    to do since. My mouth was open.
I was in the air, and all of me was shaking.
Where were you?
We don't talk about this, do we?
This is what they call love.
We keep it to ourselves, it hurts so much.
We're ashamed to say it happens over and over.
We are ashamed to let our bodies speak.
It was only an hour.
I was not asleep.
I was not here. But my body threw itself
    against the bed, against the air,
    against all common sense.
My body reached across everything logical
    and regular and acceptable.
My body is giving me messages of hate
And I take them in.
Just for an hour.
Here and there.
There are many hours in the day.
Were you at work?
Were you at breakfast?
I want to tell you all about this.
You need to know this is happening.
I'm told it's not my fault
But it's my body
Even for this hour, when I can't get up,

When I can't turn over, when I can't cry out,
When I can't say no, when I can't stop
When I can't stop coming
When my body throws itself back into another place
And I have no idea why or who is doing this
    or when it will end.
I have no excuses for this hour
I have no explanations that will dissolve the shame.
We don't hear about these things. We don't talk
    about these things.
I have promised not to hide.
What do I do with an hour like this?
I will place it in front of you.
Is it like yours?
I risk being alone with it.
Do you think I am crazy?
I have many hours left in my basket.
I do not like this kind.
But I will show it to you.
Maybe that will take the knife from its hand.
I will touch the face I have been trying
    to slap awake.
It is my face.
I will share the pain if you will share the pain.
I will not choose to be alone this time
Even for an hour. Even for just an hour.

And when I remember enough
If I ever do
If it ever makes any sense
If it ever comes to my waking day
I will place this hour in a box
    on the mantle in the living room
To remind us it has come and gone
Like yours.
Where were you then
For that brief time
Which is no different from any other time?
Where were you?
Talk about it.

invocation to the west

daddy
i will find you
and i will hurt you
and i will leave you

i'm going back to my mother

i will walk into you
and i will walk over you
and i will walk away from you

i'm going back to my mother

i will sing to you
i will sing angry
i will sing after you're gone

i'm going back to my mother

watch me
watch me fly out of the water that made me
watch me climb out of my own burial
watch me harness the wind
and blow your body away
blow your eyes closed

i am in the storm
i am of the storm
this time i welcome her
angry and pure she comes through me
i will open my legs
and my mouth and my heart
i will make love to her
i will let her come through me this way
i will move like the water that made me
i no longer hesitate
i do not equivocate
i do not borrow what is not possessed
i am going back to basics
and know this: know that
old casings—torn, pieced, shriveling—

will not survive this time
fury meets her match and dances there
the tide grabs my ankles
i kiss her face
later on there will be opportunity
    for wonder

Did You Touch Me That Way or Was I Dreaming?

Laurie York

Toolshed, 1985, 17″ × 21″ × 3½″, mixed media construction

MY EARLY MEMORIES have always been like a pile of rubble in the back of my mind—a childhood collapsed in disaster. As a child I loved to draw on paper napkins and make things out of the scrap materials my family would throw away. Looking back now, I believe that being creative helped me focus and separate myself from the emotional turmoil that kept my family in constant crisis.

In my late teens and early twenties, I abandoned art-making for a series of sexual relationships. I began doing artwork again in my late twenties. At that point, I took several classes at an art school that stressed technical proficiency and aesthetics. I felt frustrated painting still lifes when there was no stillness inside me. But whenever I'd let my anger out on canvas, I judged the work ugly and painted over it.

Five years ago, I found some scrap pieces of wood, and without a specific idea in mind, I began hammering them together in irregular ways. I followed my intuition, working spontaneously, gathering shards of memories, piecing them together. Soon I felt this piece was conjuring up memories of my father's toolshed and the relationship I'd had with him as a child. After several weeks' work, *Toolshed* was completed, and it was clear to me that I was beginning to explore a secret I'd never told anyone: I was an incest survivor.

While I sawed and hammered and glued and nailed these random materials, I was putting a shattered part of myself back together. These images spoke out for that small part of myself that had never been able to say, "My father molested me."

For years I felt incredible shame, weighed down by my father's unclaimed guilt and confusion. I began to ask, "Why do I feel guilty? I was an innocent child! Why is it my job to carry my father's shame?" When I let myself feel anger toward my father, I began making *Toolshed*. The feelings that had paralyzed me were now inspiring me to create. I see that making healing art validates my fear and pain, and through this process I've gained self-confidence and faith in the power of transformation.

Toolshed, detail, 1985,
17″ × 21″ × 3½″, mixed
media construction

Being molested demolished my trust. I put up my guard to
defend myself and held in my anger and grief because I seldom felt
safe enough to express my feelings with anyone. Being invisible
felt safer than risking being seen or heard. Surprisingly, the art
I've made for healing is about wanting to be seen and heard. My
art has helped me believe I can change, grow and heal.

It's taken a tremendous amount of energy to keep this incest
experience a secret. As I release these secrets, I feel that energy
flowing into my work. I believe these particular pieces are especially rich and emotional because they reconnect with the power
that was taken from me as a child, the ability to speak the truth.
Through these pieces I am reclaiming the potential given me at

Toolshed, detail, 1985, 17″ × 21″ × 3½″, mixed media construction

birth, and I see my art as a means to recreate my life.

The trauma and chaos I endured as a child yanked me from myself. Feeling unsafe to be in my body, I lived like an outsider looking in. Many of my drawings and paintings are from the perspective of someone near the ceiling looking down into the room. Living with my father, who was an alcoholic with an explosive temper, I understand why I felt threatened at home and in my body. In the art I've done dealing with incest, I've noticed house-shapes being repeated over and over. I believe these house-shapes represent the longing I feel to return to my body, my home. For me, healing from incest has been about reclaiming the parts of myself that were injured or taken from me. As symbols of healing show up in my artwork, I believe they reflect stages of emotional healing happening inside me.

My construction pieces are rough, raw and narrative—they tell my story. In *Toolshed* a doll's head with a wide-eyed shocked expression on her face rises up out of the roof of the building. A piece of glass covers her mouth. On the glass are the words, "DID YOU TOUCH ME THAT WAY OR WAS I DREAMING?"

I was molested when I was eight, and for many years I believed I'd just had a bad dream. I was taking a nap with my father and woke feeling his hand touching my vagina. I was embarrassed, shocked and terrified. I pretended I was sleeping and soon it was over. Ten years ago, my closest childhood friend told me my father had molested her as a child. My niece and cousin came to me with similar stories. I was horrified and relieved. I wasn't dreaming! My father was an exhibitionist and a repetitive child molester. I have felt incredible rage and pain knowing these things about my father who I loved and protected for so many years. I see now that protecting him left me emotionally powerless. Releasing these secrets has strengthened me. Sawing and hammering these construction pieces has connected me to a lot of painful feelings I've held inside my body. I'm still searching for ways to let go of this pain. I often feel a release of physical energy while building these constructions. Sometimes I'm flooded with grief and I let myself cry. Through the pain of incest I've found my voice again!

Toolshed was followed by *Escapegoat,* a construction piece that explores the guilt and shame I've carried for my family. In this piece my father mows the front lawn in his underwear (which is what he actually did!) while the rest of my family sits nonchalantly on the white picket fence as See-No-Evil, Hear-No-Evil, Speak-No-Evil. Inside my room I sleep curled in a fetal position on a bed of nails.

When Mother Left Home is a mixed-media wall construction. In the foreground of a three-dimensional wooden house-shape stands my mother, eyes closed. Behind her, rising out from her body, is her ethereal spirit, translucently ascending through the house in several stages, until you see her arms rising up and out of the chimney. There is a small image of me as a toddler with arms extended to my mother, who is beyond my reach. Behind my mother is a bright red angry window and inside that window is a chaotic drawing, which for me expresses what it was like growing up in that home. *When Mother Left Home* takes me back to my relationship with my mother, who was an invalid from the time I was five until she died when I was thirteen. My mother was bed-ridden most of my childhood, and although she complained of my father's exhibitionism, I never told her about the incest. After a series of brain surgeries, my mother was left unable to protect me from a father I didn't trust. Most of my life, my sorrow for my mother covered up my sorrow for myself. *When Mother Left Home* expresses my pain of feeling abandoned by my mother and the grief I feel for my mother and myself.

After confronting so many painful memories, I made *Small Space—Safe Place,* a grotto-like treehouse construction. As a child I made many cardboard forts and often climbed up on my father's

Escapegoat, 1988, 22″ × 38″ × 19″, mixed media construction

Escapegoat, detail

Left, *When Mother Left Home,*
detail, 1989, 17″ × 21″
× 3½″, mixed media
construction

Right, *Small Space—Safe
Place,* 1989, 17½″ × 8½″ ×
7″, mixed media construction

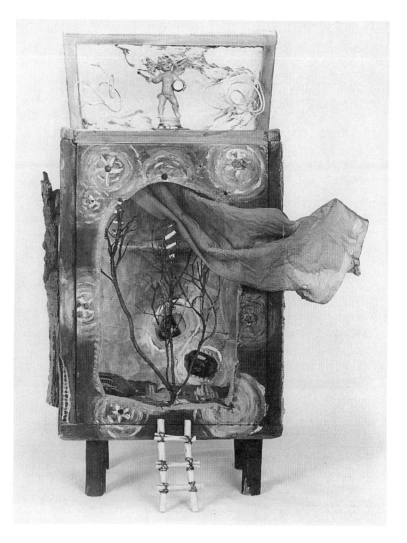

toolshed trying to hide. I longed for a place where I could be safe
from worry and confusion, a place where I could be free to play.
From that desire this piece was born, the treehouse I'd always
wanted. Because *Small Space—Safe Place* is in fact a small piece,
only a foot and a half high, I feel myself looking into it with the
eyes of a child. Inside the floor is blanketed with remnants from
one of my favorite old cotton scarves. A peep-hole through the
tree trunk reveals the message: TRUST YOURSELF. There's a
stained-glass-window effect where the back wall is cut away. I
feel a reverence for this little room. Images of me in my small San
Francisco art studio holding Nana, my kitten, line the inside wall.
The ceiling of the piece is open to the sky, where floating pillow-
like clouds pass slowly through the heavens. On the roof of the
treehouse I placed a guardian angel, symbol of safety to protect
me.

In September 1989, I joined three other artists in a show in Mendocino, California called, "Art for Healing and Empowerment—A Show of Women's Work." The public was extremely receptive and I could sense a real hunger for art that facilitates healing. At the show an older woman confided in me: "What a relief that we can find creative ways to express our pain. There aren't many places we can talk about these things." After a brief silence she continued, "When I was sixteen. . . "

Another person told me, "Incest is a trauma we can heal from. The problem is that we've had to hold the secret inside." A young man came to me and shared that he had grown up with a mother who had been molested as a child. From her pain he'd felt the effects of incest on his own life. In our guest book he wrote, "Thank you for the courage to create the beautiful out of the nightmare."

Singing Is Never Quiet

Louise M. Wisechild

MEMORY ALWAYS MAKES me change my mind about who I am. Before I came to terms with Memory, I thought I was defective and bad and that other people would figure this out if they looked at me too long. With Memory I came to honor the voice that incest had overshadowed.

For years, my secret desire was to be a folk singer. I remember now that all sorts of people told me I had a nice voice, but I didn't believe them. I couldn't take confidence from what they said, because the incest made me feel ugly and false, and songs were beautiful and true.

I assumed that some day I would stop singing—even though for many years I loved singing more than I loved people. But folk songs left with the 60's. I rolled up the full-length poster of Joan Baez that had hung over my adolescent twin bed. It seemed that most people stashed their guitars in dusty attics or picturesque corners upon adulthood.

But the more difficult challenge to my singing lay in my persistent feelings of inadequacy. How could I sing and be the shy, silent, terrified person that I was, lacking the power and confidence I imagined singers to be blessed with.

Memory tells me, however, that I was not always the quiet, self-conscious child I thought I was. In fact, I started out quite loud: howling, cooing, hiccuping, crying, screaming and babbling with a satisfying array of 'b' sounds. My earliest voice was punished or ignored, so I sought words like a shipwreck victim looking for a plank. But words were not just words, they were also sound. I spent many hours making my voice go high and low, shrill and many shades of whisper. I loved the feel of my voice bending around my lips. I liked to string words out loud into stories that I told Barbie; I liked to hum and bounce and talk over my crayons. I talk-sang to the cat, the grass, the snow-ball tree and myself. My voice was a blanket I could weave around myself. When I sang I wasn't lonely.

My devotion to my own voice was in direct conflict with my family's insistence that children be "Quiet!" My mother took to yelling, "Don't breathe so loud, you're doing that on purpose! Do you want a spanking?" My breaths got very small, measured anxiously through my nostrils. Smaller again, as I searched for air between the hairs of my grandfather's pubis.

The abuse affected my songs and singing profoundly. Sperm gummed my throat and I could only sing my way through its blockage in private. I left my body when I sang in front of others—whether I was singing in church, at high school hootenannies or for friends. My knees wobbled, my jaw locked rigid against invisible threats, my mind blanked out the lyrics at crucial instants. In anticipation of public appearances, I came down with sore throats and laryngitis, becoming hot and feverish—replicating the way I felt after each experience of sexual abuse.

I was terrified of being seen and of what disaster might befall me when I was sighted. When I was seen my voice floated away from me on a string and lost the wholeness it had when I was private. I was sure the audience was just pretending to listen and that they wished I'd get it over with.

The false public self I'd fashioned to hide the abuse learned to master speech, but only my private self could sing. Melody reveals emotion in a way that talking does not. Singing is played on the instrument of the body; but my body was clothed in shame and disgust, a bucket for the loathing of my grandfather, uncle and stepfather. For twenty years, I vowed after each embarrassing, terrifying performance, that I would never again sing in front of people. But when I sang by myself, my voice took me to a place of healing and hope. And in that place, I pretended that someone else was there to hear.

Memory says that for as long as I have sung, my music has wanted hearing. Even in the years when I barely spoke, my music defied the silence.

The first song I remember singing to an audience was about incest. I was six. I stood in the middle of a circle of knees, the recipient of rare mass adult attention. My uncle asked if I would sing a song. "Grandpa's candy tastes icky," I began, hopping about to give it the rhythm, and because in the beginning, I always moved when I sang. Before I got too far, my mother began talking to my uncle and another line later my grandfather's hand fell on my head like a lid and he said, "That's enough, Loueezy." I have had to learn to move again when I sing.

When I was in junior high, I was sodomized and tortured by an uncle, who at one point put a noose around my neck as he penetrated me anally. I wrote a song called, "The Misfit Song." It had three verses and a chorus. Even now I remember the song, "I'm just a misfit, lonely little thing/ I travel through this world 'cause I like to sing/ Nobody loves me and nobody cares/ It doesn't matter 'cause I'm not theirs."

I sang it over and over to myself, and the music soothed all the places that hurt. I remember thinking that this song was truer than anything else I knew. Even though it was a very sad song, it made me feel better to sing it. It was a tune I could find myself in, a home for my feelings.

When I was fourteen, I ran away, hoping to escape the continuing abuse by my uncle and the escalating verbal abuse from my mother. My second foster home was not much better than my family and I was very miserable, hugging my guitar for long hours alone in my room. I wrote songs about peace and "brotherhood," using my voice to sing a vision I longed for in the world around me—a vision that had everything I was missing within it.

The social worker decided I was suffering from poor self-esteem, a rather placid description given the violent suicidal fantasies I was preoccupied with. She decided that the solution was for me to make a recording of my songs. I sat in the living room while a man held a penis-shaped microphone in my direction. I promptly went to float on the ceiling while the ghost I'd left to mind my body sang in a thin, shaking voice. I felt that some part of me was being stolen. I was painfully aware that no one was really listening to what I was singing, for how could they act as they did if they were really hearing my words? Later, my mother would ask me to sing for her and then turn on the television when I began.

But still songs trickled out from me. Never so many songs as poems or stories. But songs that always described exactly what I felt the most deeply, born from a place of passion and inner truths I often did not fully comprehend. Songs that appeared line by line requiring the repetition of melody to help the words come out. Songs that refused to be thought out first within the quiet and safety of my head. Songs that insisted on noise and feeling. Songs that flew out from inside of me, shaking loose cellular truths with their vibration.

In my periodic high school conversions to Christianity, I wrote many songs to a Father, trying to conjure up divine protection and a caring I could not find in my family. Just as singing connects body and feeling through the voice, so my songs have always sought a larger spiritual connection, because they come from a drive for wholeness. When I dropped Jesus, I stopped singing. I could no longer find myself and God didn't seem to help. What was there to sing about?

But when I started therapy at twenty-four, the songs came again, after five years of silence. This time, my songs were about change and the inner journey I had embarked on. Memory and home were repeating themes, as well as imagery that celebrated my connection to nature. Each song began when I was deep in feeling; I would start humming and stroking my guitar. Each line moved me from feeling overwhelmed by emotion into trusting in my own direction and path.

I wrote "The Everything Song," as I was getting ready to meet some people I was scared would reject me. The song came from a calm place in my body, securely in my abdomen, lower within me than the fear that ate at my stomach. In this song, I knew absolutely that I was connected to a support that was more sure than the God or the family I had inherited. In "The Everything Song," I finally knew that I belonged, that I was a part of a larger whole where there was no rejection. A place where incest no longer set me apart.

"Ballad of a Survivor" came as I was in the middle of weeks of incest memories involving my stepfather. In writing it, I moved from despair to a conviction that I would throw off my stepfather's body, even as I composed this song on the guitar he had given to me when he married my mother. It still took several months before I could sing the word "penis" without tripping over it. But having this song meant that I could sing my way through the feelings of grief and anger into determination whenever I needed to remind myself of what I was doing in this healing and why it was important. I became increasingly aware that singing and songwriting involved all of me: my body, my young selves, my story and the transformation of ugliness into beauty.

Still I was shy about singing in public, the long familiar split between my public false-self and my private feeling-self a terrifying chasm I was not sure how to bridge. I stumbled upon singing classes taught by April Leona. I had done some movement work as therapy, but had never before combined movement with voice work. I was astonished that I could learn to relax my voice and jaw by sticking my tongue out and sighing. Moving my pelvis while making sound gave a depth and support to my singing I had never had before. I learned to listen to how my body wanted to move and to find sounds for the movement. My voice began to become more complex, to interact with my body.

April had us stand in front of each other and sing, then confess the judgments of our critic, and then sing once more. I learned to stand in my songs as I sang them. I took private lessons and explored the fears which came full-blown to the surface when April said, "Now sing me a song." What would I do with my eyes, with all this emotion and intimacy, what would she think?

After my book, *The Obsidian Mirror* (1988), came out, I began reading, lecturing and teaching on healing from incest. Some of the short songs that my younger selves made up on car rides snuck themselves into my workshops, so that teaching a song or two became an integral part of my work. I told myself that it was educational and that must be why it suddenly seemed a lot easier to sing in front of others. Then I started singing as a part of my lectures and reading. At first, I'd sing really well for one performance and then find myself sick and leaving my guitar in its case for the next three readings. In work with April, I continued to uncover specific areas of physical holding from the years of fear and abuse I had experienced, using my voice to speak for my muscles.

Then a remarkable thing began to happen. I stopped being so nervous. Time after time, in singing for an audience, I had the sensation of riding a vast wave of energy, as if my voice was a wind blowing through me, a wind of increasingly complex tones free from much of my earlier inhibition. As I sang publicly, I felt a new solidness and largeness in my body. Songs seemed to be made of colors that filled my body and the room in which I sang. The audience also became a part of this wind, so that my singing felt supported by the feelings of those who were watching.

I understand now why my family could never hear my music, how frightened they must have been by the power that is inextricably linked to song. A power that comes from the honest connection between the singing and the feelings of the singer. This honesty is why it took me thirty-four years to write "Home," my first love song. It is a song that celebrates my relationship and the safety I have found in our home.

Last night I dreamt that Joan Baez was in our living room. I was fourteen in the dream and felt my familiar shyness mixed with a deep love for her and for the hope her voice had always given me. Joan moved to the kitchen and began singing as she washed the dishes. When I woke, I realized how integral singing is to the most daily parts of my life. How I have come to love she who is the singer within myself.

Today I took my songs to Suzanne Grant, in order that she might translate them into written music. As I waited for the ferry, I developed a sore throat. I spoke with the fourteen-year-old self who had felt terrorized at recording her music. I drank Throat Coat tea from my mug in the car and arrived at Suzanne's studio, guitar in hand.

I said, "I don't know how to do this, I'm still an amateur."

She said, "Sing me your songs."

I fretted for only a moment. Then I fell into my singing, into the home that is better than any I have had before.

Ballad of a Survivor

Chorus:

I have the rain in my necklace,
The sun in a jar.
I have a circle of clouds round my head.
Just now I feel like running,
But everywhere's too far.
Sometimes it's hard to bury the dead.

1) The dark was a home for his shadows
That lurked in my room with might.
There's goblins and terror not far from here
And I wait for the end of the long raped night.

2) His body was heavy and sweaty on me,
My legs were tied with a belt.
His penis shone red in the moonlit sea
And I could not scream against his mouth.

Repeat chorus

3) By day he was solid and quiet,
A good man they agreed,
But at night he was monsters who grunted at
        my fall.
The step-daughter lay — "Dad" he was
        called.

4) Well it's only lately remembered,
Only recently reknown,
But it's tied my life to a heavy stone.
Must be why I never spend the night at home.

Repeat chorus

5) Yes, I'm a survivor; yes, I'll sing the call
And I'll never be gotten again.
For I'm woman and I'm mighty and I'm rising
        to scream
And this time, I'm thowin' off him.

I had the rain in my necklace,
The sun in a jar.
I had a circle of clouds round my head
But I won't be taken as captive
And I won't be told to stay
And still it's hard, to bury the dead.

© 1985, Louise M. Wisechild

Ballad of a Survivor

LOUISE M. WISECHILD

grunted at my fall. The step - daughter lay.

"Dad", he was called. Well, it's on - ly late ly re -

mem bered. On ly re cently re -known. But it's tied my life

to a heavy stone. Must be why I nev- er

spend the night at home. I have the rain in my

neck lace, the sun in a jar. I have a cir cle of

clouds round my head. And just now I feel like

run ning, but ev - ery where's too far. Some times it's

hard to bu - ry the dead. Yes, I'm a suf

viv - or. Yes, I'll sing the call. And I'll nev- er be

got- ten a - gain. For I'm wo man and I'm

might y and I'm ris - ing to scream. And this time, I'm

throw ing off him. I have the rain in my

neck lace, the sun in a jar. I had a cir cle of

clouds round my head. But I won't be ta ken as

cap - tive. And I won't be told to stay. And still it's

hard to bu - ry the dead.

The Everything Song

Chorus:

I am ahead of you,
I am behind,
I am a part of you,
Walk, we walk.

1) I am the mountains, the rock and the sand
I'm solid like granite and gentle like the lamb
I run with the lions, I laugh with the sea,
For I am the Everything, you're traveling
      with me.

Repeat chorus

2) I am all passion, that lives with delight
I revel in mudpuddles, I bathe in moonlight
There's lover's aplenty, so touch to explore
We're magnificent creatures, we needn't be
      bored.

Repeat chorus

3) The whales are sister, the kinfolk are trees
The wind is a messenger with tales of shes
There's birth all around us; death changes the
      parts
But get to the living, for growing's an art.

Repeat chorus

© 1985, Louise M. Wisechild

The Everything Song

LOUISE M. WISECHILD 217

Home

Home is where the water turns to glass
As the sun goes down, to a farther shore.
The moon's a slip of finger in the sky,
    painted yellow, making orange
And shadows of the evening
Clothe our walls.

Walls of books and pictures
    that whisper to us truths,
An altar on the piano
    and a photograph of you.
We have a kitchen stocked with spices
And a bathtub with a view.
You know, I've spent many years of time
    alone,
But now coming home means being here with
    you.

Home is where the alders shed their leaves
As the fall comes near, in days of grey.
The gull's a fleeting whiteness on the Sound,
    calling, "Gather spirits round,"
And bones of sea-washed creatures find our
    shore.

Bones and rocks and feathers,
    our windows framed with drums,
A bed upon a platform
    and a basket filled with toys.
We have meals made with laughter
And evenings soft with skin.
You know, I've spent many years of time
    alone,
But now being home means gently touching
    in.

Home is where the spider weaves her silk
And the ground turns rust with needles of
    pine.
The wind's a mighty cellist taking boughs,
    making symphonies of howls
And clouds with changing features dance on
    high.

Dancing like your fingers
    weaving iris leaves to cord,
Picking salad from our garden,
    making mornings loud with song.
We have a cat for every doorway
And crayons, herbs and pens.
You know I've spent many years of time
    alone,
But now being home means playing house
    with you.

© 1989, Louise M. Wisechild

Home

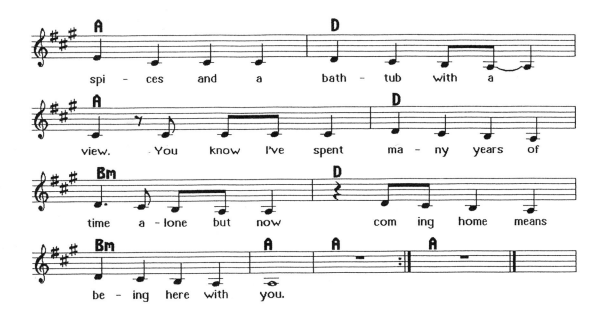

spi - ces and a bath - tub with a view. You know I've spent ma - ny years of time a - lone but now com ing home means be - ing here with you.

Emotion Goddesses

Shey Bird

HEALING, FOR ME, has meant following my creative path. I have sculpted clay goddesses, made and played drums, and other various creative projects usually inspired by my inner child. And I write: healing stories, an article, a few poems, a letter to the editor, a handful of children's books, and simple journal entries. My intention has been to heal and to share heaing with others.

I was beaten, raped, and abandoned, in the name of anger and of love, before I could walk and afterwards, as well. I learned that feelings were dangerous and that they hurt. I had to ignore my feelings to keep myself safe. Of course, that didn't always work, but sometimes it did, so I became very good at it.

Even now, I fall into habits that help me avoid feeling, but I'm beginning to see that there are dire consequences in my life when I ignore my feelings and therefore my creative self. I become irrationally angry at or critical of others or myself, and I am lethargic to the point of being unable to accomplish what I set out to in a day. The unfelt feelings weigh me down.

My healing has been the process of making contact with all the feelings my addictions and my shame hold down. I shake and rage and sob. The shame makes me feel dirty. I feel better when I can create something with the feelings, when I can put them outside of myself into some form and thereby "trans-form" them.

But that process is hard. All my habits come back, and my shame. As a young one, I clung to those habits that kept me from feeling, and the shame that said the abuse was my fault for having feelings. If it was my fault then I must have some power, but the only power I could find was to hide my feelings. I'm sure that saved me a time or two. But now I am safe to feel and express, and as I learn to trust myself, I let my feelings out.

I began the *Emotion Goddesses,* a set of painted clay masks, from that place of self-trust. I gave myself permission to make the ugliest forms I'd ever created. I felt as if "ugly" was all I had in me to express, and I had been spending lots of energy trying not to express it.

As I wedged the clay, I began looking inside. I noticed Fear first; my heartbeats felt huge and wild, leaving no room for my breath.

"What does this fear look and feel like?" I asked myself, flattening the chunk of clay. Following my images, I made a naked, white-skinned figure. She had no body below her waist; her arms were cut off just below her shoulders. Her lips and nipples were bright orange, and purple lightning bolts erupted from her bald head. A severed hand grabbed nothing. A foot sprinted, frozen up on spread toes.

When I heard a voice inside my head, I realized that Fear was talking to me.

"Run!" she whispered. "Ow! Don't feel; that hurts. I didn't do it!"

My dad, as he used to be, was running after her, growling, "You little snot-nosed brat, you know better than to get into my tools. Wait til I get my hands on you."

He grabbed her and tried to lift her up with his hand on the back of her neck. She screamed, writhing in mid-air. One of her arms fell to the floor. No one noticed. She kept writhing until he let her to her feet.

He led her to his toolbox, there, beside the TV. She placidly went where he wanted her to go, whimpering, trying to raise her shoulders enough to ease the pain of his still-tight grip on the back of her neck.

He threw her down by the toolbox and said, "Put them all back!"

Her white face looked up at him, eyes round and then flinching, round, flinching. He kicked her, yelling, "Now!"

She began to replace the tools as fast as she could, but he suddenly threw her out of the way. "I have to do it myself; you're so stupid."

She went to hide. She knew her arm was still gone, even though she could see it hanging from her shoulder. She crawled under the bed, using the arm that worked. She sucked her finger and hoped against hope that her nice daddy would be back, soon.

As an adult, I have used anxiety and mistrust to disconnect from myself, out of my chronic fear of intimacy. Fear agreed to consult with me about how to stay safe when I take risks with others, so she became my Goddess of Courage.

I went through a similar process with the next three masks. The accompanying poems illustrate my learning process with each one.

Shame was bulgy-eyed and open-mouthed. Her tongue hung out in a perpetual gag. Her large hand, fingers spread, cupped her chin to catch her own vomit. Shame showed me that places inside where I feel shame are parts of myself that I was taught or forced to hate, so she became my Goddess of Self-love.

Rage was bright red, sharp-toothed and snarling. She had snakes for ears and bright orange lightning bolts shooting out of her cheeks. Rage showed me my belief that I have to change someone else to have power. She agreed to help me consciously channel my anger rather than blaming or manipulating, so she became my Goddess of Personal Power.

Sadness was the most difficult mask to give form to, and has been my most powerful image. Pink and red dots crowd around her huge, sagging lips, flared nostrils, round watery eyes, and crumpled eyebrows and forehead. My own hair falls down one side of her head. Sadness showed me that I use sucking habits, like smoking, drinking caffeine and eating sugar to avoid feelings. She showed me that I must let go, let myself feel, in order to receive comfort, and that letting go is beginning, so she became my Goddess of Change.

As I attempted to access these emotions in myself, I developed an inner part of myself who could mediate between all my emotions, between my head and my body. She nurtured me and kept me grounded. She was my wisdom and compassion, my higher power. I named her Moon. To create a physical image for her, I sat naked in front of a large mirror, cross-legged. I made a simple line drawing of my body, with each upturned hand resting on an inner thigh, holding a disk. Her/my head was an oversized, empty oval, an empty mask.

I made dozens of copies and filled the empty mask in different ways at different times. This *Mask Meditation* drawing has been a simple tool I can use to create a visual image for an emotion, sensation or character inside me that feels overwhelming. The image of Moon contains the feeling; I can draw it as ugly and as intense and as big as possible, but still it is grounded by this meditating image of a part of me, Moon.

Because I learned that Moon could keep the feelings safe, true and sacred, I let the Emotion Goddesses come to me in a visualization.

I had been feeling irritable and easily angered. I needed to get as ugly as I felt moved to get, without drawing someone else in; my emotions needed to act out, but without conscious attention from me, they were lashing out instead.

I relaxed in a warm room, lying flat on the carpeted floor, arms and legs spread. I individually invited each part of my body that felt tense to let go of the tension, to become totally relaxed. I invited my whole body to maintain this relaxation and to experience safely whatever sensations moved through. Then, with Moon for support, I allowed myself to look at my feelings.

"Shut up!" yelled Rage, "It's her fault that I don't feel loved. It IS her fault. It has to be. Ooooohhh," she swung her fists, pacing. "She'll really have to prove she loves me now."

She wanted my partner to contain and nurture her, but couldn't ask for that.

"Who are you protecting?" asked Moon.

"I'm protecting her, the keeper of the weak emotions." Rage pointed to a corner where someone was crouched, retching into her hands.

Moon looked closer. "Who are you?" she asked.

"I am Shame," was the reply. "I am everything they hate. Oh, yuck." Shame stood up, trying to brush off the green slime that covered her arms and legs.

"What do you do as keeper of the weak emotions?" asked Moon.

Shame looked up. "I hold down fear and sadness. I let them know that they're bad, that they have to hide."

I felt my heart beat faster; my breath was tight; I knew the internal truth of what Shame said.

Moon said, "Let me see Fear."

Shame nodded. Fear appeared, narrow-faced and pink, with a tiny round mouth and tiny pink hands disconnected from her body. Though they were much too small to protect anything, the hands tried to cover the head, as if she was expecting a blow from above.

Moon looked startled. "Why are you pink?" she asked.

Fear whispered her reply: "Because I'm weak, like a girl." Her eyes darted side to side; her hands hung limp. "I can't do anything. I'm useless."

Tears grew in my eyes as Moon reached out to touch Fear's face, but Fear's eyes opened wider, her hand covered her mouth, and she disappeared.

In her place was a watery indigo mass. It contained two especially watery pools that might be eyes, and two limp, dripping hands.

"Who are you?" asked Moon.

"I am Sadness," came the muffled reply. "I am drowning in my own tears. Beware of me, for to touch my surface is to be drawn into my depths of despair."

Fear came back then. "Yes, yes," she exclaimed quickly, "Listen to her. Go back. It's dangerous here." Her hands were wide open, waving wildly.

Shame came back, too, pulling green slime out of her plastered hair. "How can you be looking here, you naughty girl? You're bad; you're weak; you're vulnerable. Oh, something smells awful. Don't talk."

Then Rage was there, with big red fists, her lips pulled back from her sharp teeth. She grabbed Shame's neck and shook her. "You're not doing your job, you stupid mucus-face. Keep those two down so I can get them the nurturing they need." She shoved Shame toward Fear and Sadness. Shame gagged and spit up.

My heart beat so fast that I couldn't get enough breath. This violence was occurring in my own body. This was my internal resistance to the peaceful, cooperative living that is my ideal.

Rage was yelling now, "It's her fault. I hate her. It's her fault I feel this way. I will hate her until she takes care of me."

Rage was directing herself at my partner, maybe even my mother. She stomped her feet and continued, "It's her fault I feel bad. I will push her away until she holds me hard enough. It's her fault. I will bite and scratch her until she makes me feel better. It's her fault."

Moon walked over to Rage, kneeling down. I was surprised to see that Rage was the height of a three year old. Then I noticed she WAS a three year old, wearing a big, red Rage-mask. She was still yelling. "You better not get too close to me because I might scare you or hurt you. I'll never be cozy with you. Yuck! You'll have to FORCE me to be cozy with you. I'm too tough for that."

"You are pretty tough," Moon nodded. "So am I, but I still like to get cozy, and sometimes I feel scared or sad. You can be tough and have feelings."

She put her hand on the child's arm. "Really?" asked the child, her mask changing to Fear. She looked away and back to Moon's face, away and back again.

"All children have feelings, even the most wonderful ones, like you," said Moon.

Tears ran down my temples as I watched tears fill the child's eyes, her mask turning to Sadness. A wave of energy surged through my body and came out of my throat as a sob. I watched the child dive into Moon's arms, felt the soft holding and rocking.

Suddenly the child jumped out of Moon's arms and I was suffocating. The fear mask was back and its tiny round mouth could pass no air. I felt so scared, alone and choking. My body tingled, then got cold.

"It's O.K." said Moon softly. "You can breathe now." She put her hand on the child's chest, softly rubbing downward. My breath came back a little at a time as I watched the child slowly relax. I remembered the pneumonia I had around that age, how crying had felt like drowning.

"It's O.K. to cry," said Moon, holding the child again. The sobs undulated through my body. I felt so sad and alone. The holding and rocking let me know I was safe in those feelings.

As the sobs subsided, Moon held the child out at arms length.

"You can come here to be with me whenever you want," she said to the child.

"I want to every day," the child replied seriously.

"O.K., then you need to tell her," Moon pointed at me.

"I want to come here every day," the child said to me.

One last sob came out as I replied, "So do I."

I held the child, and Moon held us both, rocking slowly, like the earth.

The Goddess
of Change
Speaks:

The Goddess of Change, 1989,
painted clay, mixed media

I am Sadness. I rule
the heart, the hands, the lymph system,
birth,
the element water,
the creative self.
I come not only with outer changes
also with inner changes,
even desired ones.

Honor me by letting go
from your bones out let go
into nothingness. Everythingness.
Stay there, sobbing, draining,
as images, words, and feelings
disengage from your organs,
drain from your muscles and bones.
Do not look for a new beginning
as you let go of everything
that made your bones
your bones. Let go. Let
go. The new beginning is you.

The Goddess
of Self-Love
Speaks:

The Goddess of Self Love,
1989, painted clay, mixed
media

I am Shame. I rule
the stomach, and throwing up,
the eyes, and looking down,
the clitoris, masturbation,
the element earth, dormant volcanos,
pimples, the inner adolescent.

I am the secret. Honor me
by sharing openly, however horrible,
with ones who will listen and know
the power. Share the secret
until you don't
gag, until it comes out easy,
like morning mist on water.
Say it to every branch
and leaf, even the bark.
Notice the sunshine then, the leaves
turn greener. Say it again
until the rocky soil
begins to crumble, turning to loam.
Feel the roots stretch and grow
for they are your own.

The Goddess
of Personal Power
Speaks:

The Goddess of Personal Power,
1989, painted clay, mixed
media

I am Rage. I rule
the solar plexus. I beat
my chest. I rule
the jaw. I show
my teeth. I rule
the fists, raised. I rule
the element fire. I throw
fits, stomp and scream. I rule
the inner two year old.

I am over loaded
with hurt, violated
too many times. I see
through red eyes; snakes
hiss in my ears. I can give
a burst of strength
in times of physical violation.
Use it to protect yourself
and your loved ones.

To honor me, give me a safe place
inside your head. Listen
to me, and share
honest feelings with me:
I am you, as a young child.
Compromise with your small self,
meet her needs, to discover a fair
and consciously–chosen expression.
In return, I offer
you
your own power.

Look Mom, No Hands!

Julie Blackwomon

I AM SIX YEARS old and dreaming I am asleep atop the counter of a smoke-filled bar. The bar is made of heavy mahogany wood, and I am cradled in my own familiar bedcovers. But for some reason there is a brown beer bottle at the entrance to my vagina.

When I awake I find I am in my father's bed along with my seven-year-old brother. My father is on top of me. The beer bottle at the entrance to my vagina is his penis. The sensation is not unpleasant.

When I was eighteen and about to graduate from high school, I was hired, to my great surprise, as a journalism trainee by the publisher of a now-defunct Black newspaper in Philadelphia. About six months later, the boss decided that I was a nice enough girl who had no talent. She fired me. For three days, I moped around the house feeling sorry for myself, but then decided the boss was right. I didn't have any talent. Hoping I would be steered towards college, I went to the employment office to take aptitude tests to determine which were my strongest skills. But after a battery of aptitude tests the counselor said that I was good with my hands and should seek employment in a factory. A writing block soon followed that sprawled through the next eleven years of my life. It would be almost twenty-five years before I would become conscious of how incest played into this and subsequent writing blocks in my life.

In the early seventies I went into therapy. At the time I was thoroughly disgusted with myself because I had been on welfare for almost two years and was afraid I could not support myself if I got off it. Worse yet, being on welfare afforded me the opportunity to write, but I wasn't writing either. I had not yet attributed my failure to write to a writing block. I concluded that I was on welfare and could not/would not write because I was dumb. I'd never gone to college and therefore never had a piece of paper that said I had the right to put my thoughts down on paper and be taken seriously. Within a year of ending therapy, I got a good-paying job in the bulk-packaging department of a sugar refinery. I got off welfare, wrote a few poems and I began to think of myself, not as a writer but a poet.

I am six? seven? eight? years old and playing jacks on the steps in front of Aunt Lucy's house on Carpenter Street in South Philadelphia. My father and several adult males are standing around lollygagging on the steps. My father is high on alcohol, and I hear him tell the men that I was playing with his "thing." The men think it's hilarious and ask "who?" in amused disbelief as my father points me out on the steps. A man whose name and face I cannot recall, his breath reeking of mint gin, tells me not to do that again because it's not nice.

In the late seventies I began to write poems in earnest. Poetry became an expression of primal pain and joy. It was a gut instinct; a survival mechanism. I could write poetry and not be something as threatening as a real writer. To write poetry was to inhale a breath of fresh air and breathe out a poem. I didn't write prose, I told myself, because I didn't know how. But poetry was different. It was not something I needed to learn to do, it was just there—the physical expression of joy and pain, like crying, like laughing. When an inner force compels me to begin working with issues I am not yet ready to face, it comes out in the form of a poem. Poetry has often been the safety valve that has kept me from exploding. Or contemplating suicide. It has also served as the x-ray film through which I could chart the scars that incest has carved into my psyche.

In the early eighties I again entered therapy to deal with depression. This time I explored not only the incest, but also the connection between my writing, which feeds my emotional health, and my physical health. The challenge to my physical well-being comes in the form of a fear of stomach cancer. I would routinely run to doctors looking for the cancer I felt was predestined for me. If I was diligent, I felt, I could catch it before it became fatal. I left therapy, again convinced that I had found the root of my problem and could cope on my own. I stopped spending money on x-rays and continued to drink milk, which produced the same symptoms that sent me to doctors looking for cancer. I told myself that the rumblings in my stomach were only gas, not the cancer I felt I deserved. By not going to the doctors to check out the "gas" in my stomach (which might in reality have been cancer) I was playing a passive Russian roulette with the cancer I feared. It was my tradeoff.

Over dinner in December, 1990, my publisher at Seal Press informed me that a woman was putting together an anthology on incest and asked if I'd like to contribute to it. I explained to her that I had a long-standing writer's block around nonfiction prose and, although I believed in the value of the project, I doubted that I would be able to write the essay that was required to go along with my incest poems.

By then, thanks in large part to several years of therapy with an excellent therapist, I had peeled off several layers of the onion that is incest and gotten in touch with some of the necessary pain of healing. I had also been writing poetry at will and had written at least three poems that I knew were about incest. Seal Press had just published a number of my short stories. I privately marveled that the publication of *Voyages Out 2* had not brought on another writing block and was grateful for whatever it was that freed me to complete the eight stories that went into that collection.

I was writing constantly: getting up at four and five a.m. to write before getting washed and dressed for work, falling asleep at night with material I had been editing in my hand. Weekends I got up at five and wrote until noon or so, or until my lover indicated I'd better start acting like I knew that I, too, was responsible for helping to clean the apartment. I was working simultaneously on a book of short stories and on a novel, and had no idea which I would complete first. Most importantly, I was confident that I could do as I had promised, and send my publisher a manuscript for my second book by my self-imposed deadline of March first. I had no intention of looking my hard-won success in the eye to see who would first blink. I didn't want to risk bringing on a writer's block by trying to write an essay about incest.

Then I got a letter from Louise Wisechild that included a re- quest for the dreaded essay. Worse yet, there was a deadline in- volved. I wanted to write the essay. I didn't know that I could. I felt a strong debt to other survivors whose broken silences have helped me begin to heal. The women behind the voices, who along with the help of my competent therapist, have repeatedly in direct and indirect ways spoken the words I have so desperately needed to hear in my gut as well as in my head: that it was not my fault, that I was not, that I *am not* guilty. I wanted to do my share in spreading the word to the hurt child in other survivors that it was not their fault either. I wanted to do it, but I didn't know if I could. I answered the letter, explaining how I had a block about nonfiction prose. I yanked "Ghost Story II" and "Ghost Story III" from a nearby copy of my poetry book *Revolutionary Blues and Other Fevers* and sent it off, knowing that more was required. So there, my civic job done, I returned to my real work—getting the manuscript done for Seal. I did not enclose a self addressed stamped envelope. I didn't care if Louise Wisechild failed to con- tact me again. I certainly had no intention of contacting her.

I am fourteen years old and am spending the summer in Virginia with my paternal Grandmother. My father lives down the road with his common-law wife but comes often to visit. It is a Saturday in August so my grandmother is off from work. I have completed my few chores and have gone upstairs into the bedroom that used to be my father's. I am asleep on the bed with the windows open when I stir and am suddenly awake. Still half asleep, I blink and recognize my father standing in the doorway watching me. I stare back at him. Watch him pull down the zipper to his khaki pants and slide his hand inside. I can see his white jockey shorts where the zipper is open. Fully awake now, I lay motionless on the bed, barely believing my eyes, watching my father fumble in his pants for his penis. Eventually my father turns and leaves the room. To this day I am not sure why he left. I didn't tell anybody about that. Not until much later. It would be a long time before I figured out why I never told.

The marriage of my parents dissolved when I was seven or eight. For years I thought I hated my father, not so much for the incest, but for his loud absence from my life. When I first wrote "Ghost Story II," I had no idea I had written my first poem about incest. I thought the poem was about loss, about what I viewed as my father's rejection of me. It was not until last year when I wrote "Keeping Daddy's Secret," particularly when I was able to read it aloud before an audience, that I have begun to get in touch with how angry I have been with my father.

I am twenty-seven and visiting Virginia with a male lover. We have been "home" for three days and are preparing to leave. Our bags are packed in the back of the car, and we are heading out route 33 when I realize I cannot, as planned, leave without trying to see the man I used to call daddy. I drive back to my uncle John's, ask him to lead my lover and me to where my father lives.

It is a warm morning in mid August 1971. My father meets us in the front yard of a weather-worn shack. He will not invite us in, he says, because the place is a mess. He is sitting on the springs of an old hassock; one of his drinking buddies is sitting nearby on a rusty milk crate with a fifth of gin. As we are about to leave, my father embraces me, then kisses me full on the lips. Before I can pull away my father pushes his tongue into my mouth.

I sent my poems off to Wisechild on Sunday, January 20th, 1991. By wild coincidence, two days later I was scheduled to visit a gastrointestinal specialist at 10:15 and had not planned on going to work. I got out of bed that morning at 6:45 and walked the few feet to my office with the intention of working on the manuscript to be sent to Seal. Three and a half hours later, I was still at my desk, crying my eyes out. I had written the first draft of this essay.

Six days after I wrote my first essay in almost twenty years, I discovered I did not have stomach or rectal cancer. I sat down and cried again in relief in joy and in wide-eyed disbelief.

The journey back to my writing has been a long, painful process spanning almost thirty years. Sitting crying in my office that January morning, I pieced together the reason it had always been so difficult for me to write prose at times: I had been saving my own life. I am now discovering over and over again that I can write, that I am not dumb and that I am a good and worthy person. I am understanding better why I constantly need to be reminded of these things.

Somewhere within me there's a little girl who believes she's guilty, that she's done something "nasty" to her father for which she must be punished. If she ever gets both her writing and her romantic life in sync at the same time—so that she's writing regularly and in love with someone who loves her in return—then she will die. This is my legacy from incest: the feeling in my gut that I am undeserving.

Now, intellectually I can laugh with my therapist about this. I can joke with my friends who assure me they'll be dead and gone while I'm still searching for cancer. But in my gut there still remains the suspicion that I have done something for which I must be punished. And the punishment is death by cancer.

There are many ways in which I still do not know how all this ties in, if it ties in at all. I know only that it has taken me almost thirty years to finish half a book, and I have written the first draft of an essay that was not assigned to me as part of a class project.

Healing from incest is like slowly pulling off scabs and letting the wounds get some sunlight, because things do not heal in damp, dark places. One of the problems of writing about it is that at some point, you are forced to look yourself in the eye and decide if you really want to put all your family crap out there for the world to see. But I keep writing. I have developed sudden, inexplicable anxiety attacks and my lover complains that I am cranky and start silly arguments. But I am still writing. Because I have to. I have to do it for all those guilty-feeling six year olds, the embarrassed teenage girls and the confused, shame-faced women whose suffering needs a voice. And I have to do it for me.

I am surviving. I have survived writing blocks, depression and anxiety, and the recurring nightmare that is incest. The excitement I feel at being able to write this piece is like watching my little six-year-old self riding a bicycle for the first time. She is grinning from ear to ear and saying "Look Mom, no hands!" My adult self is applauding wildly for her.

Ghost Story II
(for my father)

I feel you moving
through my rear passageways
returning through doors marked one way
this way out and exit only
your persistent footfalls echo
along my narrow corridors
constricting   drawing in my center
You are a blind vagrant who returns to me
because your cane remembers the way
and there is no place else to go.
I hear the splinter of wood
the clatter of falling hinges
as you assault doors that open into yesterday
seeking sunlit rooms
in which I used to call you daddy.

Ghost Story III

Needing to make peace with your ghosts
I am training them to walk on short leashes
so they will not embarrass us.
Well behaved, they no longer spring
from my nightmares, fangs dripping to frighten people.
Instead, they come properly dressed
to dine with me, sip tea with my friends.
No more wailing and braying at full moons.
They sit quietly now, smiling
in white tie and tails
while audiences marvel at how well-behaved they are.
yet,
      imperfect still
when I leave the room
your ghosts whisper behind their hands saying,
pay her no mind, saying
she was always an imaginative child.

Keeping Daddy's Secret

I

She kept his secrets hidden
in pockets of cotton dresses
where she tucked the soiled tissue
on which she wiped her six-year-old nose.
He was the good father
She was the nasty child who touched her father's thing
of course she could not tell.

II

For forty summers she kept his slimy secret
carried it, cocooned
in pockets where it stained her clothes,
gnawed like rats at her self esteem
while pigeons cooed
on the window ledge of sunlit rooms
in which she used to call him daddy.

III

And when grownups asked why,
when they wondered aloud why he
placed her in bed with him
she would not tell.
She bit her lower lip and stared down
at her patent leather shoes
refusing to let it out.

IV

He was the good father.
She was the nasty girl who touched her father's thing
while pigeons cooed on the window ledge.
You think she dared to tell?
and later playing jacks on the steps with a cousin
She heard him tell,
        his version
stupid with shock she listened to his voice

slurred with gin,
   saying:
"Yeah, and when I woke up
she was playing with my thing!"
The men nearby
their faces awash with amused disbelief ask
   "Who?"
and he smiles repeats the lie
   his voice ringing with fake shock
   "Sis! he said, "Sis did it!"
and he points her out on the steps
while she stares back
   ashamed,
clutching the jacks in her hand
   ashamed
and the droppings of pigeons cake
the window ledge
seal in her guilt
   the way he sealed her to the mattress.

V

For forty years
she has been scaled by his blame,
held his slimy shame to her bosom
as if it were her own
she has been the nasty child
who played with her father's thing
the dirty one,
Laminated in the filth that spread
from the window ledge.

VI

I have grown weary of keeping your secret
Have gone back to the attic and turned on the light
not caring that pigeons startle
and scatter in fright.
You were not the good father
I was not the naughty child
there was no sunlight in that room

only lies and shame
that settled in my pores like soot
on the window ledge.

To set the record straight
I have only to write it down on paper
speak the words aloud
      name it
incest incest
      shame, shame
your shame,
      incest
your guilt
      shame.

You were not the good father.
It was not something I did to you
it was something you did to me
I had no control
not then
I do now
      Now, I see the truth and know
      the shame belongs to you.

      It was you
    pedophile, pedophile
      shame

Incest, Incest.
      Shame
May god forgive you for I shall not.

Woman Giving Birth to Herself

Jacqueline Carr

ART HAS BEEN a part of my life for as long as I can remember. Even as a child, I spent a lot of time and energy on art. As time passed, this attraction grew more intense within me, until by the time I was eleven and twelve, I had become very passionate about creating art. Two significant things stand out in my memory from this time in my life. I began seeing an image of myself standing in front of an easel with a crayon in my hand. I would put the crayon on the paper ready to draw, but I would draw so hard I would rip the paper down from the easel. I felt no piece of paper could hold the intensity of my feelings, but I didn't understand why. Also around this time, my father increased the frequency and intensity of the sexual abuse, an abuse that I later discovered had been occurring since I was about five. Looking back at these events now, I realize my art became an outlet for the sexual abuse at a much earlier age than I had always believed.

Art has been a powerful catalyst in healing from incest. During my most difficult times of struggling to confront and understand the sexual abuse, I was able to release my feelings secretly and express my most intense emotions through art. Creating art helped me become more in touch with myself and face my emotions surrounding the incest. My artwork also pinpointed different periods of time in the healing process for me. I could flip back in my sketchbook and look at my earlier art to see what I was feeling and working on at a particular time. Looking at it helped me realize that I was making some progress in the long journey to wellness that often seemed far off in the distance.

The *Mandala Shield* is a significant work for me because it represents my pain and anger at not being protected from the sexual abuse. It is about my twelve-year-old inner child who stood silent but full of secrets, wanting so much to share the pain with someone. It is about the sharp hurtful edges inside of me that resulted from holding in the suffering. It is about the awareness that I grew into knowing: that I have the ability to protect myself.

Both as a child and as an adult, I frequently had nightmares

Mandala Shield, 1989,
16″ × 20″, tempera paint &
India ink

that related to the sexual abuse. An image in a dream would terrify me and become branded in my mind so that I couldn't close my eyes without seeing it. At times, the image would be so strong that even with my eyes open I would see it. I became haunted by the image and I couldn't seem to banish it from my vision. This happened frequently when I was working on healing from the sexual abuse. During that time, I tried drawing the terrifying images in my dreams. I found that by putting the scene or image from the dream down on paper, I was able to release the image and emotions that haunted me. Looking at the image after I drew it helped me to deal with the fears expressed in my dreams.

Like the images from my dreams that branded my mind, the repetition of certain sounds relating to the sexual abuse also imprinted my memory. In the piece *Washing His Hands of Me,* I illustrated an extremely shameful memory of my father washing his hands after he sexually abused me. Every time my father finished

touching me, he walked directly from my bed into the bathroom. As I lay in bed, I could hear him pull out the faucet, grope for the soap, rinse his hands under the running water, push back in the faucet, dry his hands and walk quickly out of the bathroom. The sound of his running the water always made me shudder. I desperately wanted to shut out the noise and disappear. I believed that I must be dirty for him to want to go wash his hands immediately afterward. It was very healing to express this secret of feeling unclean that I had carried around for so many years.

Creating art about the incest often triggered pain, horror, rage and deep sadness, while at other times it helped free me from the blackness that I struggled to escape. Sometimes I was afraid to work on art because I knew it would bring on emotions in such a pure form that it might be too much to handle. I was afraid that in feeling the rage and pain I might get out of control. And being out of control was not acceptable to me, because it was a leap into the unknown. The following is an excerpt from my journal. It describes what happened after I worked on art that triggered buried memories and emotions.

> I drove home after class and came home to an empty house. I was relieved that I didn't have to deal with anyone. I ate my Rocky's pizza and watched M*A*S*H because I was afraid of facing myself. All day long I had been haunted by imagery of the large vertical wound or gash that ran the length of my torso. I hated it because it became indistinguishable from the opening of the vagina. I wanted to draw, but I kept making

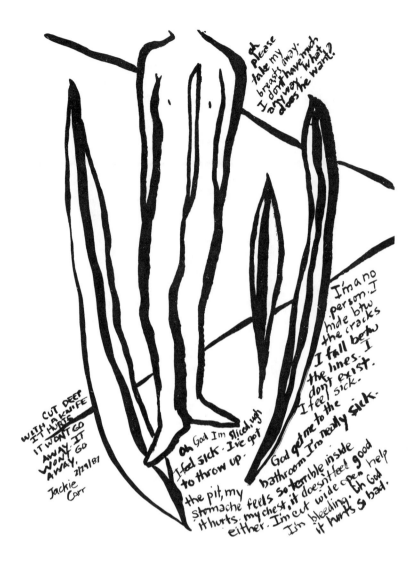

The Gash, 1987, 11″ × 14″,
India ink

excuses to myself. After I finally got my shit together, I was at the table and painting with India ink. I drew the gash image. It was very painful and scary. I wrote down a lot of feelings. I remember how I wrote about wanting to throw up. After I finished that piece, I felt like I needed to do another drawing of the same thing, this first one just wasn't good enough. So I painted another gash—an adolescent female figure just like the first one, and then I lost it. I went out of control for a good hour and a half. I screamed, sobbed, pounded the walls around me and hit my head against the wall. The pain and rage felt too much to bear. I finally was able to pick up the phone and call my friend. I told him I was afraid of myself and needed him to come over as soon as possible. It took me quite a while to calm down, but after a while my friend convinced me to go out for a drink. It's hard to believe I became calm enough to do that. God, was I wiped out that night. It's so strange, it's always been my worst fear to go out of control. But I did I experienced one of my worst fears and I'm still O.K. It's really amazing.

Creating the piece *The Gash* (described in the excerpt) and allowing myself to lose control and get in touch with my rage was a turning point in my healing process. Before *The Gash* I had worked only in black and white. After, I began creating art in color, using oil pastels. I found an intensity in color that I had never experienced before. After working on two pieces in color, I wrote in my journal about the excitement I felt.

> I'm doing my second piece in the color series—Oh it feels wonderful.
>> Each piece is beautiful and precious
>> Each color represents a special part of me
>> Some of me is bruised, blue and brown
>> Some is filled with fury and fire
>> Some is silent and blue
>> Some is screaming for words to describe this feeling of being silent and helpless.
> But throughout it all there is black lifting up and out. At times it's only in my head—on paper it still is not there yet.

> Colors mix and weave themselves into one another. Some colors some say they don't belong with one another, but I can make them work.
>> Some of me is dark, still so unsure and scared
>> Take it slow—Savor this quiet happy period
>> Fear, wonder... what will happen next
>> My art speaks of who and what I am becoming
>> I want it to be beautiful.

The gash symbolized the pain of the sexual abuse for me. It continued to be a part of the artwork I did. At times, I would examine it up close, or include it in the background of a piece, or display it repeatedly as part of a nude adolescent figure. As time passed, the wound or gash became smaller and my drawings of female figures became more round and womanly. I was able to draw a bare-breasted woman without wanting to destroy it, and then slowly I began drawing nude self-portraits. It felt scary at first to draw myself nude, somehow feeling that this was not O.K. to do. The most recent piece I have done in this series was a full nude of my-

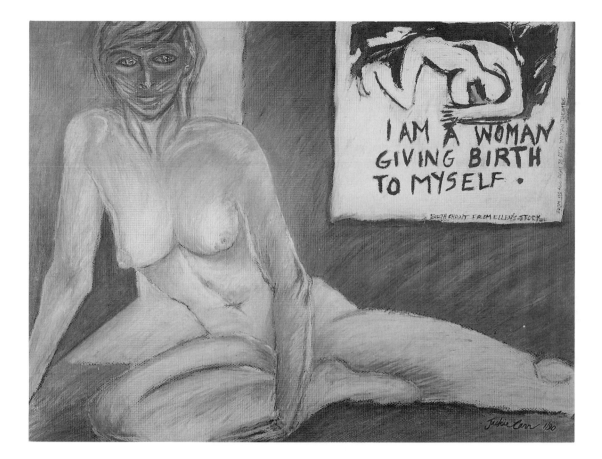

I am a Woman Giving Birth to
Herself, 1990, 25″ × 19″, oil
pastel & India ink

self larger than any work I had done. It was exciting because I felt
for the first time an acceptance of my body and felt unashamed to
draw it. I struggled with the face and finally felt at peace with the
cat-like quality I had given it. I love the symbol of the lioness; for
me she is the beautiful, strong mother-leader. There is no gash in
the lioness-woman's body. She is open and beautiful. The words
on the piece say "I am a woman giving birth to myself." I felt
those words were appropriate after experiencing the long and
very painful process of healing from incest. Giving birth is a very
painful process, but the result is a celebration of new life. The new
life is what I feel I am beginning to live.

A Rising Phoenix

Lalla Lepeschkin

I
N JANUARY OF 1987, I dreamt I lit the gas heater in my home
studio and exploded the entire structure. I found myself flying
over what had been my home. Nothing was left. I was
amazed at the sight of an empty grassy field with trees. Nature
had survived the explosion, but nothing man-made remained. In
the months afterward, I had no insight into the dream, yet I experienced a growing anxiety.

A year later, I was plunged into what seemed a very dark
cave. There was no light at the end, and though my mind strained
to find hope and distractions to ease my pain, I was in a deep depression and terrified. Oh, there were triggers, of course. My
third marriage had failed and I had filed for divorce. I felt betrayed
and needed to take control out of fear of more abandonment.
During this time my first husband, the father of my three children, had died awaiting tests for a liver transplant. He had bled to
death from advanced cirrhosis caused by alcoholism. I sat with his
bloated body for an hour, forcing myself to be with death for the
first time in my life. As a child of seven, I had refused to look at
my father's dead body, and had not attended his funeral. He had
been killed in a furnace explosion. On the day of my ex-husband's
memorial service, my daughter-in-law went into labor and gave
birth to premature twins. I had excitedly anticipated my first experience of grandmothering and had expected that the joy of new
life would lift me from my losses. One granddaughter died in five
days and the other was due to die any day from a cerebral spinal-
fluid hemorrhage and infection.

At fifty-one years of age, with all the intellectual knowledge,
experience and theories I had accumulated over thirty years as an
artist, wife of three different men, mother of three, grandmother,
therapist/therapee, and book junkie, I felt I knew nothing. The
belief systems that fabricated my identity had crumbled. I knew I
had lost control.

I went into my studio and gave myself permission to paint
whatever my inner child directed me to do, thinking I had nothing to lose but probably nothing to gain. My despair felt ultimate,

The Hurt Child, 1990, 10″ ×
10″, ink wash

yet my hands seemed to move with a life of their own. I began by
making messes with paint on the canvas. Then the colors and
shapes seemed to grow with a force of their own making. Figures
emerged, tormented, angry and in terrible pain. I was shocked at
their expressions and postures. I could not recall living through
these pictorial dramas in real life. What surfaced were my denied
feelings, buried from childhood. My body trembled in fear, my
stomach clenched itself in revulsion and shame as these powerful
images sprang forth from my hands. My eyes filled with wonder.
My inner child was portraying on canvas and paper clearly what
she had felt and experienced as a victim of incest. Pride and a
fierce self-determinate independence had always been my closest
intimates. Again and again, my head fought for control and lost.

Compartments of rationality and understanding had little
bearing on what my body was expressing through these images.

Throughout the years, I had lost touch with my terrified inner child and would not surrender to her. My mind had minimized or effectively blocked out these painful experiences, and it wasn't until I gave myself full permission to paint the emotional integrity held in my body, without preconception or control, that these past experiences could come forth. These paintings were the beginning of my journey of recovering memories, releasing my rage, fear, pain and grief into healing.

I sat with a pencil, staring at the images and wrote:

Stepfather giant demon sniffs at me like a frantic furtive dog
hoping to find a bitch in heat.
My body rages in terror and humiliation.
Like a cat, I slink off
silently screaming indignities.
In confusion with my body's desires,
I squirm and burn inside.
Penis snakes writhe everywhere.
I am obsessed by their power.
I quake with shame.
The more I hide, the more he seeks.
Moma tells me I'm making it all up and that once
     upon a time,
she thought bad things like that about her stepfather.
I have no safety anywhere.
I turn to my older brother who attempts to confront
HIM
My brother is shouted down in roaring denial
and leaves to survive.
I turn to a bottle of aspirin. I want to die.
I find no sweetness only bitter acid.
I turn to a Catholic priest who says, "Go do 100 Hail Mary's
and sin no more."
I turn to marriage at 18 and weep in fear of men,
shamed of my sexuality,
my womanliness.

After several months of painting and writing, I began to open up to myself and own my reality. I, who could never do it right, make it right, make it go away or fix it forever. I, who grew to recognize and attend to other's pain and vulnerabilities. I, who had a love/hate relationship with pain, serviced it with shame. I, who sabotaged any successes that came my way by withdrawing from personal recognition and focusing on others. I, who could not face the appreciative mirror I held, always turned towards others. Pitiful, but pity isn't healing. Anger and grief are.

From this experience, I envisioned the "Recovery Show." I shakily called friends, therapists, strangers—professionals and novices in imagemaking, to ask if they had interest in helping me create a recovery show. Many were from incest survivor 12-step groups and were closet artists, processing their inner worlds privately in poetry, painting, sculpture, photography and music. I wanted to expose my inner child's reality to the light of day. I was known for my beautiful abstract landscapes, not my figurative horror images. I felt the fear of people's judgments. We all did.

With the help of a core group of incest survivors, we scoured the community for financial and in-kind support to make the "Recovery Show" happen. The call for entries brought over two hundred responses, more than the exhibit space could hold. Three sets of jurors were selected, all of whom were in recovery from childhood abuse, and each juror was an expert in one of the categories: poetry, visual art and performance pieces. The jurying process was difficult, at times painful. The catch-22 was that by not including all who submitted their work, we'd be re-stimulating and creating feelings of rejection. In the process of jurying we had to open our hearts to the message each work expressed and to each other. We had to suspend our personal aesthetic judgments as artists and let the images speak to our imaginations. There were times when silence spoke to the gravity of feeling resonating from the work. We did not include work that expressed surface perfection or exquisite technical proficiency without a crack into the emotional depth and vulnerability of the creator. Out of this process, two "Recovery Shows" came about that touched and embraced the frightened isolation and vulnerability of all who participated.

To be there with my very personal secrets and those of others—put out there, hanging on the walls, being seen, read and listened to by strangers—was terrifying and exhilarating. Fear and excitement feel the same to a fast-beating heart. This experience opened me to a deeper compassion for humanity, mine and others. We held together in strength and in honor, belonging to ourselves and to the creation of a community of survivors. We celebrated the release of our shame to a deeper healing and trust in our own being. We celebrated our right to express, to be seen, heard and take up space in the world. Some participants initially responded to seeing their work on the wall by wanting to hide, and then felt moved, honored and amazed when hearing people comment, "I'm blown away by the guts it must have taken to do this, to deal with their pain so openly!" For some it became a stepping stone to gaining more strength to carry on the process of recovery, and for others an all-time first in taking themselves seriously as artists with something important to say and moving on

Right, *The Origins of War— Personal,* 1988, 18" × 24", monotype and craypa

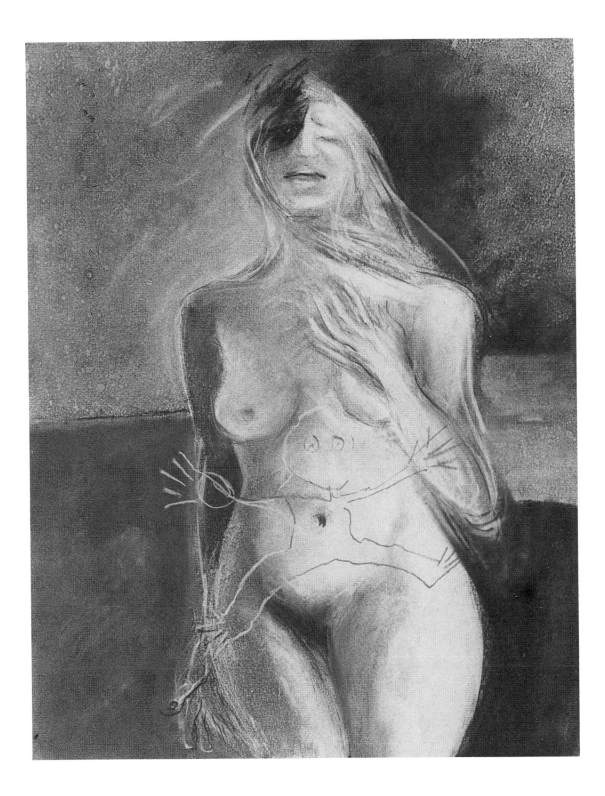

to careers of professional art making.

The "Recovery Shows" became community collaborations, events by risk-takers, who responded to the call and revealed their emotional truth with heartfelt courage to over 1,500 people. Many came to Santa Fe, New Mexico from both coasts of the United States to experience these two events and were moved to begin their own journey into recovery. My vision is to inspire this event throughout the world as community.

The Promise

Yoná Flemming

I DID NOT REMEMBER being molested until I reached the age of forty-one, having completely repressed conscious memory of the sexual and other physical abuse inflicted on me as a young child by my father.

I grew up to be a very dysfunctional adult, living a dramatic and tortured inner life and a passive fearful outer life. I was aware of an incredible grief at the center of my being, with no clue to its cause. Because there seemed to be no reason for so much pain, I was critical of having it. This made me feel crazy. I was shy, self-conscious, introverted and subject to long, deep depressions. Injustice and pain in the world deeply affected me, especially where children, Third World people and women were involved. I strongly identified with oppressed peoples.

At age twenty-one, I met and married a man who was eighteen years older than I and a practicing alcoholic. We set about creating a life built on denial and fantasy. We became part of a colorful but nonproductive subculture, living mostly in rural areas in abject poverty. In looking back, I can see that we could barely cope with the realities of adult life, including the care of our two sons. Although I was spared addiction to alcohol, the chaotic lifestyle of alcoholism and poverty engulfed me throughout nineteen years of marriage.

As I prepared to leave my marriage, disturbing but vague and disjointed images started coming up, but I had no idea what they portended. A few weeks after I left, I had a devastating memory, and my denial system cracked open.

Since then I have been immersed in an effort to understand and heal, which has meant allowing the terror and agony of memories to emerge. This process, though necessary to my healing, is disabling and absolutely hellish.

I do have a gift, a saving grace as they say—something that kept me alive, or kept alive that part of myself that wanted to live: I love to create. Throughout my life, I have been passionately involved in different art forms: painting, music, filmmaking and writing.

I have written poetry since I was ten, but the meaning and source of my often tragic-sounding work had eluded me. As memories came, the meaning finally became clear. The poems were recordings of the psychological effects of my childhood experiences and, in some cases, descriptions of the healing process that was to take place.

The Making of *Boneseed*

In spite of shyness and introversion, my creative drive sometimes compelled me into situations that required considerable skill in dealing with the public and with groups. Over the course of my life, I have been a member of a women's art group and a women's writing group. I co-founded, co-directed and performed as a drummer in a music and dance troupe, and, most recently, I wrote, directed and produced this theater event I call *Boneseed*.

Other forces propelled me into this project. After years of an intense struggle with the realities of my childhood, I had begun to recognize the extent of the damage done to me, and the enormity of the issue of incest in general. I felt I wanted the world to know; I needed to publicly break my silence and, in doing so, perhaps help other victims of incest. I became absolutely committed to the completion of this work.

The project started with a simple idea. I picked the poems of mine that meant the most to me and wrote a narrative around them. I asked a friend to read the material publicly and maybe even sing some of the poems. Another friend became interested. As we met and talked, more women were drawn to the project. Some were dancers and drummers, students of African culture, as I was. We decided to incorporate the drum, which had a great significance in my life, and dance into what was becoming a theater piece. We eventually included slides, a clip from a movie I had made, a simple set and costumes for the dancers.

The project had grown to include more than eight women and incorporated all the creative forms I'd worked with. It pushed me far beyond what I thought were my limits. I had no experience directing, and most of the members had no experience acting or performing. Half of us were incest survivors in various stages of recovery. Besides classic group dynamics, the content of the play regularly provoked pain, despair, terror, rage and, in some cases, incest memories. At least half of each rehearsal was spent processing myriad complicated, painful issues. In spite of these difficulties, no one left the project. We created rituals at every rehearsal to help ground and protect us. We confronted, comforted and empowered each other. As we worked together, we overcame to a large extent the distrust that is ingrained in incest survivors. A deep bonding took place. We also began to feel like warriors. We made masks and wooden spears together for the triumphal Spear Dance at the end of the piece.

Each time we worked with the poems, I saw more and more clearly that they contained an irrefutable inner wisdom. The poems "The bells of her youth" and "All I have loved" describe the death of the child, of hope and will. The poem "Base and longing" reveals the perversion of sexuality—the mixing of the longing to be loved with sex, pain and shame. The poem "The madwoman" tells of self-hatred and the neurotic behavior necessary to maintain denial. The poem "Down here" speaks of the survival through psychic exile to a place where my artist's self thrived. The poems "Preludes" and "She falls" foretell remembrance, and the poem "She rises" describes the breaking of silence in all its implications.

A major memory emerged during the work on *Boneseed*. It was connected to a memory I had had long before of a brutal violation by my father when I was five. In therapy, I noticed I was keeping my fingers crossed on one hand. When we explored this, I had the following memory: When my father was done, he got me to my feet and started straightening my clothes and hair. He was kneeling in front of me on one knee as he did this. I was standing, with my head down and my hands behind me. He made me look up at him and told me never to tell anyone. "Cross your heart and hope to die," he said as he made an x with his finger over my heart. I lowered my head and nodded yes. But behind my back, I had crossed my fingers! My promise to him was voided. I was making a promise to myself that someday I would tell. The play was the fulfillment of that promise.

Through this work, I experienced many things: extreme satisfaction at the validation of my words and experience; immeasurable gratitude for the dedication of this group of women; admiration, even awe for their willingness to open up on such vulnerable levels; and a deep sense of completion of mission, especially when the audience was moved, supportive, enlightened and encouraged.

What I didn't realize until a new group of us did the play again, was that I had become a good teacher and wise leader. I had learned patience, acceptance, belief in the good in people, and had been opened to the power of ritual as spiritual practice.

I continue to deal with new memories, as they seem to have a life/birth rate of their own, and I continue to create, lead and teach. I am not certain of what lies ahead, but I have come to believe in the element of prophecy in my poems.

In the poem "Mountain," what at first seemed impossible becomes a healing path that leads me "above the tree line," a place untouched, pure, bare, with magnificent sweeps of sculpted rock and clear, cold streams banked with small gardens of lush grass, wild herbs and flowers. It is the paradise of the joyful child who is loved and who loves—a child I am able to envision who trusts, who is fearless, who feels at home in the universe and with herself.

Boneseed
A Ritual Theater Event

Notes

"Boneseed" is the word Joan Halifax uses in her book *Shamanic Voices* to describe the initiation process of the shaman. "For the hunting and gathering peoples, bone, like seed, represents the very source of life... Where there is dismemberment in the beginning, there is remembrance in the end..."

The poems I wrote before remembering incest will be marked with an asterisk.

In the first production, there were three actors/musicians, four dancers, six technicians and many advisors and contributors.

The set was plain, black backdrops with a tree in one corner and a moon.

I have combined the scripts of the first and the second productions.

Boneseed was written in 1986 and performed at Sonoma State University in January and November of 1987.

Boneseed Script

Dark stage.
Ritual bell is sounded.
Wind sound offstage.
Lights up to dim.

Messenger appears
dancer with spear
seems to be urgently
searching for something.
Low drumming offstage.
Stage darkens as figure
exits.

*

Sung offstage in   The bells of her youth are silent
darkness.

She is the sea virgin
locked on the curve
of her own beaches.
blood-bird on the sand.

It is the stone beneath her hand.
The blinded heart of innocence.

*

Dim light. Actor to   Sorrow shall mark the roots of life
one side. Four figures   and henceforth
move slowly in group   all joys shall know the undertone
at back of stage.   of grief—an echo of existence.

*

Light comes up   All I have loved
slightly.   or was fixed in me
is twice undone
All the furies spent
all the weeping battles lost.

*

Light all the way up   Preludes in a forest of reserve
actor urgently addressing the dam is heaving outward
audience. All run offstage, the hill is trembling,
at end.   the frozen river is cracking
its ice.

The rumbling of a loosened world
clouds the horizon.

*

She falls like a prophet crying.
The winded night fills
her thoughts.
She lies face down.
in the crook of her own arm
in the dawn of her own thoughts.

She falls.

I remembered when I was 41.
After leaving a long, sad
marriage, after a lifetime in
darkness, after bearing and
raising two children, after a year in
therapy.

I remembered with a flood of emotions,
a river breaking the dam covering
the lowlands with a lake of sorrow.

My grief was as deep as when I was a
child, as if someone I loved had died.
I raged but still could not fully believe.

There was no safe place, no justice,
no appeal, no end to awful possibility.
Where were the lines of right and wrong
if my father had none? Where was a
foundation to stand on? Why, why had
this little girl not been protected?

I began to understand the pain and
confusion that had plagued and
baffled me all my life.
I had a context at last... a kind of
justification.

Stage darkens.

*Lights up, one woman
sings through
once. One at a time
others form semi-
circle. All sing a
second time. Stage
darkens. All exit.*

Narrator. Lights up.

*Parts of this last
line are repeated
by others offstage
as stage darkens.
Slides of us as
children shown.*

Lights up.

I WASN'T CRACY.

Fade.

*Lights up. Actor
stands at back
of stage.*

My outrage, even at age five, had
been so great. I had sworn to murder
my father and make my mother pay for
her weakness. But stronger than my
outrage was an intense mortification.
I was used against my will.
I was here to please my father.
I had no power.

The world became empty and terrifying.

Instead of murdering him, I murdered
myself.

*

Another actor.

Base and longing
dragged to tender treasures
of the flesh
rejoice and foul regret
the child and the dead
so shamed for loneliness.

*The last poem and
Outrage section before
it are interwoven
here.*

Narrator.

The soft joyful child was
extinguished, locked away in a
deep cavern. In that moment of
death, I left my body and split
into many selves. One was the
warrior who lived at the bottom
of a huge lake of sorrow, roaming
about filled with seething, murderous rage and unbounded grief. Another
was the mourner, who knelt at the
lake's edge weeping piteously and
endlessly into the bitter grey waters.
My conscious self grew up secretive,
manipulative, living in circles of
fear, haunted by nameless bottomless
longing—one who lived a humorless
life of poverty and bewildering des-

pair, out of context, unable to
perceive the world or her own
feelings.

Crazy laughter offstage.

*

In the thorn bush
a madwoman drinks her dregs.

Actor leaps on stage.

She loves her cage
and forbids the forgiveness
of her crimes.

She lives in the pit of disaster
pain to pain
impotent with the passions
of her sorrow
and revenge.

Stage darkens.

*

Daughter of braided hair
holds a knife of fire.

*Spot on actor with
knife. She steps out
of spot at end.*

Her head lowered
seemingly submissive

She waits for the right moment.

Stage darkens.

Instead of murdering him,
I murdered myself.

*Whispered by all
offstage.*

*Slides of powerful
female shamanic
images.*

*

Down here
in my underground caverns
I wear simple white clothes

*Actor puts moon up as
she talks.
Mist.*

Wind and anger walk with me.

YONÁ FLEMMING   261

Bells sounding
water roaring
trees rooted deep inside,
their leaves,
my dreams.

Here, I am like the deepest river:
my own myth lives
unchallenged.

Stage dims.
Bells begin.
Dancers do "Down Here"
dance.

Narrator.

I became an artist and writer
at a young age, working with urgency
and moments of deep joy.

The memories and feelings locked so
fiercely away swam up into my work,
messages from the warrior and the
mourner. They spoke of what had
passed, what was in progress, and
what was to come, their meaning
undeciphered but compelling.

This poem interwoven:

Yesterday, I began
to practice
how to be alive.

And the journey was begun to find
knowledge and freedom—the truth at
all costs.

Death

Journey

Stage darkens.

Recognition

One light silhouettes
figure moving
towards us as if
on a tightrope. Four
actors stand to side
and speak sections
separately.

The little girl is finally here,
a vision or a nightmare

She stands with dark all around her
alone and abandoned.

As she approaches,
she casts bolts of light

radiant in her innocence
and power.

Yet she wants to die.
She has finally arrived
and wants to die.

Lights up. Figure
starts to convulse
and collapse. Four women
circle her, wailing.
Abruptly, wailing becomes
single wolf howl. Stage
darkens. Slides of wolf.

Movie clip.
At end, bells start
and dancers line up
at rear of stage.
Bells fade.

She rises like a prophet.
She rises and comes running,
running here to wash in our river,
in the magic water of rivers,
in the earth's blood.

Lights up. Poem
started by one actor
She is joined by
two others who add
their voices to the
poem. All have masks.
At the last line,
actors back off to
drums at side of
stage.

She comes running.
her body washed with blood,
her hair wound with wings
and thunder.

Messenger rushes on
stage and spears
spot with triumphant
scream.
Deep bottom drum
sounds. The dancers
begin "Spear Dance."
At end, stage darkens,
mountain slides are
shown.

Mountain,
quest for myself
lost so young in life.

Poem is sung and then
spoken by actor who
joins singer on
stage. Use spot.

Dancers stay down at
rear of stage.

I see the peak now
lit with rising sun
I climb above the tree line.

The approach is breathtaking,
The stumbling becoming surefooted

Fade to darkness.

The mountain becoming friend.

Spoken on stage in
darkness.

This is the dark one
the one who brings messages
of memories and pain.

Ritual bell is sounded.

the ghoul of truth.
the one
who will set you
free

END

More notes

    After each performance we offered a sharing circle to the audience. We did this because we needed to connect in person with them and we wanted to hear their reactions. It was a very moving experience. We sat in a circle, did a grounding ceremony and then passed a "power object" one by one to allow each who wished to, to speak.

    The piece lasted about 35 minutes.

To Be Seen Speaking:
Artists Healing Together

Louise M. Wisechild

OVER TWO YEARS ago, I facilitated an eight-week group for women on healing from incest through creativity. As a survivor, I had found that working with my own creativity allowed me to go deeply into my memories and emotions and to make meaning from this inner territory. In creativity, memory moves between metaphor and reality and between what was and what might be. The act of creating releases pain, rage, inspiration and power from the body into a medium of expression, into a form. I knew that creativity also allowed women to break the taboo on telling. By making telling a creative process, I believed that survivors could remake themselves as well, finding image and language not only for what happened, but also for what heals.

As a professional teacher and bodyworker specializing in work with survivors, I hoped that my skills and experiences would lay a foundation for the group to continue on its own as a peer support group. I wanted to provide a common experience in which the group could establish safety and explore creative methods of working with incest. Because of the number of survivors needing long-term support groups, it seemed essential to me that groups become ongoing without continuing to pay a facilitator. Acting as a seed person rather than a long-term group leader also enabled me to work with several groups instead of devoting my energies to one ongoing group. As a feminist, I believe that this continues the work that consciousness-raising groups began—by suggesting structures where each woman's creative voice is valued, where each woman is empowered in speaking what is most true for herself and where each woman can learn, from other women, important truths for her own healing.

In preparing for the group, I realized that although I identified myself largely as a writer and increasingly as a singer, I had, in fact, drawn on a number of creative media in my personal healing work. I wanted to encourage women to explore artforms that were unfamiliar as well as those they were already involved with. Our meetings included movement, body awareness and visualization exercises directed toward helping each woman increase her awareness of her own inner journey as an incest survivor; a journey involving memory, inner children, emotion, body and survival. To express this journey, I drew on a variety of creative media—including sand trays, in which objects are intuitively placed in baskets of sand to represent the internal landscape and shields, in which a paper plate is decorated with power symbols and worn over a vulnerable area of the body. Mandalas, drawing, poetry, rhythm, music, ritual and exercises that combined visual art with words were also used as creative forms for expressing this journey. "Check in," group sharing of what had been made in the group or the process of making it, and time each week for one woman to share what she made outside of the group were also integral parts of our work. After four meetings, each member also brought an exercise to teach the group.

As the facilitator, it was my job not only to structure these initial meetings but to lead the group in the creation of a safe place in which each woman's journey and art would be respected and valued. Incest is an incredibly intimate issue, fraught with our deepest fears and vulnerabilities—and art also comes from this deep, sensitive place. The group included women sexually abused by their fathers, mothers, uncles, siblings and by cults. One of my requirements for the group was that each woman have other support—to have been or be currently in therapy or to have a strong support network for her work as a survivor.

Each week, as I cleaned my apartment and lit the candles for our meeting, I felt a growing excitement about the work these women were doing and the observations they had about their creativity and their journey. In addition to sharing healing, we also had fun together (a word seldom associated with healing from incest, but often associated with child-based creativity). I enjoyed the company of these women and missed them when our eight weeks was completed and they moved on to meet in their own living rooms.

Four of the initial six group members continued to meet once a week for a year and then biweekly. I attended their first reading and show and read with them at Kim Newall's art show at Pacific Lutheran University. Both times I was impressed with how they created an atmosphere of healing and empowerment—both with their art and with their use of woman-centered ritual to create a sacred space for their work and the women viewing it.

So it was with a sense of awe and a bit of nervous apprehension that I went to visit this group again and question them about what the group had experienced in their two years of meeting without me. Kim Newall, Shey Bird, Joanne Barrie Lynn and Judy Bierman were seated in Judy's living room when I arrived, amidst candles and with a fire in the wood stove. As I sat again in this circle, I felt the warm feeling that comes from sitting in a group of strong women who respect each other while sitting each one solidly within herself.

"What have you gotten from meeting and working together?" I wanted to know. "How has it been important to you?"

"What I say about incest is taken seriously here," Joanne said. "Here is a sacred place and time to work on the incest, to make from it. It's a place where I can bring new poems. A place where I am both public—because I'm speaking and sharing my work—and private, because I know that what I say won't go outside this group."

"I know that as a professional artist, I would have shown my art anyway," Kim said. "But here I've developed a commitment to a public presence that says clearly, 'I am an incest survivor and this is what my work is about.' It brought me directly to the challenge of being seen speaking. I've developed my commitment to a public presence in being public with this group, with the support of this group in doing what I do individually and with a language learned in this group.

"We also do projects together that I wouldn't do by myself but that I've wanted to do—like the body tracings we're doing together now. I'm able to share my feelings with the group as I draw on and write about this full length image of my body."

"For me it's been a validation of the linkage between art and healing," Shey said. "Because in this group, I see us healing. For all of us, to speak the incest out loud in a group is against everything we ever learned. I've been able to move to defining myself as an artist and a writer as well, because it is valued here. I like to be active too, and here we 'do' instead of just talking."

"I'm still making the transition to defining myself as an artist and writer," Judy said. "Five years ago, I had never shared my writing with anyone, it was entirely private. Now, when I'm writing with the group, I know I'm a writer and I can feel that broadening, especially when we read and show our work together."

As is true for many women in incest support groups, the group spoke also of the importance of having a safe place to talk about being survivors and to exchange information on the issues they were dealing with. Yet it was also clear that coming together as survivors working with art encouraged each member to connect her art with her healing and to be public with her work. Joanne noted that Kim's profound respect for her own art and insistence that those around her also respect their art had taught her a lot about taking her creative work seriously.

Over a year ago, the group created a mural together, which they hung at their first reading. "I remember when we made that, we were all so careful not to get in anyone else's allotted space," Judy said. "Now we're doing the body tracings on separate pieces of paper, but more of our imagery is coming together."

"Yeah," Shey said, "all of our pictures have beaks and two of them have wings—even though we didn't look at each other's papers as we were working."

"I've wondered if we're tapping a more universal imagery," Kim added.

"I also have never drawn, and I wouldn't do it anywhere else," Joanne said. "But here we're drawing and writing about what we've drawn with the goal of having our work be both healing and with eventually presenting it publicly."

"When we're working on the body tracings—even though we're each working on our own piece of paper—I feel like the group's working together. It's a different feeling than the one I had when we were working on the mural," Judy said.

"And now," she continued, "if one of us is tired of writing or drawing, we just say so and then we do something else."

"It takes a lot of comfort to say, 'I want to do something else now' while everyone else is scribbling away," I commented. "And clearly, as we talk, you seem to have an ease about saying what you feel and think in front of each other. How did you get to this point?"

The group agreed that the initial group had been useful in creating a sense of safety and trust and in suggesting alternatives that they might explore. In transitioning from a facilitated to a peer group, they spent several sessions just talking about who they were, what they were experiencing as survivors and creative artists, as well as sharing ideas for how they might proceed. Shey's hot tub and their conversations held in moonlight to the hooting of owls helped them deepen the trust they needed to continue taking risks in working together. After this they spent some meetings just writing together, but always with some time for "check in."

Each woman also became increasingly aware of her own patterns within the group and they addressed these with each other, tracing the roots of the fear and isolation survivors often feel in group situations.

"There were several times when I felt like I couldn't keep doing this," Kim said. "But I just kept trying and putting out the issues as they came up."

"We learned that when something comes up, we need to go to that place," Shey said.

Everyone agreed that the decision to be public as a group was very significant in their evolution as a group. Yet the group did not decide on this as a primary focus until after their two public presentations.

"We kept meeting after the readings," Judy said, "but we sensed that something was missing. We discovered that even though being public raised a lot of issues for us, we were all committed to it. We wanted to make something to share together and we needed that focus."

"So we started the body tracings," Judy continued. "We wanted an ongoing project to commit to, something with a long-term public angle. We're thinking of creating a book about this work or of offering a workshop."

"The body tracings have made it easier to come to group as well," Joanne added, "because I know what we'll be doing. And here writing, drawing and talking are all part of the same project. I'm glad we've decided to be public with our work as well. As a survivor, I feel that I must be public in order to protect and honor myself, my inner children and my own children."

"I wonder if we were able to make being public as a group the focus because each of our individual work had expanded outside of the group. We were further in our own process and looking for a structure to push along our creative process as a group," Kim offered.

"So how might other women do this?" I wondered. "If you were going to give advice to other women in setting up a group like this, what would it be?"

"Be conscious about making a safe place," Shey said, "and know that each woman has to know and ask for what makes her safe."

What is most characteristic of this group is their respect for themselves and each other and their willingness to be honest about how they are feeling. This honesty allowed the structure of the group to continue changing to meet the needs of its members. Each woman was also able to feel supported by the group and to offer support without abandoning herself to caretaking someone else. An absolutely essential ingredient for an ongoing group around this issue is that each woman be centered in herself. They are also very conscious about leadership issues and are careful to make decisions by consensus. It is a group where equality is valued, even though the members are at different stages in their development as artists. As writers, visual artists and incest survivors, they were able to come from mediums and situations that are normally isolating into working collectively. "It's the link between art and healing again," Judy added, "that our focus is on finding creative ways to heal."

"I think one of the key elements is commitment," Kim said,

"to equal time for everyone and room to grow. With that is a clarity about power; that the object is not to have more power than anyone else, but to be empowered by every other woman in the group. I think this requires some awareness—that each woman must have done some work on herself and understand enough of her own issues to bring them up, so that the group has an ongoing vulnerability with each other. Asking herself, what can I do or not do? What should I say? No matter what happens in bringing this up, I'm going to at least try. There's also a commitment to making art and making art as survivors as well as to sharing publicly. This has given us the energy as a group to move toward something."

As I got up to leave I recalled standing with this group of women in their second group performance at Kim's show. Reading and singing with them, I felt profoundly part of a great transformative energy that was everywhere with us in the room. On the walls with Kim's paintings, in the words of Judy, Joanne and Shey and in the faces of an audience deeply moved by what they were witnessing and with which they were joining.

Once again, I felt incredibly cheered as I gathered my tape recorder and notebook and hugged everyone good-bye. The remark I hear most often from survivors is, "No one wants to hear my story." But here, as each woman makes her story, she is both seen and heard and encouraged to speak ever more loudly. Here she is encouraged to take her story seriously and to make art and herself from a place of deep knowing. We are only just beginning to find the power in sharing healing art with each other. The power of standing with each other and sharing our work with an audience. And, as in this group, the power of making art together; giving voice to what is collective and universal from that which is personal.

Contributor Notes

Judy Bierman is a forty-year-old lesbian who lives in Seattle. Three years ago, when her son was two, she began to recover the truth of her own childhood. Her writing and music have long offered her a private window into parts of her life that have felt too dangerous to touch directly. She has been a teacher for almost ten years and believes that teaching is an opportunity to give something back. She is happy to be able to share the process of growing up again, this time more gently, in the company of so many fine children and caring friends.

Shey Bird has been working for seven years to tip the balance in her life away from addiction and denial to greater feeling and freedom. She was beaten, raped and abandoned throughout her childhood, and must work with her early basic patterns and beliefs in order to affect her healing. She has no formal training in art or writing, but is guided on her creative, healing path by her feelings.

Becky Birtha is an African-American Quaker lesbian-feminist poet, fiction writer and mother. She was born October 11, 1948, in Hampton, Virginia, and grew up in Philadelphia, Pennsylvania, where she now lives. She began writing as a child with the encouragement of parents who loved literature. She has a degree in Children's Studies, a Master of Fine Arts in Writing and years spent in wonderful women writers' support groups. She worked for ten years as a pre-school teacher and another ten as a law librarian. She is author of two collections of short stories, *For Nights Like This One: Stories of Loving Women* (Frog in the Well, 1983) and *Lovers' Choice* (Seal, 1987), and one collection of poetry, *The Forbidden Poems* (Seal, 1991).

Julie Blackwomon was born in Virginia and raised in Philadelphia. A year ago when she was still keeping her father's secret, she felt it was her responsibility to shield her reading audiences from pain. Then she heard Sapphire, a strong African-American poet who is also a survivor, read her survivor's poems. Sapphire's words, which caught Julie at a time when she was able to hear them, made it possible for her to come out of her last closet, the one around incest. She hopes that this book and her work will help other survivors in a similar way. Julie's short stories appear in *Voyages Out 2.* (Seal, 1990).

Jacqueline Carr has been an artist from the time she was very young. She received her B.A. in Studio Art and continues to work with art in her free time. After graduating with an M.A. in Public Policy and Administration, she has chosen to focus her work on the social-economic aspects of women and minorities. She currently acts as an independent consultant for several evaluation firms and is enjoying co-parenting her lovely baby daughter. Born in Illinois, she now resides in Minneapolis, Minnesota.

Debby Earthdaughter is a thirty-year-old woman from German/unknown roots. She has recently moved from Boston to a women's campground near Tucson as a result of becoming disabled with environmental illness. Currently involved in disability activism, she is also finding out what it's like to be homeless, to live on welfare and deal with bureaucracy, and to have many spaces and events inaccessible due to toxins. Her energy now goes toward survival and creating access. Her dream is a land trust for lesbians with disabilities and their allies, and energy to create her art regularly again.

Heidi Eigenkind lives in Winnipeg, Manitoba, with her marriage partner and co-conspirator, Pat Treacy. She currently co-manages a women's bookstore, Bold Print Inc., and works on the publishing and editorial collectives of *Contemporary Verse 2,* a feminist poetry journal. In her un-scheduled time, she draws, writes, reads and indulges her Dragonish Self in the company of like-natured beings. Her work has appeared in two other anthologies: *Celebrating Canadian Women* (Fitzhenry & Whiteside, 1989) and *Living the Changes* (University of Manitoba Press, 1990), as well as in various Canadian feminist journals. Until 1989, her work was published under the name Heidi Muench.

Yoná Flemming continues her struggle with incest on a personal and political level. She is cur-rently compiling her writings and starting a book. She teaches conga drumming classes for women, performs and has a cleaning business. Twice a grandmother, she will celebrate her fifti-eth birthday this year. She lives in northern California.

Lynne Yamaguchi Fletcher is a Japanese-American poet who would love to connect with other Asian survivors. Her poetry appears in *The Forbidden Stitch: An Asian American Women's Anthology* (Calyx). She is also co-author of *Lavender Lists: New Lists about Lesbian and Gay Cul-ture, History and Personalities* (Alyson), and poetry co-editor of *Sojourner,* the feminist monthly. She lives in Massachusetts with the love of her life, and misses the Arizona desert deeply.

Ayofemi Folayan is an activist concerned with saving our planet and creating a world of peace and harmony. She pursues the end of all forms of violence and oppression through her creative energy as a writer. Her work has also been anthologized in *In a Different Light: An Anthology of Lesbian Writers; Spring Street; Lesbians at Midlife: The Creative Transition; Indivisible; Riding Desire;* and *Blood Whispers.* Her columns, essays, book reviews and short fiction have appeared in many publications. She is currently working on a new performance piece, "The Talking Drum," and finishing her novel, *Onyx.*

Judy Grahn is author of a ground-breaking Gay and Lesbian cultural history, *Another Mother Tongue: Gay Words, Gay World* (Beacon) as well as a number of books of poetry and a novel ex-ploring the goddess and the history of women in Western experience. Her newest poetry uses multitrack tape and effects for what she calls "virtual poetry." She is currently writing a book on how menstruation created the world. Her tape, *March to the Mother Sea: Healing Poems for Baby Girls Raped at Home* is available for $10.00 through Lavendar Rose Productions, Box 11164, Oak-land CA 94611.

Katherine F. H. Heart has utilized bodywork, creativity and spirituality within a womon-identified healing frame for more than ten years. She holds a masters degree in Health Education and certification in Psychophysical Therapy and maintains a private practice providing consul-tations and workshops for survivors and healers, as well as coordinating training programs at Pittsburgh Action Against Rape. She's shared her artwork and writing at exhibits, speakouts, conferences, universities and through the media. She is currently working on a book about the spiritual healing of incest. Katherine lives in Pittsburgh with her partner, Bern, and their furry family of four.

Beryl-Elise Hoffstein, a longtime resident of the Boston area, was born in 1953 in Philadelphia. A graduate of Brandeis University and a professional proofreader and copyeditor, she is currently working as a secretary in the Brandeis Department of English, hoping to pursue her literary interest. At home with her plants and three cats, she indulges her love of watching things grow and develop around her, including, unfortunately, items in her refrigerator and laundry hamper. She would like to thank Tanya Gardiner-Scott, Rick Reinkraut and her writing teachers Judith Grossman and Olga Broumas for their support and encouragement.

Catherine Houser lives on a small island off the southern coast of Massachusetts, where she is working to complete her novel, *To Be Worth Diamonds.* The work is slow, as she spends most her time teaching writing at Southeastern Massachusetts University, trying to get her students to open up to and write about the truths in their own bodies.

Jena was born and raised in Southern California, where competitive swimming was the focus of her life until she entered college. Majoring first in Advertising Illustration and later in English, she supported herself through eight years of college working as a bartender, bookkeeper, prep cook and bus driver. Eventually, she graduated with a degree in English, a newly raised and politically correct consciousness and a lot of school loans. After two years of eking out an existence as a swim coach, she accepted a teaching position in Japan, where she has been living for the past five years, and where memories of childhood abuse first surfaced. She plans to return to the United States and to continue painting.

Lalla Lepeschkin is an artist, writer, art therapist/psychotherapist and producer/director of the Recovery Shows in Santa Fe, New Mexico. She has worked with sexually and emotionally abused children, adults and groups in private practice since 1978. She has worked as a Civil Rights Specialist for the state of New Mexico and has been a professional painter for twenty-five years. Her work is in corporate and individual collections in the United States and Europe. She is the mother of three children and three grandchildren. She has also written a manual, *How to Create a Recovery Show.*

Patti Levey has used self-portrait photography as an artform as well as a mean of self-examination, empowerment and healing for eleven years. She has a masters degree in Clinical Psychology and Feminist Therapy and has worked with women survivors of childhood abuse, both as a therapist/intern and as a phototherapist. She has lived in San Francisco for nine years and is in the process of developing a practice using self-portrait photography as a healing tool with women.

Roseann Lloyd lives in Minneapolis. She works as a teacher and nonfiction writer. Her next book, forthcoming in August, 1991, was written with Merle Fossum, and is titled *True Selves* (Hazelden/Harper). She is the author of a book of poetry, *Tap Dancing for Big Mom* (New Rivers Press), and the co-author of *Journey Notes: Writing for Recovery and Spiritual Growth* (Hazelden/Harper) and co-editor of *Looking for Home: Women Writing About Exile* (Milkweed Press). *Looking for Home* is one of the books that received the American Book Awards 1991 from the Before Columbus Foundation.

Sherrin Loyd continues to recover memory, and is healing through the uses of singing, writing, dancing and walking meditation. When she has no voice, her hands speak through clay. Individual therapy, group therapy, sculpting at a community art center and attending Quaker meetings and retreats are all important tools that aid her in reclaiming her mind, her spirit, her fat body and her shattered faith. She is now, in mid-life, beginning a new career as a speech pathologist, helping others reclaim their lost or damaged voices.

Joanne Barrie Lynn is a Canadian living in the U.S. with her husband and seven-year-old son and her just-grown-up stepdaughters, whenever they can visit. She has published articles and poems in several magazines, and is working on a poetic autobiography of healing from incest.

Bonnie Martinez is a native New Yorker who presently lives in a large apartment/studio in Brooklyn with three cats and a dog. She is a lesbian with a married daughter named Rebeca. She started painting years after receiving a degree in Psychology. She teaches Spanish literacy and High School Equivalency Diploma preparation to adults to support herself. She spends every moment when she is not teaching in her studio. Bonnie's work is shown at the Ceres Gallery in New York.

Linda Ness is a self-taught artist who has lived and worked in Seattle for over twenty years. Her early work in the printing and graphics industry contributed to her own successful graphic arts career. In addition, her hundreds of paintings over the last sixteen years are evidence of her commitment to healing from the horrors of a childhood filled with physical, emotional and sexual abuse. Her paintings have been recognized and included in numerous exhibits in the Pacific Northwest.

Kim Newall is a lesbian artist who lives and works in Seattle. For over three years, she's been remembering the events and effects of her past through therapy and artmaking. Her work draws upon unconscious images that she may not understand until months or even years after completing them. She believes that creativity and healing are one process, and she is committed to sharing what she's learned through exhibiting, lecturing and teaching. She finds being a visual artist profoundly magical and elusive, and is glad she stayed alive to arrive here.

Margaret Randall's book, *This Is About Incest,* was published several years ago by Firebrand Press. She continues to read her poems of re-memory and healing to audiences at large events, as well as with smaller groups of survivors. Her most recent book, *Walking to the Edge: Essays of Resistance,* is just out from South End Press. In it, she further explores her conviction that the invasion of a body and the invasion of a people, or the earth, are simply different manifestations of the same disease: partriarchy, capitalism, imperialism.

Nancy Redwine lives in Seattle. She shares an apartment with Mr. Crowley, the cat. She was born in Monterey and grew up in First Assembly of God churches. She first spoke in tongues when she was twelve, the same year she began thinking of herself as a writer. Currently, she is completing a novel about incest and everything else. She writes a poem about once a year and stories and things like that more often. She has been published here and there. She loves garlic, women and her own stubbornness.

Janvier Rollande was born in Manchester, New Hampshire, in 1950 to Catholic French-Canadian working-class parents. She was the last of three children and the only girl in an alcoholic, incestuous family. She left home to live in the safety of a convent boarding school at fourteen. At nineteen, she dropped out of college to marry and had her daughter, Sarah, six years later. After divorcing, she returned to school and received a B.F.A. in Drawing and a B.A. in Art History in 1983. During this time, she studied, created, worked, mothered, began therapy and explored her lesbian identity. She lives in Amherst, Massachusetts, where she creates, loves her teenage daughter and continues her therapy and healing. She aspires to earn a living, to own a home with a studio, and to get a dog.

Vickie Sears is a Cherokee/Spanish/English and adopted Quileute writer, therapist and teacher happily living with her partner and her dog friend, Tsa·la·gi, in Seattle. Her poetry and nonfiction have been published in a variety of publications and books. Her fiction has been anthologized in *A Gathering of Spirit: Writing and Art by North American Indian Women* (Sinister Wisdom Books, 1984), *Gathering Ground: New Writing and Art by Northwest Women of Color* (Seal Press, 1984), *The Things That Divide Us* (Seal Press, 1985), *Hear the Silence* (Crossing Press, 1986), *Spider Woman's Granddaughters* (Beacon Press, 1989), *Dancing on the Rim of the World* (University of Arizona Press, 1990) and *Riding Desire* (forthcoming). Her first book, *Simple Songs: A Collection of Short Stories* (Firebrand Books, 1990), was nominated for a Lambda Literary Award. She is currently working on a novel, *One of Them Kids*.

Clarissa T. Sligh has had to resist pressures to 'speak for' black people and for women. She has found that she can best oppose the power structures she confronts by speaking from her particular experiences, and her work is about confronting those experiences. Much of her work draws on her own family photographs, which she examines for latent contents. In 1988 she received grants for photography from both the National Endowment for the Arts and the New York Foundation for the Arts. Her life and work has encompassed broad and diverse experiences, including work on the National Aeronautics and Space Administration's Manned Space Flight Project, employment as a financial analyst on Wall Street, and travels around the world.

Cheryl Marie Wade is a forty-three-year-old heavy-duty gimp who writes and performs and edits books. She resides in Berkeley, where she sometimes lives in her head because reality is too real. Saving graces in her life are her partner of thirteen years, their three cats and German shepherd, a few supremely wonderful friends, a few supremely wonderful relatives, a thick down comforter, cable TV and laughter. She also has an M.A. in Psychology, although she can't remember where she put it. And her feet hurt.

Marie-Elise Wheatwind is a "coyote" of mixed heritage: She is half Chicana, one-quarter Swedish and one-quarter Russian Jew. She has a B.A. in Creative Writing from San Francisco State University and a M.A. in English from UC Berkeley. Her work has been awarded two California Arts Council Literature grants and a PEN Syndicated Fiction Prize. She presently lives in New Mexico, where she divides her time between teaching, writing and working and browsing in bookstores. Her work has appeared in numerous anthologies.

Laurie Williams lives in New York City with her boyfriend, Doug. Currently, she works for a benefit consulting firm in the Communications/Design division and is learning graphic design. She finds living in New York City challenging and exciting, and says she's grown up and progressed since moving there from California in 1988. She is also a drummer and, after working with a Caribbean band throughout 1990, is now forming her own rock and soul band. She's also an avid skier, and spends several weeks a year skiing in the Grand Tetons.

Laurie York moved from Memphis, her home town, to San Francisco in 1980. Over the last six years, working full-time, she has created a body of work that traces her Southern past and envisions her future. Her work will also be published in *Into the Light: Art work About Childhood Sexual Abuse* by Elizabeth Nees. She has recently received a grant to continue her work in New Mexico through Druid Heights Artists Retreat. She is interested in sharing her art and healing process with others through workshops and exhibitions and can be reached through P.O. Box #1, Albion, California, 95410.

About the Editor

LOUISE M. WISECHILD is a writer, musician, bodyworker, teacher and lecturer specializing in work with adult survivors of childhood abuse. She is the author of *The Obsidian Mirror: An Adult Healing from Incest* and is currently writing a book about her childhood relationship with her mother that will be published by Seal Press. In addition to her non-fiction books and articles, she is also writing a fantasy trilogy, a murder mystery and a play, each of which explores alternatives to violence based on creativity, community and cooperation. Information on her workshops and lectures for survivors and professionals may be obtained by contacting her care of Seal Press.

Selected Titles From Seal Press

The Obsidian Mirror: An Adult Healing From Incest by Louise M. Wisechild. $10.95, 0-931188-63-6. One woman's inspiring journey—the pain of her experience and the power of her healing.

No More Secrets by Nina Weinstein. $8.95, 1-878067-07-9. A beautifully written and sensitive novel for young adults as well as survivors of sexual abuse of all ages.

Getting Free: You Can End Abuse and Take Back Your Life by Ginny NiCarthy. $12.95, 0-931188-37-7. The most important self-help resource book in the movement to end domestic violence. Also available on audiocassette, $9.95, 0-93118884-9.

Dating Violence: Young Women in Danger edited by Barrie Levy. $16.95, 1-878067-03-6. Both a call for action and a tool for change, this anthology addresses the plight of teenage women who are, in alarmingly high numbers, being sexually, emotionally or physically abused in their dating relationships.

The Forbidden Poems by Becky Birtha. $10.95, 1-878067-01-x. An incantatory collection of poems by a well-known African-American lesbian feminist that explores healing from the loss of a longterm relationship.

Past Due: A Story of Disability, Pregnancy and Birth by Anne Finger. $10.95, 0-931188-87-3. A writer disabled by polio explores the complexities of disability and reproductive rights through a riveting account of her pregnancy and childbirth experience.

The Black Women's Health Book: Speaking for Ourselves edited by Evelyn C. White. $14.95, 0-931188-86-5. This pioneering anthology looks at the health issues that today's black woman faces and offers words of advice, comfort, inspiration and strength.

The Things That Divide Us: Stories by Women edited by Faith Conlon, Rachel da Silva and Barbara Wilson. $8.95, 0-931188-32-6. Sixteen stories exploring issues of racism, anti-Semitism and classism by many of today's top feminist writers.

Voyages Out 2: Lesbian Short Fiction by Julie Blackwomon and Nona Caspers. $8.95, 0-931188-90-3. In this second volume of our series designed to showcase talented short fiction writers, two fresh voices report on lesbian life in distinctive ways.

Seal Press, founded in 1976 to provide a forum for women writers and feminist issues, has many other titles in stock: fiction, self-help books, anthologies and international literature. Any of the books above may be ordered from us at 3131 Western Avenue, Suite 410, Seattle, Washington, 98121 (please include 15% of total book order for shipping and handling). Write to us for a free catalog or if you would like to be on our mailing list.

1991

306.87
W is
    WISECHILD, LOUISE M

SHE WHO WAS LOST IS REMEMBERED

DATE DUE		
NOV 2 1 1991		
2-4-92		
MAR 1 2 2008		